D1068433

Geography and Politics in a World Divided

GEOGRAPHY AND POLITICS IN A WORLD DIVIDED

SAUL BERNARD COHEN

RANDOM HOUSE
New York

FIRST PRINTING

 Published in New York by Random House, Inc., and simultaneously in Toronto, Canada, by Random House of Canada, Limited.

Library of Congress Catalog Card Number: 62-16205

MANUFACTURED IN THE UNITED STATES OF AMERICA BY
THE COLONIAL PRESS INC., CLINTON, MASSACHUSETTS

PREFACE

Political geography can be described as that discipline which treats political phenomena geographically. The purpose of this book is to present a geographical view of contemporary international politics. Recent changes in the geographical and ideological environment require that we reappraise our thoughts on current geopolitical realities. For the Maritime World in general, and for the United States specifically, the Soviet Union's rise to the position of a great power made such a reappraisal inevitable. The framework that has been sketched in this book supports the thesis of geopolitical equilibrium in this World Divided.

In considering the geography and politics of various regions, I have offered selective rather than general coverage. For our generation at least, the prime movers in international politics will remain the United States, the Soviet Union, and Maritime Europe. The text, therefore, gives emphasis to these regions and to the shatterbelts within which great power interests directly converge. It does not attempt to give equal weight to all areas.

In the field of geography, much of what is termed "political geography" lacks political substance. It is, in fact, cultural geography organized according to political units. Therefore, I have not tried to avoid the *politics* in political geography but have focused upon current geopolitical situations. Moreover, to acquaint the geographer with the approach and methodology of the political scientist, I have enlisted the assistance of an esteemed colleague and valued friend, Andrew Gyorgy, Professor of Government at Boston University. Dr. Gyorgy has prepared the section on "International Relations: Concept and Application" as an appendix to this book.

Another aim of this work is to present in simplified conceptual form a geographical study that will have meaning for students of international politics. All too frequently, the political scientist owes his acquaintance with geography and geopolitical theories to the writings of non-geographers. This situation will be remedied only as geographers and political scientists become increasingly aware of the very specific methodological contributions and points of view that each field brings to bear upon the study of international affairs.

Maps 1 and 4, the maps of the world as viewed by Halford Mackinder and Nicholas Spykman, have been redrawn on different projections to conform more closely to present geopolitical realities. Both maps were Siberian centered, cylindrical types; Mackinder's, a Mercator, and Spykman's, a Miller projection. The projection upon which they have been recast is an azimuthal type, the Oblique Aitoff, centering off the coast of Maritime Europe. This is an equal-area map, with the shape of the land masses reasonably free of distortions.

I am indebted to the late Professor Derwent S. Whittlesey who, as teacher and guide, inspired me to pursue work in political geography; to Andrew Gyorgy, who encouraged me to write this volume and who read portions of the manuscript; to Andrew F. Burghardt, who read the manuscript in its entirety and was so generous with his comments and suggestions. I am grateful to Eileen Schell, who was most helpful with her cartographic ideas and who drafted the maps in their final form, and to the indexers, Elsa Dorfman and Leonard Phillips. My thanks go also to various members of the staff and student bodies at the United States Naval War College. Since 1957, when I served in residence as Lecturer in Political Geography, I have maintained close and fruitful contact with the College through a series of lectures on geopolitical themes. While the views that are expressed in this book are my own, I have benefited from the frank exchanges that I have enjoyed with seasoned senior naval officers from the United States and a large number of Maritime countries, who live not only as observers but as practitioners in the realm of international affairs.

The final manuscript for this book was prepared while on sabbatical from Boston University, an opportunity which I deeply appreciate.

S.B.C.

Boston University
Boston, Massachusetts

CONTENTS

PART TWO—POWER CORES IN A DIVIDED WORLD

MAPS AND CHARTS

TABLES

INTRODUCTION

Ours is a politically divided world. It is divided because man wills it and because nature reinforces this will. Aspiring to be unique, groups of people organize themselves within politically ordered societies and associations thereof. These societies are territorially framed. The edges of the frame are political boundaries. A geographical approach to international affairs requires appreciation of the reciprocal relations between these political groups and their physical and cultural setting.

From the reign of Henry IV of France at the close of the sixteenth century until the First World War, the national state was the unchallenged cornerstone of the politically divided world. There were other political components—internal, such as provinces or cities, and external, such as colonies or trusts. However, such components had relatively limited functions to perform—generally, the functions were subordinate to those of the state. While pressures of arms and economics at times compromised national sovereignty, the important elements of this sovereignty were never transferred.

Following the close of the First World War, two new forms of political unit emerged: the (British) Commonwealth of Nations and the Union of Soviet Socialist Republics. Although they differed in structure and objectives, they shared a political format that embraced more extensive and more varied territories than those occupied by the traditional national state.

The Second World War and its aftermath have witnessed the creation of additional multinational units. The North Atlantic Treaty Organization, the French Community, the Warsaw Pact, the European Economic Community, the short-lived United Arab Republic, the tottering Federation of Rhodesia and Nyasaland, the announced (but still vague) union of Ghana, Guinea, and Mali—all are vehicles for grouping larger areas than those embraced by national states. The purposes of such units range from the strategic to the economic to the ideological. Most are regionally oriented, and some, like NATO and the French Community, extend beyond the bounds of geographical regions. But all have in common the desire to exploit the specific advantages that larger territorial frameworks have to offer.

Because of their varied objectives, these new territorial units differ in features and in size. Moreover, they fluctuate in area and significance, as strategic, economic, or ideological conditions change. Thus, addition of the Mali Republic has increased the area of the earlier Ghana-Guinea union by 350 per cent. Withdrawal of Iraq from CENTO has made land communications between Turkey and Iran considerably more difficult. Physical separation of Syria from Egypt made it easier for Syria to reassert its independence.

While supranational units are appearing in increasing numbers, the national state-formation process is by no means slowing down. On the contrary, over seventy new states have joined the United Nations since 1945. Many of these states have been carved out of relatively homogeneous economic or political regional organizations. This disruption of regional lines appears superficially to be turning the clock back. More probably, however, the establishment of these new national states is the first step in the creation of additional supranational units.

The reshaping of the world's political map is a result both of technological innovation and ideological ferment. Technological innovation has made it possible and even necessary for states to take a global approach to their problems of military and economic security. It has emphasized the military and economic power disparity among states, causing an increase in the number of political satellites that revolve around Great Powers.

Ideological ferment expresses itself in two ways. First, in terms of the spread of nationalism, it shatters formerly unified colonial empires into a plethora of independent political entities. Colonial empires were a means of dividing the world into broad strategic units that represented a balance of Great Power interests. The rise of today's newly independent states has shattered this balance. Long-established intra- and extra-regional economic and military ties have been swept aside without advance notice. The events of the past few years have proved that political, economic, and cultural commitments are a poor match for the fervent idealism or even the whims of small groups of men who are bent upon upsetting the *status quo.*

Second, international doctrines easily leapfrog space, thanks to modern communications and transportation. We need no longer assume that only areas that are contiguous to ideological centers are areas into which this ideology can spread. True, contiguity makes the spreading of doctrines easier. Thus Communism has been extended from North Vietnam into Laos, neutralism from Egypt into the Sudan, and Western-style cultural and foreign affairs orientation from Europe into Turkey. But absence of contiguity is no assurance against the spread of Communism into the Caribbean, Africa, or South Asia, or against the maintenance of the Western alliance in Pakistan.

Changing Geopolitical Patterns

The regrouping of political units on a regional or a national basis does not seem to be occurring in random fashion. The regional processes are strongest within the geopolitically more mature parts of the world. The national processes are strongest in the underdeveloped reaches. Older, mature states seek in regional activities a means of providing broader scope to their highly developed, specialized societies. Newer, underdeveloped states, which have yet to harness their internal forces, seek not so much to specialize as to broaden and to diversify their economies. Frequently this can only be achieved by a self-imposed form of national economic and political isolation.

How are these political regroupings affecting our ideas about the divided world? Certainly, they have altered the pattern of geopolitical relations across the various parts of the earth's surface. The clear-cut division that existed after the Second World War between the "Free" and the "Iron Curtain" worlds no longer exists. Generally speaking, there now is a threefold division—"Western," "Communist," and "neutral." This division is in a state of flux. The boundaries of the three groups are constantly changing and vast areas are shifting from one camp into another.

This new division reflects the most significant geopolitical event of our times—the post-1945 retreat of the West from positions that tightly encircled the Eurasian interior. Today, we can liken the political world to a series of concentric rings, with the Communist bloc in the Eurasian center, the West partly surrounding this region, and the neutral grouping taking up intervening positions between the two. The two inner rings have, since the Second World War, extended their areas, the Communist ring at the expense of both the Neutral and the Western-controlled world, and the neutral ring at the expense of the Western world.

Following World War Two, the prime objective of the Western alliance was to contain the Soviet landpower within continental Eurasia by keeping the littoral portions of Eurasia within the Western political fold. With the loss of China, containment became the major motif of American foreign policy. Despite our efforts, however, more of this littoral has fallen under the sway of the Communist or the Neutralist blocs. Strict containment of the Eurasian Heartland has not been possible, whether accompanied by the strategic doctrine of massive retaliation or not. This fact must be forthrightly faced by America's leadership if a new power balance on a global scale is to be achieved. Because realistic global strategic frameworks have not been proposed to the public, many in the Western world have not been able to face up to the fact that the containment policy can no longer be the guidepost of our foreign relations with the Soviet Union. Indeed, the turn of recent events has made a complete jumble of our past ideas on global strategic frameworks, leaving us adrift in a sea of confusing and frequently contradictory international policy statements and actions. Immediately after World War Two, areas that many American and Western European strategy-makers considered essential to the security of their peoples, such as China and Eastern Europe, were pulled into the Soviet orbit. Since 1948-49, North Korea and North Vietnam have been lost, and the battle for the southern halves of these countries is by no means resolved. Elsewhere along the Eurasian periphery, other losses are imminent. Pro-Western governments have been displaced by neutrals with violent anti-Western biases in such countries as Egypt, Iraq, Laos, and Indonesia. Lebanon, Afghanistan, and Cambodia may follow suit. Changes in personal or family rule may swing from the Western camp such countries as Libya, Saudi Arabia, and Jordan. Within states like Iran, Thailand, and Taiwan, alliances with the Free World may lack a sufficiently broad base of popular understanding for long-term continuity.

Thus, in looking at Eurasia, we find that Soviet influence has pushed outward from its core so that the Elbe has been reached, the northern Middle East leapfrogged, and Monsoonal Asia deeply penetrated. Waters formerly denied to the Czars, like the Western Baltic, Eastern Mediterranean, Red, South China, and East China Seas, are now open to the Commissars both for peacetime commerce and preparations for war.

But the Eurasian periphery is not the only part of the world where age-old links with the West have been broken. While Cuba is a current example, many parts of Africa south of the Sahara and Latin America are subject to violent political currents that can lead to Soviet Union or Mainland Chinese biases. Even Antarctica is the laboratory for Soviet scientific activities as much as it is for Western ones.

It may be asked whether Soviet influence throughout the world is being extended according to a broad design or strategy, or whether the extension is a blanket one that probes all areas of possible discontent and seizes upon any opportunity that presents itself. Communist ideologists discredit ideas of environmental determinism, and they discount various schools of national geopolitics as being deterministic. This antienvironmental determinism and belief in the inevitability of Communist victory seems to contradict any suggestions that Soviet strategists hold doctrines that give priority to penetration of specific areas. However, there is little doubt that the U.S.S.R. continues to show very special concern over those areas that adjoin its key population and industrial centers. These are areas from which invasions of Czarist Russia and the U.S.S.R. have been launched, and which the U.S.S.R. has attempted to secure with a great measure of success during the past two decades. Thus it was that Stalin insisted upon control of eastern Poland, Estonia, Latvia, southern Finland, and Bessarabia in his pact with Hitler in 1939, and subsequently moved into Lithuania and Bucovina. These advance positions did not stem the onslaught of the Nazi invasion in June 1941. From prepared positions in northern and southwestern Finland, East Prussia, central Poland, Silesia, and Romania, the *Wehrmacht* simultaneously launched its attack against Leningrad, Moscow, and the Ukraine. After the defeat of Nazi Germany, considerable territorial reshuffling took place in Eastern Europe. It is significant that as a result of these boundary changes every one of the positions from which the Nazi attack was launched, with the exception of Silesia and part of Romania, is now Soviet territory. In the east, Outer Mongolia and Manchuria, which presented serious threats to the survival of the Bolshevik regime in 1919-21, have also been brought into the Soviet orbit (although these frontier areas are by no means free of the threat of long-range Sino-Soviet differences). Two other areas of extraordinary Soviet concern are Turkey and Iran, opening as they do onto the Ukraine and Central Asia.

Beyond this specific concern for strategic frontier reaches, however, there seem to be no area priorities for Soviet pressures, unless we include the former colonial world as one great target for Communist ambitions.

The colonial world is, in Soviet eyes, on the threshold of the second, and socialist, revolt against the "Capitalist-Imperialist" world. The nationalist revolt has succeeded for the most part without Soviet intervention. It is not likely that the socialist revolt will be conducted against a background of similar Soviet, or at least Chinese Communist, restraint.

In 1923 Lenin said, "The outline of the struggle in the last analysis depends upon the fact that Russia, India, China and so on, constitute a gigantic majority of the population of the globe . . . and it is precisely this majority which is being drawn with extraordinary rapidity in recent years into a struggle for its own liberation."[1] Lenin's hopes for the world Communist victory were, to a great extent, based upon the sheer numbers of people who had been under colonial rule; they were not based upon the presumed strategic significance of the U.S.S.R. in a global location sense. From what has happened since Lenin, it appears that most Soviet probings into the former colonial world are based upon moments of opportunity. Therefore there is little reason to suspect that Soviet pressures against Thailand or Syria would have a higher priority than those against Indonesia, Guinea, or Cuba. In the face of American pressure, initial Soviet agreement to dismantle missile bases built in Cuba during the fall of 1962 is evidence of the secondary strategic value assigned Cuba by the U.S.S.R.

During the Containment-Massive Retaliation era, the policy of the Western alliance was to try to maintain the *status quo* in a spatial sense, without apparently attempting to ascribe priorities to different parts of the world. This *status quo* has been broken. What is now called for is the recognition that new global geopolitical divisions exist. They are based upon the strategic needs and capabilities of both the U.S.S.R. and the United States. We are not suggesting that static global equilibrium or balance of forces exists or is attainable. Static equilibrium is contrary to the essence of geopolitical life, which seems to be change. We are suggesting, however, that the world is divisible into broad groupings, and that within these groupings today's two major powers can find economic, political, military, and psychological security. We speak, then, of a divided world, not referring to a twofold division of isolated, self-contained parts. We seek to describe, rather, a framework of partition across which various forms of interaction, competition, and contention will continue to flow, in keeping with the dynamic changes and needs of the major power cores.

The Strategic Value of Space

Political relations among states are influenced by an area's strategic value. These relations in turn affect this value. We can

[1] Quoted by Bertram Wolfe, *Khrushchev and Stalin's Ghost* (New York: Praeger, 1957), p. 50.

view the strategic importance of parts of the earth's surface in terms of three dimensions: space, time, and national vantage points. The term *space* includes natural resources or location with respect to the lines of movement that carry these resources. But the endowments of areas change, in time, with technological innovation. Moreover, what is considered strategically important to one state may be unimportant to another. The Suez Canal is a highly strategic area today. If, within the next decade, the Canal remains too shallow for giant tankers, or if North African petroleum supplants Middle Eastern supplies within the Maritime European market, then the Suez Canal will lose much of its strategic significance. Moreover, Suez is important to Maritime Europe and indirectly thereby to the United States. However, it is of secondary importance to the U.S.S.R. and India, and of trifling importance to Latin America.

Finally, an area's strategic significance cannot be assessed in terms of the needs of a single power core. Two parties, and frequently more, will be involved. Thus, Mainland China, the United States, the U.S.S.R., Japan, and Australia are all directly concerned with Korea and Southeast Asia. While Eastern Europe is of primary concern to the U.S.S.R. and to Maritime Europe, as is North Africa to Maritime Europe, the fate of these regions is of secondary importance to other power cores of varying sizes and strength.

In the following chapters, the salient political geographical characteristics of the major power cores of the earth—Anglo-America, the U.S.S.R., and Maritime Europe—will be discussed. Background for the discussion will be global strategic frameworks within which these power cores can function and interact in relative stability. Stability by no means implies harmony. It does suggest a dynamic equilibrium in the political and economic relations that each of these cores may be expected to seek with one another and with other parts of the world.

While the world is constantly shrinking in a time-communication sense, some of its components are maturing economically and politically at a rapid rate. Such a maturing process enhances the prospects for the striking of a global strategic balance built upon a multiple-core base. Unlike those who believe in the inevitability of one-power world domination—a belief best articulated by nineteenth-century German philosophers—the author holds that coexistence is geopolitically possible. A global geopolitical balance is a practical goal for the statesmen of our time. One basis for such a goal can be found in the distribution patterns of the earth's physical and cultural environment.

This book is in three sections. Part One discusses the earth's geopolitical foundations and provides a contemporary view of the global geographic setting from which a framework for dynamic geopolitical equilibrium is formulated. The essence of this framework is a division of the world into geostrategic regions. As background to this contemporary discussion, the nature of political geography and a short history of geographical thought along geopolitical lines are examined.

Part Two deals with the major power cores. Emphasis is upon the three strongest powers of the earth (the United States, the Soviet Union, and Maritime Europe) and the changing geopolitical environments within which they function.

Part Three treats the Middle East and Southeast Asian Shatterbelts, and the African, South American, and Offshore Asian portions of the Maritime World, focusing upon zones of contact and influence from the standpoint of Western interests.

Part One

GEOPOLITICAL FOUNDATIONS OF A DIVIDED WORLD

·1·

POLITICAL GEOGRAPHY

Concept and Application

The Nature of Geography

This volume is a study in political geography. As such, its themes rest on a spatial approach to international affairs. Thus, while political geography has much in common with international politics in terms of its concern with the relations among states and other political entities, it differs in its method. Political geography belongs to the field of geography. Its manner of inquiry, spirit, and purpose is geographical. Geography can be defined as the *science of area differentiation.*[1] Its essence is to observe, inventorize, map, classify, analyze, and interpret patterns of earth-man relationships over different parts of the earth's surface. We may wish to emphasize contrasts from place to place—or we may wish to point out similarities from place to place. In so doing, geographers are concerned with the uniqueness of given areas. Geographers seek out subdivisions within the physical environment (climate, soils, vegetation, and landform) and subdivisions in the cultural or man-made environment. Finally, they

[1] Introduced into American geographic literature by Carl Sauer, this definition was adapted from Alfred Hettner's concept of geography. It is quoted in Richard Hartshorne, *Perspective on the Nature of Geography* (Chicago: Rand McNally, 1959), p. 12.

search for correlations between and within the two sets of environmental patterns.

Thus, the geographer relates densely populated areas with soil, mineral, or water supply distribution patterns, or with favored focal points of transportation. He measures the distribution of housing types against the background of climate, building material sources, or place of origin of the builders of such houses. He observes how cities have grown, noting the relation of residential areas to prevailing wind patterns or agricultural land use, and manufacturing areas to rivers, highways, and less desirable soil areas. If no valid case can be made for the interrelationship of patterns of the physical and human environment, then the geographer has at least fulfilled one valid function in pointing out the distribution of single-featured elements, regardless of the causes for this distribution. But it is the search for correlations that tests the geographer's mettle. During the Middle East's Khamsin periods (the hot, dusty, desert-born winds), human energy and productivity decrease. Knowing that humid coastal areas are even more adversely affected by such winds than higher plateaus helps us to understand people's actions during that period. Or the geographer may point out that in as volatile a region as the Middle East it is noteworthy that no revolts have broken out in recent years during the month of Ramadan, while revolts have broken out in non-Muslim lands elsewhere in the world during this period.

Differences among peoples within a country may have developed or become accentuated because of isolation imposed by the terrain. The Basques did not accept the language and way of life of the people of the Spanish Meseta, because of the isolating effects of the Pyrenees. The Kurds, in northern Iraq, are a mountaineering, grazing people, who differ racially, linguistically, and culturally from the Arabs of Mesopotamia. They constitute a separatist element in modern Iraq. Often such differences make it difficult for a state to achieve strong, centralized control.

These and other examples can be cited, but the essence can be summed up thus: people and their activities differ or are similar from place to place. Often, although certainly not always, these differences or similarities can be explained in cause-effect terms that stem from the study of geographic relationships. However, in examining the cause-effect relationships between the earth and man, many have been tempted to overinflate the influences of the environment. A popular example that is cited to point up man's relative insignificance in relation to nature, is to note that were it possible to pack all mankind into a box, like sardines, such a box would be small enough to fit into the Grand Canyon. And the story attempts to heighten man's insignificance by suggesting that if the box could teeter on a knife's edge at the lip of the canyon, the wagging of a dog's tail could push the box and all mankind with it into oblivion.[2]

While such an example emphasizes the grandeur and scale of the physical environment in relation to man, it is not especially appropriate because it tends to cast a shadow over the role of man as an active agent in molding the environment. Thus, to use the size of the Grand Canyon to express nature's dwarfing of man is not particularly apt. Man can dam the Colorado and fill the Canyon with water if he is so disposed. He can, with nuclear energy, blast new holes of equal magnitude or fill present ones. He can bridge the Canyon or fly over it. If he desires and is willing to pay the price, man *can* move mountains. This is stressed not because man is likely to move many mountains, but to point out that nature only overpowers us with its immensity when we don't want to go through or over it. Obviously man's sights, desires, and capabilities differ from place to place over the earth's surface. What we can think of and are capable of carrying out in the United States is far different from human aspirations and capabilities in Mozambique, and part of what we are is a product of our physical environment. When, therefore, we consider man and his activities in relation to his environment, we have to take into account his specific framework of thought and activities. Let us not make the mistake, however, of underestimating man as an active agent in relation to nature.

The Nature of Political Geography

Hartshorne has defined political geography as "the study of the variation of political phenomena from place to place in inter-

[2] Hendrik Willem van Loon, *Van Loon's Geography* (New York: Garden City Publishing Company, 1940), p. 3.

connection with variations in other features of the earth as the home of man."[3] Whittlesey said that "the kernel of political geography is the political area . . . the political significance of any area bears a well-defined relation to its climate, landforms and natural resources."[4] Jones, for whom the political area becomes a "field of interaction" of forces, has pointed out that man's political ideas generate political forces within specific areas, the area first being an inactive recipient of these ideas. As the areas become political in character, they in turn begin to shape political ideas and processes.[5]

These definitions have in common the thesis that the essence of geographical thought is area differentiation. As such, the differentiation of political phenomena from place to place is the essence of political geography.

Political area, or space, is multidimensional. Space is *horizontal* as viewed from the standpoint of the shape, size, location, and natural resources of one political unit. Space is *vertical* as viewed from the interplay of man's objectives, laws, and economic and cultural tools upon the horizontal plane. Space has a third dimension, *time,* which considers the interaction of horizontal and vertical space at any given period. Thus, time can be thought of as a series of points that constitute a curve along the horizontal and vertical space axes. These three dimensions are not absolutes because the selection of the criteria for their measurement and their interpretation are subjective. Space dimensions vary according to the point of projection, or point of view, that is applied to them, just as maps vary in size, shape, and data with their cartographic projection and timing. Distortions occur in maps that reproduce space frameworks; distortions also occur in the analysis of spatial relations. For political geographers, this point of projection varies with national or regional outlooks. To a lesser extent, it varies with a number of other subjective ele-

[3] Richard Hartshorne, "Political Geography in the Modern World," *Journal of Conflict,* IV, No. 1 (March 1960), p. 52.

[4] Derwent Whittlesey, *The Earth and the State* (New York: Henry Holt, 1944), p. 585.

[5] Stephen Jones, "A Unified Field Theory of Political Geography," *Annals of the Association of American Geographers,* XLIV (1954), pp. 111-23. This, in a sense, is an extension of Jean Gottmann's recognition of ideas and circulation as the two main and contradictory factors that shape and reshape the political map.

ments, which are bound to temper any process of inventory and analysis.[6]

Four Approaches to the Study of Political Geography

Geographical study of the political environment rests upon survey and analysis within a cartographic framework. Various approaches can be employed in such studies. Hartshorne recognizes four distinct ones within the field of political geography: 1) power analysis; 2) historical; 3) morphologic; 4) functional.[7] Power analysis refers to "an analysis of political units of power and the relations among them."[8] These are units that are defined in space, whose internal character is influenced by space, and whose relationship with other units is conditioned by space. Historical political geography has, as its focus, the political landscapes of the past. The morphologic approach examines political areas according to form and features. Functional political geography is concerned with the functioning or operation of political areas.

(1) THE POWER ANALYSIS APPROACH

The power analysis approach is very commonly used by non-geographers, some of whom like to define geography as one of the several power resources in international relations. One such study, for example, divides national power into five components: geographic, economic, political, sociological, and military.[9] The geographic element is defined as "including the location, size and shape of the area which comprises the nation . . . the extent to which it provides access from, and egress to, the world community . . . the degree to which the land is arable or barren . . . the effect of climate, not only on the fertility of the land,

[6] Harold and Margaret Sprout, *Man-Milieu Relationship Hypothesis in the Context of International Politics* (Princeton: Princeton University Press, 1956), p. 16.

[7] Preston James and Clarence Jones, editors, *American Geography Inventory & Prospect*, Association of American Geographers, Syracuse University Press, 1954. Chapter by Richard Hartshorne, "Political Geography," pp. 167-226.

[8] *Ibid.*, p. 174.

[9] U.S. Army War College, *Power Analysis of the Nation-State*, Discussion Topic 2-B, Carlisle Barracks, Pa., 1960, p. 2.

but also upon the hardiness and energy of the people, [and] the reservoir of natural resources with which the land is endowed."

This, however, represents a limited geographical approach, for geographers do not isolate geography as a determinant of national power. A fully geographic approach would make an inventory of pertinent categories and relate this inventory to politically significant phenomena. Let us enumerate the inventory categories, and then cite examples of their political applicability. The categories include:

1) *The physical environment* (landforms, climate, soils, vegetation, waterbodies, etc.);
2) *Movement* (the directional flow of the transportation and communication of goods, men, and ideas);
3) *Raw materials, semi-finished and finished goods* (employed and potential, in both time and space terms);
4) *Population* (in its various characteristics, particularly qualitative and ideological);
5) *The body politic* (its various administrative forms, ideals, and goals in their areal expression, such as county, state, national and international bloc frameworks).

Physical Environment. An example of this first approach would be to measure the Norwegian coastline and to indicate how the high ratio of useful coastline in combination with fertile fishing grounds and poverty of land base has influenced Norway's development as a commercial, fishing, and NATO-oriented state.

Movement. An example would be to measure the reach of Radio Cairo within Africa, with reference to its impact upon emergent nationalism.

Raw Materials and Goods. An example would be to measure the distribution of Maritime Europe's coal, iron ore, and limestone resources in terms of the economic and political impact of the interchangeable use of these resources by various national steel industries. Thus, Saar coal is more rationally used by French steel makers in Lorraine than by German steel makers in the Ruhr.

Population. An example would be to map population by ethnic characteristics in Iran. Such a map would show the majority of the population of Khuzistan to be Arab. This would help explain why the oil-rich province that borders Arab Iraq has been a tension area in Iraqi-Iranian relations, with the unresolved Shat-al-Arab border dispute as the major irritant.

Body Politic. An example would be to analyze the effects of the internal political organization of national states upon land use-patterns. The division of England into electoral constituencies enables the relatively small rural population (10 per cent of the total) to exercise a disproportionate political influence on the national level. As a result, grazing obtains tax benefits and rough land areas that might otherwise be lost as a utilizable resource continue to have economic and recreational value.[10]

While these five categories are all viewed from within a spatial framework, geographers also work with space as a sixth and distinct category. In this sense the location, shape, and boundaries of political entities are analyzed, as well as the impact of space upon the internal character and external relations of such political entities. An example can be drawn from an examination of Israel's boundaries.

The length of Israel's land borders relative to its total land area is in a ratio of one mile of border for every thirteen square miles of land area. As a result, an inordinately high expenditure of national energies is needed to secure this border. One way to secure a border is through fixed military garrisons. An alternative to garrisons are farm settlements. The path that Israel has chosen has been to encourage border farm settlements in poor, as well as fertile, agricultural areas, thus draining off capital that might be invested elsewhere in manufacturing pursuits.

It is not difficult to collect data for the power inventory. The difficulty lies in the sifting and weighing of the data. The fact of the matter is that not all available data need be taken into account in comparing specific political areas in terms of geography-strategy interrelations. Indeed, much comparative analysis suffers from including all features of the physical and cultural environment, regardless of their pertinence or their comparability. The crux of the problem is to search out the elements that are germane and can be fruitfully applied.

For example, we have become increasingly concerned with

[10] L. D. Stamp, *Applied Geography* (Baltimore: Penguin Books, 1960), pp. 151-60.

space and numbers in assessing the relative strength of nations and blocs. China and India especially loom important on the power scene to those analysts who feel that the weight of their populations may tip the balance of world power. The geographer has to concern himself with space and numbers—but not as the statistician does. Instead he searches out meaningful relationships. Sheer numbers are translated into population densities. These densities are expressed in terms of arable land (which in turn reflects climate, soil, slope, etc.). The numbers are expressed in terms of urbanized population—a good index for reflecting technology. The raw material base can be expressed by such a factor as steel production.

While the power inventory is generally a method of comparative analysis that has been reserved for the national state, it is becoming increasingly important to examine its applicability to various levels of regionalization, and to include indices of growth or development rate to insure a reflection of areal dynamics in any study that is undertaken.

Tables 1 and 2 suggest how the power inventory might be made in simplified terms. Table 1 draws together the basic data and the index.

Table 2 shows that there is no single answer to the power base, but rather a series of answers that depend for their selection upon the intelligence and experience of the analyst (for which no electronic computer can substitute). Using one grouping, Maritime Europe is the leader; using another set, the United States leads; and a third points to the Soviet Union. By comparing data over different periods, an appreciation of trend can be obtained.

But this method cannot quantify the ideological strength, motivation, policies, and goals of the political units. It can only give the framework in which to study these aspects. And even quantifying certain elements presents pitfalls. For example, steel, aluminum, and petroleum might be selected as indices for evaluating national strength. However, shall these industries be measured in terms of output, or in terms of capacity? If capacity is selected because it best measures potential and can be regarded as a stored resource, do we have common yardsticks for measuring capacity from state to state? Also, we accept urbanization as a measure of national strength. And so it is, because urbanization usually reflects greater national cohesiveness, more effectively

TABLE 1

*An Inventory of National Power**

	Total area in square miles	Pop. density per sq. mi. arable land	Total popula-tion	Urban popula-tion	% of urban to total pop.	Cultivated land in square miles	Steel produc-tion in tons
United States	3,657,630	240	180 mil.	125 mil.	70%	700,000	93 mil.
Maritime Europe	1,219,300	1,050	300 "	180 "	60%	285,000	98 "
U.S.S.R.	8,650,140	235	212 "	102 "	48%	900,000	66 "
China	3,767,751	2,100	700 "	100 "	14%	330,000	15 "
India	1,269,506	845	440 "	75 "	17%	520,000	3 "
Canada	3,851,809	125	18 "	12 "	67%	145,000	6 "
Brazil	3,286,344	310	65 "	25 "	37%	210,000	2 "

Same Data Translated into Index Terms

United States	3	8.8	10	10	5	4.9	46
Maritime Europe	1	2	16.7	15	4.3	2	49
U.S.S.R.	7.2	8.9	11.7	8.3	3.4	6.2	33
China	3.1	1	38.8	8.3	1	2.3	7.5
India	1	2.5	24.4	6.2	1.2	3.6	1.5
Canada	3.2	16.7	1	1	4.8	1	3
Brazil	2.8	6.8	3.6	2	2.6	1.4	1

* Steel production is for 1959. Other data are for 1960.

centralized authority, and higher productivity per man effort. Highly urbanized societies are now more stable politically, showing a lower proportion of revolutions, for example.[11] Nevertheless, there are exceptions, such as situations where larger numbers of urbanized people mean greater instability rather than stability. The size of Naples, as a measure of urbanization, bears little relationship to manufacturing strength and political stability. This is because the economic base of the city is so narrow. Consequently, hundreds of thousands of persons are affected by unemployment or underemployment, and society is far from

[11] Hans Weigert *et al., Principles of Political Geography* (New York: Appleton-Century-Crofts, 1957), p. 307.

TABLE 2

Index Base for National Power Inventory

	Average composite index	Average index excluding total population	Average index excluding total pop. and urban pop.	Average index for total area, cultivated land, urban pop.
United States	12.5	12.8	13.5	6
Maritime Europe	12.8	12.2	11.7	6
U.S.S.R.	11.2	11.2	11.7	7.2
China	8.9	3.9	3	4.6
India	5.8	2.7	2.1	3.6
Canada	4.4	4.8	5.7	2.4
Brazil	2.9	2.8	2.9	1.9

stable. And in the restless, underdeveloped, rural countries, revolutions are generally fomented and led by urbanites or by military juntas that exploit the presence of urban mobs to gain and maintain power.

These qualifications do not mean that power indices cannot be used. They simply mean that indices must be weighted and then employed with judgment and skill. The final results can be no more than useful guides for comparative analysis.

(2) THE HISTORICAL APPROACH

Historical political geography has as its focus the past, both for the sake of understanding the past better and for analyzing current problems. Whittlesey's discussion of the evolution of the French national state in *The Earth and State*[12] is an outstanding exposition of the historical approach. He traces the growth of France from its seat of political origin in the Île de France to the attainment of its current territorial form. The sequence of state growth in relation to the physical and cultural environment is carefully sketched out. This discussion covers a range of varied elements in earth-state relations. One is the defensive significance of a series of outward-facing limestone cuestas to the security of

[12] Whittlesey, *op. cit.*, pp. 129-65.

Paris. Another is the focal significance of Paris in an over-all physiographic and transportation sense. The location of Paris helps to explain both the step-by-step growth of the French national state and France's high degree of political and economic centralization.

While much that now exists can only be understood in terms of what existed in the past, most studies in historical political geography have their greatest value in explaining the past. To rely upon them as guides to projecting the political roles and activities of states today can prove fruitless and even misleading.

(3) THE MORPHOLOGIC APPROACH

The morphologic approach studies political areas according to their form—that is, their patterns and structural features. *Pattern* refers to the arrangements formed by the association of political units, whether national states, regional blocs, global alliances, or internal administrative divisions, as expressed by location, size, and shape. *Structure* refers to the spatial features that political units have in common—i.e., population and economic cores, capitals, components, boundaries, and underdeveloped or otherwise problem units.

Italy's pattern, for example, can be understood within the context of the country's location within the broader European economic union. As a component of E.E.C., Italy has gained steel manufacturing advantages through the introduction of international rail through-rates on scrap shipments from Lyons to Turin.

Its geopolitical pattern can also be viewed from the standpoint of its location and shape within the Mediterranean. Italy is especially concerned with the co-ordination of NATO naval activities in the Mediterranean. While France's withdrawal of its naval units from the co-ordinated command affects all NATO countries, it particularly affects Italy. On the one hand, Italy is more vulnerable to Soviet submarine activities; on the other hand, Italy becomes NATO's Mediterranean mainstay and its navy the recipient of a greater share of allied material and training support.

Among Italy's geopolitical structural features are:

Population and economic core area. The Po Plain concentrates within it not only the bulk of Italy's manufacturing but also its most productive farm areas. Proximity of this core to the Alps means readily available hydroelectric power for industry, in a country poor in fossil fuels. Such a location also favors trade exchange with Northern Europe.

Capital. Rome, a very large city, is removed from the economic core area. Absence of a broad Roman manufacturing base, as well as the presence of the Vatican, helps to explain why Rome is relatively immune from Communist mob pressures. Rome lives from such industries as tourism, government, and movie-making. Its workers are not strongly organized within the framework of Communist- or Socialist-controlled trade unions. Much of the local Communist strength is derived from clerks, shopkeepers and intellectuals, whose challenge to the Church and government comes in nonviolent forms. As a result, the central Italian government has been able to operate within a general atmosphere of stability and security.

Boundaries. Italy's northern boundaries are a traditional source of instability. In modern times, the boundary line has fluctuated in all directions, northeast, north, and northwest. The Yugoslav border dispute over Trieste was settled less than ten years ago. Following the end of the Second World War, France annexed minor territories, providing it with strategic control over those areas from which Italy had invaded France in 1940.[13] Alte Adigo has been Italian since World War One. It remains, however, a major irritant to Italo-Austrian relations.

By and large, modern Italy is strategically exposed to threat of attack from Alpine-based neighboring states. After the *Anschluss* in Austria, for example, Nazi Germany was in a far better position to dictate to Mussolini than was the case prior to 1938.

Underdeveloped unit. Italy can also be analyzed according to its north-south internal regional units. The underdeveloped South, plagued by soil poverty, lack of water, and tenancy, is rurally overpopulated. Unable to support its population, the South has

[13] Some of these changes were essentially defensive, giving France the Little St. Bernard Pass and command of heights that overlook Briançon and the Briançon-Modane Road. Others are potentially of offensive significance, such as the Mont Cenis Plateau that overlooks Turin and furnishes it with water power; and Tenda-Briga, whose hydroelectric plants supply the Italian railways in Liguria and South Piedmont.

had to export people to such areas as northern Italy, France, the United States, and Germany. Many people of the South consider themselves to be unfairly exploited by the industrial North, which receives the bulk of Italian national investment, and have turned to political extremism, both Communistic and Monarchical-Fascistic. This turn to extremism applies in particular to Southerners who migrate northward. Thus, Italian political stability suffers from the vast disparity in the resource base and economic levels of the north and south.

(4) THE FUNCTIONAL APPROACH

The functional approach, as conceived by Hartshorne,[14] is concerned with the functioning of an area as a political unit. Every political area is subdivided into subordinate areas of organization, each with its own governmental functions. These subordinate areas must have stronger political associations with the state than with one another or with outside states. For the state to function properly, it must have unity. Homogeneity, coherence, and viability are basic requirements for such unity. Viability of the state is related, not only to domestic economic considerations, but to economic, strategic, and political relations with other states.

Thus, the functional approach would study state-strengthening or centralizing forces, and state-weakening forces as they are related to space. Within the United States, one of the functions of the state is to guarantee freedom of passage across interstate lines. In theory, therefore, none of the fifty subunits, or states, can interfere with such passage. In practice several do. The fact that such interference occurs in Southern states is a fact of distribution. That these states have a set of White-Negro race relations that are reciprocally related to the physical and cultural environment is also geographical in nature.

Another example of the functional approach can be drawn from a state's external economic relations. The function of the state is to create or to maintain economic viability for its citizens. Laws on foreign trade, including subsidies, tariffs, and embar-

[14] Richard Hartshorne, "The Functional Approach in Political Geography," *Annals of the Association of American Geographers,* XL, No. 2 (June, 1950), pp. 95-130.

goes, are tools used by the state to promote this particular function. For example, the desire of the United Kingdom to increase its sales in automobiles and chemicals to Maritime Europe may force the United Kingdom to become more intimately associated with the Common Market countries to the detriment of trade with the United States. In most cases, laws that relate to foreign trade cannot help but have internal ramifications. For example, United States tariffs upon men's shirts from Japan protect eastern seaboard manufacturers. Higher shirt prices in the East will be offset by the jobs provided directly and indirectly by the shirt-making industry. This will not be the case in the Pacific Northwest, however, where domestic shirt manufacturing is unimportant. A counterpressure might be exercised by the Pacific Northwest to raise imposts on Japanese tuna and salmon. As a result, the Northwest and the eastern regions would have worked out a *quid-pro-quo*. At the same time, both regions might look dimly at continued U.S. aid to Japan. The Middle West, on the other hand, might find its interests better served if there were no tariff on Japanese shirts and tuna. Moreover, it might regard continued United States aid to Japan as being of particular benefit in stimulating United States-Japanese trade in machine tools.

In all of these approaches, we face the problem of measuring and describing the distribution of political phenomena as they *exist in space*. This presents dangers of relying upon static elements to describe inherently dynamic situations.

Change Through Movement

Space and man's use of it are dynamic. The constant process of change vitally affects international politics. One way of indicating change is through mapping political processes and phenomena *in time*. Such a sequential approach has long-term usefulness. Thus, as we view the shifting of the energy sources of the United States from Appalachia's coal to Texas petroleum to Venezuelan and Middle Eastern oil we gain an appreciation of change that has political implications. Similarly, the move of a country's capital, such as Brazil's from Rio de Janeiro to Brasilia, or the greater weight recently assigned to non-European states within United Nations councils, reflects this process.

But examination of change through time is a slow process. It is much faster to seek such an appreciation through analysis of the movement factor.

Halford Mackinder recognized movement when he spoke of the "man-travelling" element in geography, thereby referring to the variable mobility of man, ideas, and materials over different parts of the earth's surface. Using the term *movement factor* as a translation of the French *circulation,* Jean Gottmann pointed out that "analysis of the movement factor as it applies to a position . . . helps us to understand easily the motives and imperatives of the policies . . . emanating from that position. Movement, however, makes for fluidity and change." [15]

Gottmann has presented movement and national ideas as the two main forces in political geography. Movement refers to current status in traffic, communications, transportation, and trade. Without movement, there can be no international relations.

We view the movement factor as consisting of three elements: the channel, the field, and the arena. Channel refers to pathway or means of movement; field, to the specific areas that include the origin, transit route, and destination of the channel; arena, to the general medium of space-land, sea, or air within which the fields and their channels lie.

CHANNELS OF MOVEMENT

Some channels are two-way; others are only one-way. Some channels can be used for a multiplicity of purposes; others have only single-purpose functions. Some channels have no competitive channels; others have. What is important is first to recognize the nature of the channel and then to define the reciprocal impact that movement through this channel makes upon the fields within which the movement flows.

For example, pipelines are two-way; they are multi-purpose; they have competitors. Those pipelines that carry ocean-transported crude oil from the eastern seaboard to the interior of the United States can be reversed to carry products from the refineries of the interior to the east coast's cities. A pipeline that

[15] Jean Gottmann, "Political Partitioning of Our World," *World Politics,* IV, No. 4 (July 1952), p. 515.

carries oil can be converted to carry natural gas, water, or powdered coal in slurry form. An oil pipeline has to compete with road-carried trucks and rail cars, and with water-borne tankers. On the other hand, a radio transmitter is only one-way; it has one purpose—to transmit sound; in underdeveloped countries where the percentage of illiteracy is high, the radio may have no competitors as a propaganda weapon.

We cannot disregard the possibility that geographical variability may loose its significance within or between specific channels of movement. Certainly, in the age of the intercontinental ballistic missile, there is no practical difference between a channel that extends for 4,000 miles and one that extends for 3,500 miles for rockets with a 5,000 mile range. The time lead that the latter distance presents to its user over the former might be no more than one minute. Also, electronically controlled automobiles traveling on expressways at 100 miles per hour could provide the traveler with the same ease and speed of movement as the crack express train or monorail. However, in most instances, movement channels have geographical variability owing to distance, physical features, and cultural distinctions.

In the case of the Soviet radio propaganda that is beamed to Latin America, it is not distance, but rather the amount of capital investment and broadcast time, and the choice of language and topic, that provide the advantage over the efforts of the United States Information Agency. The impact of the Soviet and American efforts can be compared by number of man-hour listeners; the relative effectiveness can be analyzed through public opinion polls. With American and Soviet technological capabilities assumed equal, it is possible to foresee a reversal of the present trend to one that is favorable to the United States, considering such other elements as distance, trade ties, availability of Spanish- and Portuguese-speaking peoples in the United States, and capital expenditure potential.

FIELDS OF MOVEMENT

Movement occurs within specific areas, and its effects are frequently felt outside these operational areas. Stephen Jones has suggested that such areas as are affected by movement be called "fields," and has pointed out that what occurs within the "fields" influences political units as a whole.[16]

We can cite, as an example of field, the area which is soon to be affected by the Mont Blanc Auto Tunnel. This includes Lyons and much of surrounding southeastern France, the tunnel itself, the Val d'Aosta, and Turin. The effect of the first all-weather auto-truck route across the Alps will be to increase the exchange of passengers and goods. Both Lyons and Turin are likely to benefit industrially. Many of the sleepy Alpine villages, too, will realize new prosperity from the motels, gas stations, and restaurants that will be built to serve auto passengers. Movement within this field is bound to affect the entire political area. For example, greatly increased trucking through the tunnel probably will come at the expense of traffic that now moves in roundabout fashion via the ports of Genoa and Marseilles. Some provisions, in the form of subsidies or alternative sources of business, might have to be made by the states to the ports adversely affected by the tunnel.

ARENAS OF MOVEMENT

Arena of movement refers to the three space media (land, water, and air) through which movement takes place. As long as human habitation is restricted to land, our concern with the other two space media is as they are used for movement to the settled portions of the earth. From a political geographic standpoint, arenas of movement are important for their variable uses in projecting political, economic, and military power.

Previously, it was safe to generalize that land was the primary arena of movement for continental interiors, water for the Atlantic and Pacific shorelands and islands, and air for the Arctic. In fact, however, such a generalization is now apt to be misleading.

Land is the primary space medium for such continental interiors as Eurasia, North America, Africa, and Australia. However, water is a significant secondary medium in North America, and air, of some importance to all continental interiors, is heavily utilized in North America and in the U.S.S.R.

[16] Jones, *op. cit.* In all, Jones sets forth five elements: political idea-decision-movement-field-political area, as a unified chain through which political ideas operate to affect political areas.

Water is the key medium interconnecting Eurasia's rimlands and the remainder of the Atlantic and Pacific ocean littorals and islands. But air has achieved significant stature as a connecting medium for the North Atlantic.

Finally, while the Arctic is almost exclusively the domain of the air space medium, we must look to the future when nuclear-powered polar submarines and Soviet Arctic surface vessels, spearheaded by nuclear icebreakers, will make water a secondary medium.

Unity or Change?

Basically, the movement factor exercises a unifying influence as men, goods, and ideas move via channels to connect fields. However, we should be mindful that movement can act as a unifying force upon one field at the expense of other, formerly unified elements. Specifically, movement that unites fields in different countries may divide fields within one country. Communism has unified some Russians, Italians, and Frenchmen, but at the same time has created greater cleavages within Italy (the Industrial North versus Rome) and within France (the rural countryside versus the industrial cities). The movement of Jamaicans and Pakistani into Liverpool and London may not be a factor that will lead to greater unity between the United Kingdom and Jamaica and Pakistan. The racial antagonisms that have been stirred up as a result of these immigrations can become, on the contrary, a source of friction.

Therefore, rather than state that movement exercises a unifying influence, we prefer to say that movement is the greatest inspirer of change, bringing with it unity to some fields, but disunity to others.

Because movement reflects change, the political geographer must be alert to the ramified political consequences of such movement—those tending to unite and those tending to disunite.

Let us take certain critical parts of the world and touch upon movement developments that have important political significance. First we can cite the 480-mile pipeline that has been completed between Edjele in eastern Algeria (near the Libyan frontier) and the Gulf of Gabes port of Skhirra in Tunisia. The pipeline is the channel, and the field includes the Algerian oil deposits, Tunisia's ports and cities that may benefit from transporting or using the petroleum, and France's refinery areas. The political areas affected include Tunisia, Algeria, and France. Arena in this case embraces land and sea. In agreeing to the decision to construct the pipeline and thereby give France a second and alternate oil-carrying route from the Sahara to the Mediterranean, the Tunisian government has undertaken certain risks. Algerian nationalists may some day oppose this venture in French-Tunisian co-operation, perhaps to the point of cutting the line. France, too, has assumed a political risk in handing to Tunisia a weapon—i.e., the threat of pipeline take-over—that can be applied against France. What were Mr. Bourghiba's motives in assuming such risks? Were they based on economic need and anticipated revenues from this line, as well as a counter-pressure against the French presence in Bizerte? Or was Mr. Bourghiba so firmly committed to the concept of a French-Arab North African Community that he deliberately wished to tie his country more intimately with France despite the attendant risk of intra-Arab conflict and greater economic dependence on France? While it is only a thin line in the desert, this channel of movement reflects a reciprocal relationship between France and Tunisia that is fraught with dangers and yet with hope.

A second movement development that might be cited has to do with the construction of two railroads between the Soviet Union and China. The first, completed in 1955, from Tsining in North China to Ulan-Ude (east of Lake Baikal) on the Trans-Siberian Railway, crosses Mongolia at Ulan-Bator. The second is near completion and will connect Yumen in Kansu Province of Northwest China with the Turksib Railway near Lake Balkash. This railway crosses Chinese Sinkiang at Urumchi and enters Soviet territory via the low, grassy Dzungarian Gate. The first line traverses 500 miles of desert; the second, over 1,000 miles of desert. These lines are strategically important because they represent the fastest and most secure routes for transporting bulk materials between the U.S.S.R. and China. Viewed in the context of possible Sino-Soviet friction, however, they suggest channels of tension.

All of these areas named are fields of movement. Chinese

settlement in Inner Mongolia and the relative proximity of industrialized North China could place Eastern Outer Mongolia and the Lake Baikal region under considerable Chinese pressure (as these areas were once subject to Japanese threats). The proximity of a string of modern, industrialized Soviet centers along the Turksib Railway could pose an equally strong threat to China's control of Sinkiang, most of which is more than 1,000 miles' distance from Lanchow—China's present northwest frontier. Expressed in different fashion, China's pioneer fringe in Inner Mongolia and the Soviet pioneer fringe of Turkestan are in a position to move forward along the new transcontinental railroads. The expansion of these respective frontiers poses mutual threats to the Soviet-dominated Mongolian People's Republic and to Chinese Sinkiang. It also heightens the mutual vulnerability and thus the interdependence of the two countries.

The twentieth century has given unprecedented breadth and sweep to the movement factor. As we have advanced from the automobile and radio age to the age of television, manned aircraft, and guided missiles, the political impact of events in one part of the world upon another has become more direct. However, our ability to predict the consequences of this impact is less certain.

Movement developments need be considered in economic as well as technological terms. For example, jet aircraft make it possible for statesmen to span the North Atlantic in six hours. The effect has been to help to centralize power in the hands of the few, and personal diplomacy on the highest level has become the rule. However, jet aircraft play another vital role in movement. They have displaced slower propeller-craft along many runs. The latter, though less desirable and less economical for regular commercial flights, are more than adequate for charter flights. The chartered airplane has made it possible for hundreds of thousands of American students and middle-income persons to become international travelers. It may not be premature to suggest that the acceptance of the concept of a North Atlantic Community by an American generation that knows Maritime Europe well, will be an indirect product of the jet air age.

An International University in Moscow or an African students' airlift to the United States are as important an element of the movement factor as is the prospect of increasing the range of radio-telecommunications through the use of earth-girdling satellites. If we accept a university and its environs as the field of movement, then we must be prepared to recognize that there is a geography to this field. Thus, the nature of the distribution of African students within American universities has important political implications. Where such students take up locations in small college towns, residing in dormitories with their White counterparts, they are most likely to be integrated successfully into the university milieu. Where they take up residence in large city-based universities where housing may be available only in segregated Negro sections of the city, the results may be disastrous.

Having thus discussed the nature of geography and political geography, particularly the movement factor, we will turn in the next chapter to the political organization of areas on an international scale.

·2·

GEOPOLITICAL PERSPECTIVES

Ancient and Recent

Frameworks of Analysis

The essence of geopolitical analysis is the relation of international political power to the geographical setting. Geopolitical views vary with the changing geographical setting and with man's interpretation of the nature of this change. On this last point, Mackinder commented: "Each century has its own geographical perspective. To this day, our view of geographical realities is colored for practical purposes by our preconceptions from the past." [1]

In this century, our view of the geographical setting, and hence of geographical "realities," is a combination of landform distribution and patterns of movement. In the nineteenth century, the prevailing view of the geographical setting was the distribution of continents. Previously, climate and regional landforms served as the basic framework. Current debates suggest that tomorrow's geographical "realities" will weight population dis-

[1] Halford J. Mackinder, *Democratic Ideals and Reality* (New York: Henry Holt and Co., 1942), p. 29.

tribution and resource complementarity far more heavily than has heretofore been the case.

What purpose does geopolitical analysis serve? Harold and Margaret Sprout feel that such hypothesizing "may serve purposes of contemplative research or of policy-making and propaganda, and that whatever the avowed interests of the authors . . . [their geopolitical writings] have tended to serve both kinds of purposes." [2] We could cite modern works, ones of a dispassionate geographic nature as well as those of the German geopoliticians, to prove this point. But let us reach back into antiquity to Aristotle, who held that their temperate-zone location qualified the Greeks for world dominion over northern and southern climate people.[3]

Granting the truth of the observation made by the Sprouts, we would simply add that the geopolitical analyst is validly fulfilling this dual function so long as he does not deliberately distort the geographical setting as *he sees it* and as long as he does not lay claim to being the practitioner of an empirically based science.

Geopolitical analysis has two major aspects: 1) description of geographical settings as they relate to political power, and 2) laying out of spatial frameworks that embrace interacting political power units. It is more difficult to attempt such analysis today than in the past. Because of the spatial overlap that exists among great power blocs and the process of constant political realignment, sharply defined global political divisions cannot be easily rationalized. Moreover, the exercise of political power may be the measure of a man's daring or a people's desperation, rather than a resultant of the cultural and physical setting.

Formerly, geopolitical analysis could be more safely attempted. Until the late nineteenth century, major power blocs were associations of European-based empires. The core of world power resided in a tightly compressed area—the European and Mediterranean maritime-influenced landscape. For over 3,000 years the nodes of this power were such localized points or areas as

[2] Harold and Margaret Sprout, "Geography and International Politics in Revolutionary Change," *Journal of Conflict Resolution,* IV, No. 1, p. 152.

[3] Aristotle, *Politics,* Book VII, Chapter VII, p. 291. Translated by B. Jowett (New York: The Modern Library, 1943).

Mesopotamia, the Nile, Western Persia, Hellas, Carthage, Rome, Byzantium, Baghdad, Spain, Portugal, France, England, and Germany. This was "the world that mattered"—a world whose highly endowed geographical setting enabled its inhabitants first to develop their local environments in maximum fashion and then to reach out to less favored parts of the earth, exploiting their specialized resources for the benefit of the home base. Whether it was Aristotle referring to Athens, Polybius to Rome, or Pope Alexander VI to Iberia (at the promulgation of the papal bull dividing the Discoveries between Spain and Portugal), "the world that mattered" consisted of the coastlands that bordered the Mediterranean and the eastern North Atlantic.

With the latter half of the nineteenth century came a change. Some analysts felt that "the world that mattered" now had come to embrace the entire Northern hemispheric landmass, from 30° to 60° North Latitude. Others felt that world power was shifting to the continental sectors of this belt only—i.e., to North America and to Russia.

James Fairgrieve, for example, used the term "the world that counts" to describe those areas to which *place* and *distribution of energy* have given power primacy. Fairgrieve pointed out that "the history of the world is mainly that between 30° and 60°, and the peoples of these lands have naturally taken the lead in the world." [4] Within these latitudes, the United States, Europe (including Russia), and China, interconnected by sea and land routes, constituted Fairgrieve's "world that counts." Interestingly enough, Fairgrieve, writing about future possibilities in 1915, did suggest that the intertropical latitudes might one day become the world that counts because "the nearer the equator one goes the greater are the potentialities of saving energy." [5]

Today, we are far less confident that any one part of the earth (specifically the "north temperate" zone) possesses the material and human advantages to monopolize world power. Such factors as population and national will are beginning to claim equal weight with location, climate, and resource patterns in the world-power ranking process. Thus, China, India, and Brazil have

[4] James Fairgrieve, *Geography and World Power* (University of London Press, 1915), p. 357.

[5] *Ibid.*, p. 358.

emerged as states that aspire to world power. And the temper of our times is such that the analyst who would suggest that these states lack the prerequisite geographical setting to compete with existing power nodes is apt to be accused of deterministic thinking.

The second aspect of geopolitical analysis—dividing the world into power blocs—is much more complex because of the spatial overlap of great power interests. Because communication has conquered many of the restrictions formerly imposed by distance, West Berlin and Cuba can, at least temporarily, stand as enclaves within mutually conflicting power spheres, and Thailand and North Vietnam can belong to separate spheres.

In the light of the foregoing, can we no longer speak of "the world that matters" and "the world that does not matter"? Must we refrain from suggesting that certain parts of the earth's surface are destined to remain, essentially, within the spheres of influence of major powers?

Our answer is "No." We believe that geopolitical analysis still retains its validity. Place, accessibility to resources, and qualitative use of these resources through historically derived cultural advantages continue to give power dominance to certain parts of the earth. If relatively weak and depressed states have begun to exercise considerable influence on the world political scene, it is not because they possess power, but because of the stalemate between the North Atlantic and Soviet blocs. This stalemate has presented weak states with the opportunity to play one force off against the other. Abuse of this opportunity may well backfire, as the major powers come to realize that the issues between them will be solved only through their own actions.

A case in point is the attitude of the Soviet Union towards the sensitivities of others in such matters as the Hungarian revolt and the resumption of atmospheric nuclear testing. When the U.S.S.R. concluded that its national interests would be best served by taking unpopular measures, it did so with complete disregard for what others might say. Whether the resultant propaganda "defeat" for the U.S.S.R. has been a real liability in the East-West conflict is doubtful. The U.S.S.R. suffered a propaganda "defeat" in Hungary. The United States gained a propaganda "victory" over the Suez invasion. Basically, these victories and defeats are only relevant as they affect Great Power relations.

It may well be that our reluctance to use such terms as "the world that matters" stems from the fact that the East-West stalemate has caused both sides to exercise power in halting fashion. However, this does not do away with the fact that the ability to exercise this power does exist, and that many nations do not have it.

Naturally, the ability of weak states to take advantage of the international stalemate and to exercise political voices far in excess of their power abilities is not without political significance. For this reason we might wish to revise our description of the divided world into "the world of direct power capability" and "the world of indirect power capability." Major power areas are capable of international action on their own initiative; weaker states can only act when the major powers afford them an opportunity.

With such a view of the world, a sense of political clarity can be maintained. Without it, we in the West run the risk of losing our sense of what is important to us and what is not. If we feel that every part of the earth is of equal weight in the power struggle, we shall exhaust ourselves economically and emotionally, as well as militarily, in the struggle to attain some form of global power equilibrium.

Geopolitical Perspectives of the Ancients

Geopolitical theories to explain the political partitioning of the earth or to rationalize a change in the existing pattern are as old as the Old Testament. When Abram and Lot, upon returning from Egypt, found that the land of Canaan could not support their combined flocks of sheep, herds of cattle, and tents, they agreed to partition the land.

The basis of partition was water. Lot selected the well-watered Jordan Valley, whose physical qualities were reminiscent of the favored Nile Valley; Abram retained the grassy hills of Canaan.[6]

In the ancient and classical times that followed, there developed wide cultural and technical disparities among peoples. Some became gifted irrigation farmers; others had horses, or used

[6] Genesis, Chapter 13.

iron, or possessed location advantages; still others were driven by an especially harsh environment to conquer territories as a means of survival. Whatever the reason for their strength, the strong were able to press their political and military advantages over the weak, because the movement of ideas, men, and resources was so limited, and the advances made by one group were not readily acquired by another.

Geopolitical views, at first, were limited both as to the extent and the character of the geographical setting. The partition of Canaan between the Jordan Valley oasis and the western Palestine hills was quite representative of the times. River valleys like the Nile Valley and Mesopotamia were natural units, unified control of which was the major geopolitical objective. Adjoining landforms like deserts or hills were treated as separate areas, which at best served as barriers against invasion, and at worst as breeding grounds for warlike incursions.

When man began to seek broader geopolitical horizons, in this period, he did not consider as his major goal the combination of major valleys, desert, and mountain into one complementary unit. He sought rather to unite various river valleys and their divides into one geopolitical region. He was oriented to one major landform. Thus, three to four thousand years ago, Middle Eastern rulers aspired to unite the Nile and the Fertile Crescent, from Thebes to Ur. The setting for this unity of space was the irrigable lowland agricultural world, with primary land (the Fertile Crescent) and secondary sea (the Levantine ports and Crete) ties. The desert and mountain regions remained distinct and separate geopolitical units. When the Pharoahs of Egypt became locked in combat with the kings of Anatolia's Hittites, their goal was to clear the latter from the Syrian frontier—not to try to enter the Anatolian plateau and annex it to their empire.

The Greeks began to employ broad climatic patterns as their bases for dividing the known world geopolitically. Hecateus, in the sixth century B.C., drew a map dividing the world in two parts: Europe (including Siberia) and Asia-Africa. Climate was the basis for this political partition, Europe representing the cold areas of the north and Asia-Africa the warm areas of the south. The Asia-African environment, more favorable for settlement, was considered the major power locale. A century later Parmenides proposed his theory of five temperature zones or belts, one torrid, two frigid, and two intermediate. Building upon Parmenides' temperature zones, Aristotle claimed power pre-eminence for the intermediate zone inhabited by the Greeks. Such a broader view tended to see in the geographical setting something more than unity of landform. However, the Greeks continued to explain local political partitioning by land-characteristic differences. Thucydides, for example, explains the rise of Attica as due to freedom from invasion. Attica's attraction is described as deriving from its qualities as a place of refuge, which stemmed from the poverty of its soils and its consequent undesirability to outside factions.[7] This Thucydides contrasts with the rich-soil parts of Hellas, which were caught up in continual strife because of their attractiveness.

Soon continental landmass was added to climate as a framework for the geopolitical setting. The Greek Polybius suggested that the Asian continent imposed boundary limitations on the Persian Empire, stating that "every time they (the Persians) ventured beyond the limits of Asia, they found not only their empire but their own existence in danger." [8]

The Roman geographer Strabo's view of the earth was continentally oriented, and European-centered. He divided the entire globe into quadrilaterals, within one of which he placed the habitable earth. This habitable earth he described as looking like a soldier's cloak lying within a parallelogram and surrounded by water. The habitable land area consisted of three divisions, Europe, Libya, and Asia, whose forms were molded by the various arms of the ocean. Strabo viewed the European continent as being "the quarter most favorable to the mental and social ennoblement of man." [9] That Strabo wrote of a "world that mattered" geopolitically can be seen from the following: "Now the geographer should attend to none but our own habitable earth, which is confined by certain boundaries [from the Pillars of Hercules to the Eastern Ocean Bay of Bengal, and from Ierna

[7] M. I. Finley, editor, *The Greek Historians: Thucydides Book I* (New York: The Viking Press, 1959), p. 219.

[8] Ibid., Polybius, Book I, p. 443.

[9] Strabo, *The Geography of Strabo,* translated by H. C. Hamilton and W. Falconer, Vol. I (London: Bohn, 1854-57), p. 191.

(Ireland) to the Cinnamon (Ceylon) country]." [10] . . . "The countries which border on the regions uninhabitable . . . have no interest to the geographer." [11] . . . "It would not serve any political purposes to be well acquainted with those distant places and the people who inhabit them, especially if they are islands whose inhabitants can neither hinder us, nor yet benefit us by their commerce." [12]

The idea of there being more than one habitable world and therefore of multiple core power regions was not considered by Strabo or by the majority of the earlier Greek writers. However, Plato had introduced such a new dimension with his "lost continent." In *The Republic* Plato conceived of an ideal state, strong enough to repel any state and located on a new continent—Atlantis.[13] Later the Roman Mela asserted that the southern temperate zone was habitable and no doubt inhabited.[14] While the theme of a great *terra australis* persisted among the ancients, it was by no means commonly accepted and did not fundamentally shake the faith and resolve of European continental supremacists.

Whereas the ancient Greeks and early Romans regarded the inhabited world as an island, Ptolemy made it fade away in the north, south, and east into "unknown land," rejecting the continuous ocean as a mere assumption.[15]

With respect to movement, classical geographers tended to think in single-feature terms, using either water or landforms as barrier boundaries. In the fifth century B.C., Herodotus subdivided Asia into *actae* (peninsular tracts of land), using the surrounding water bodies as boundaries. Strabo preferred to use land boundaries, such as the Isthmus of Suez to separate Libya from Asia and the Taurus to divide Europe from Asia. But Pliny the Elder, in presenting a unique Roman geopolitical view of the world, employed a combination of movement channels—roads

[10] *Ibid.*, p. 199.
[11] *Ibid.*, p. 203.
[12] *Ibid.*, p. 174.
[13] J. Oliver Thomson, *History of Ancient Geography* (Cambridge University Press, 1948), p. 91.
[14] *Ibid.*, p. 323.
[15] *Ibid.*, p. 342.

and sailing vessel routes—to map the Empire. He showed Rome as extending its regional influences in various directions around the Mediterranean in conformity with the extent of the Roman road system. In some cases these roads terminated at barrier rivers, such as the Rhine, Danube, Euphrates, and Nile. The terminating points of the Roman road system served as an outer-ring boundary for the Empire. However, surrounding the Roman core was another (interior) ring—the Mediterranean Sea. Complete control of the Mediterranean gave to Rome a unified, sea-based, open inner core.

Early Muslim geographers hewed closely to ancient Greek and early Roman geopolitical thought. Thus, the northern quarter of the globe alone was regarded as inhabited, and as being in the center of a vast uninhabited area surrounded by interconnected seas.[16] The continental framework was widely accepted by medieval Arab geographers, who regarded Asia-Africa as one unit and Europe as a separate unit guarded by water barriers at Gibraltar and the shores of Marmara. Islamic geographers were interested in provincial geography, as well as descriptive geography and astronomical-cartographic geography. Provincial geography, in this connection signified the political geography of specific countries, mostly within the Islamic world. The very division of the Mediterranean along north-south lines reinforced continental geopolitical orientation. Only Spain was an exception, and Moorish Spain, for much of its history, had little in common politically, and even ideologically, with the rest of Islam.

Perhaps the first major attempt to break the continentally oriented geopolitical setting of Christian Europe *versus* Muslim Asia is seen in the fourteenth- and fifteenth-century Portuguese efforts to circumnavigate Africa. Portuguese ambitions were to use the sea to gain the riches of Africa and India, and to surround the Muslim Middle East from East Africa and the Indian Ocean. Here was a new strategy, free of the bounds of continental thinking. Such strategy derived its inspiration from early Greek concepts of the insular character of the habitable world, and from the lessons of the Discoveries. This view matured into a truly global strategic view as Europe's national states began to

[16] George Kimble, *Geography in the Middle Ages* (London: Methuen, 1938), pp. 51-55.

carve out colonial empires, acquiring key islands and coastal enclaves in their drives to unite ocean basins.

Early Global Geopolitical Perspectives

With the development of modern geography came attempts to find an underlying pattern and unity of the geographical setting. Immanuel Kant expressed the belief that a "Universal International State" was founded upon the nature of things.[17] He held that nature 1) provided that man can live in all parts of the world; 2) scattered people by war so that they might populate the most inhabitable regions; and 3) by the same means, compelled them to make peace with one another.[18] Kant was European-centered. He felt that no European balance of power could be struck because the will of states to subdue each other was too great. On the other hand, he held that a peaceful European federation of free states could impose global peace.

While Kantian philosophy accepted no form of unity save a global one (i.e., the Universal International State), the founders of modern geography admitted the concept of regionality within their philosophical system of global unity. Regionality was based upon varying views of geographical patterns. Where these views had international political or strategic implications, they became the basis for modern geopolitical thought.

Contemporary geopolitical views of the earth take stock of the patterns of arrangements of land and waters and of their interconnecting lines. For example, one view centers on Eurasia and Africa, which constitute 56 per cent of the earth's total land area and include 84 per cent of the earth's populations. Encircling this huge landmass are open seas that are three times as vast as all of the land combined. Here, then, is a distinct view of what is called "World-Island." Its focus is the center of the earth's largest landmass. Another view centers on the Northern Hemisphere—i.e., Eurasia, North Africa, and North and Central America. This embraces 60 per cent of the earth's land area and 90 per cent of its people. The focus for this global view is the air

[17] Immanuel Kant: "The Principle of Progress," *Eternal Peace and Other International Essays,* Vol. 3, World Peace Foundation, 1914, p. 66.

[18] *Ibid.,* p. 91.

and ocean space that links North America and Eurasia. There are other global views, such as the one that centers on the Atlantic, and views the adjoining Americas, Europe, and Africa as the key landmasses of the earth.

From these differing views of the earth's spatial patterns have evolved differing strategic theories. One is that control of the heart of Eurasia could mean world domination. Another is that control of those peninsular lands that rim Asia, such as Western Europe, the Middle East, and South and East Asia, could mean world domination. Another is that control of the Polar world by one power could spell world control. Still another is that a world of two or three Great Powers can achieve geopolitical balance.

Regardless of the various points of view, this much is clear. Strategists, today as in the past, ascribe varying degrees of importance to various parts of the earth, so that their political and military actions are greatly influenced by their geographical views.

While most of the geopolitical concepts with which we are concerned have been sketched out within the past seventy-five years, we can trace their geographical-setting base back to the beginning of the nineteenth century.

Alexander von Humboldt and Karl Ritter, whose first contributions appeared respectively in 1799 and 1804, founded modern geography in Germany. They held to the concept of the unity of nature and to the reciprocal relations between man and the state and the natural environment. Ritter elaborated a hierarchical system of regional divisions within the unified globe. First, he divided the earth into two: the land (continental) hemisphere and the water (oceanic) hemisphere. The boundary between the two was a great circle drawn through Peru and south of Asia. Then, within the land hemisphere Ritter saw two more subdivisions: the Old World and the New World. The former possessed considerable climatic similarity because of its great east-west extension. The latter displayed more climatic diversity because of its north-south extension. Further down the scale of size, Ritter conceived of each continent as a "natural whole." Finally, in some cases, he recognized divisions of continents as individual units.

Arnold Guyot, who introduced modern geography to the

American public with a series of lectures delivered in French in Boston in 1849, did much to describe and interpret the work of Ritter.[19] Guyot presented the two types of global divisions: 1) the land hemisphere's Old World-New World landmass division, and 2) the water hemisphere's Atlantic-Pacific Ocean basin division. The Old World he described as the world of mountains, plateaus, and limited-use plains; the New World as the world of rich plains. In discussing the oceanic division, he referred to the Atlantic basin as the most maritime, where inland seas predominate and where bordering land slopes are all long and gentle. The Pacific basin is described as the most "oceanic," with land-locked seas predominating and rimming land slopes that are short and rapid.

Guyot was among the first modern geographers to stress the central position of Europe within "the ocean [that] is, in fact, the grand highway of the world."[20] While he constantly emphasized the oceanic unity of the globe, his two major geopolitical concepts stemmed from Ritter's view of continents as "natural wholes." The first concept held that the mantle of world leadership was passing from Europe to North America and its European-derived culture. The second concept sketched the grouping of continents in three double-worlds, with leadership resting within the northern continents. Each of the northern continents was seen as contributing to a "natural universal civilizing" order, with Asia as the cradle, Europe as the maturing ground, and North America as the culminating locale of this process.[21] In vague, mystical terms, Guyot saw the bonds of Christianity, race, and proximity of location as the basis for global unity of the northern continents.

The Landpower Setting

It fell to the German geographer Friedrich Ratzel to make the first systematic studies of political areas. Ratzel was not the first to recognize that differences in the physical and cultural environment contributed directly to the political division of the

[19] Arnold Guyot; *The Earth and Man,* translated by C. C. Felton (New York: Scribner's, 1889), p. 70.

[20] *Ibid.,* p. 316.

[21] *Ibid.,* p. 331.

earth. He was, however, the first to treat space and location systematically in his comparative studies of states, and it is for this reason that Friedrich Ratzel is regarded as the founder of modern political geography.

Writing at the turn of this century,[22] Ratzel based his system on principles of evolution and natural science. He viewed political geography as a branch of natural science. The two essentials of Ratzel's systematic approach were space (*Raum*) and location (*Lage*). Space he regarded as contributing to and being dependent upon the political character of groups occupying this space. Location he viewed as giving particular uniqueness to the space occupied by the state.

Ratzel's evolutionary point of view was most clearly expressed in the "geographical laws" that he sought to establish defining the effect on states of their space and location. These laws stemmed from his organic view of the state. Ratzel considered the state as an organism fixed in the soil; a spiritual and moral organism derived from the imperfect combination of men; a spiritual tie to the ground that lies in living together, in common labor, in need for protection against the outside.

Ratzel's "laws" were above all laws of space and location. The activities, character, and destiny of men and their states were held to be products of location, size, altitude, frontiers, and above all, space. He placed special emphasis on frontiers, which he regarded as the peripheral organ of the state, and, as such, evidence of its growth or decline, strength or weakness.

Perhaps the most significant contribution of Ratzel to our ideas of the geographical setting lay in correlating continental areas with political power. Ratzel felt that man's need for, and ability to utilize effectively, large space would be the political dictum of twentieth-century international politics. In this he was most deeply influenced (as Guyot had been) by his studies of the United States—the first modern state to evolve within a "great space" framework. Relegating Europe, eventually, to a minor role in world politics, Ratzel felt that history would be dominated by larger states occupying continental areas, like North America, Asiatic Russia, Australia, and South America. In this continental

[22] Friedrich Ratzel, *Politische Geographie* (Munich: R. Oldenbourg, 1897).

MAP 1. Mackinder's World—1904

approach there was, and still remains, the frequent contradiction between the advantages of large space and the disadvantages of location. This approach also is weakened when it fails to account for the qualitative and quantitative differences of man-resource ratios within comparable continental areas.

It remained for Halford Mackinder to combine great space and location in a view of the geographical setting that attributed pre-eminence to one continental portion of the world. Mackinder's geographic writings and lectures over the span of the first half of the twentieth century are best known for their influence upon German geopolitics and for the strategic counter-doctrines they inspired. Sir Halford can also lay claim to having established geography as a university field in Britain.

Mackinder was trained in biology, history, and law, as well as in topography, strategy, and geography. This explains his interest in historical analogies, as well as in the ecological studies that led him to geography and finally to diplomacy. Some measure of his philosophy can be discerned from the following quotation "Man and not Nature initiates, but Nature in large measure controls. My concern is with the general physical control, rather than the causes of universal history."[23]

Mackinder's theory, first propounded in 1904, was that the inner area of Eurasia is the pivot region of world politics. (See Map 1.) He warned that rule of the heart of the world's greatest landmass could become the basis for world domination. Mackinder felt that it was entirely possible for the landpower that gained control of the pivot area (be it Russia, Germany, or even China) to outflank the maritime world. Eleven years later, James Fairgrieve was to point out even more forcefully that China was in an excellent position to dominate Inner Eurasia.[24]

It can be seen that the pivot area, as defined in 1904, was that part of eastern Europe and northern Asia characterized by polar or interior drainage.

What many critics have failed to note, as they have elaborated on Mackinder's theories, is that his views of the world kept changing. As a geographer, Mackinder was more aware than

[23] Halford J. Mackinder, "The Geographical Pivot of History," *Geographical Journal,* XXIII (1904), p. 422.

[24] Fairgrieve, *op. cit.,* p. 332.

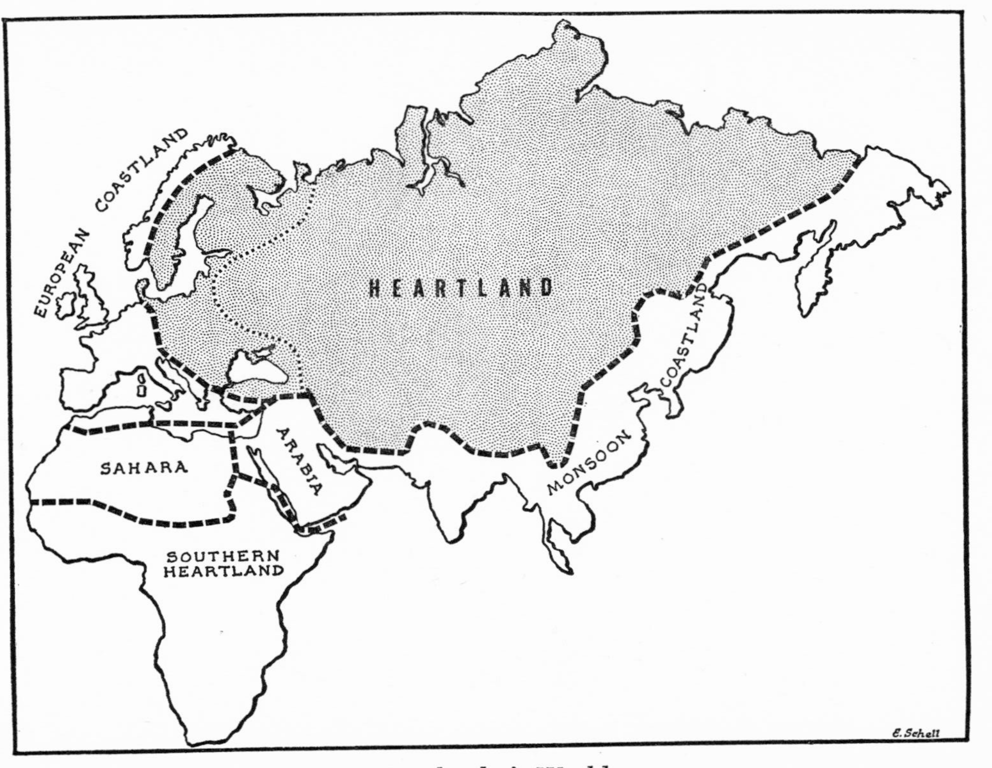

MAP 2. Mackinder's World—1919

most of his critics that man's use of the physical environment constantly changes, and that even the environment itself changes, albeit at an almost indiscernible pace.

Mackinder's 1919 map demonstrates his changing views of the world. (See Map 2.) The Heartland, as defined in 1919, was revised to include the Tibetan and Mongolian upland courses of the great rivers of India and China. Also, while not labeled Heartland, Eastern and Central Europe were introduced as a strategic addition to the Heartland, and for all practical purposes are considered Heartland. Mackinder's new boundary took into account advances in land transportation, population increases, and industrialization. Because of these advances, he felt that the Baltic and Black Sea land areas had become strategically part of the Heartland. These areas essentially lie within the Eurasian Lowland Plain and within the winter snowline. The term *Heartland,* incidentally, was not actually introduced by Mackinder, but by James Fairgrieve in his 1915 work, *Geography and World Power.*

It was in Mackinder's 1919 volume that he enjoined the statesmen of the West to remember this saying: "Who rules East Europe commands the Heartland: Who rules the Heartland commands the World-Island: Who rules the World-Island commands the World." [25] Thus, the middle tier of German and Slavic states, from Estonia to Bulgaria, becomes, in Mackinder's opinion, the key to world domination—a key then as available to Germany as to Russia.

Seldom have one man's theories been so exposed to critical examination as have those of Mackinder over the past decade—after years of passive or uncritical acceptance. But when all is said and done, most Western strategists continue to view the world as initially described by Mackinder. American foreign policy of containment in the postwar era, with overseas alliances peripheral to the Eurasian landmass, is an attempt to head off Soviet-controlled Heartland's dominion over the World-Island.

German Geopolitics

German geopolitics adopted the word *Geopolitik,* and much of its organismic-Hegelian philosophy, from the Swedish political

[25] Mackinder, *Democratic Ideals and Reality,* p. 150.

scientist Rudolph Kjellén. For its views of the geographical setting geopolitics seized upon diverse and occasionally contradictory concepts that had been sketched out by Ratzel and Mackinder. Led by Karl Haushofer, the geopoliticians preached conflict, strategy, and total war. They made household slogans of such words as *Lebensraum* (living space) and *Autarchy* (economic self-sufficiency) in a post-World War One Germany which ached for the restoration of the *Reich* to world power status.

Three geographical settings kept recurring in the literature of German geopolitics: 1) Ratzel's large states, 2) Mackinder's World-Island, and 3) north-south combinations of continents. Haushofer, harking back to Ratzel's laws on the spatial growth of states, saw large states as the wave of the future. Mastery of Germany over smaller states to the west and the east within Europe was regarded as "inevitable," and the conflict needed to bring this about as completely justifiable, because continental mastery in Europe was the goal.

Haushofer saw in Mackinder's World-Island the spatial framework for German hegemony over the new World Order. The German geopoliticians had two objectives in World-Island: 1) dominance of Russia to achieve Eurasian mastery, and 2) destruction of British seapower to gain complete World-Island rule. Haushofer held that landpower possessed a fundamental advantage over seapower. He looked to a German-Russian alliance as the core of Eurasian union with a broader transcontinental bloc that was to include China and Japan. Indeed, during most of the 1920's and 1930's, Haushofer called for Japan to accommodate itself with China and the Soviet Union, just as he propagandized for German-Soviet friendship.

Ratzel's correlating of continental areas with world power status influenced the geopoliticians in two ways: 1) their Pan-European concepts, and 2) their pan-regional concepts in general. The geopoliticians spoke of Eastern Europe as lying within the "European law of geopolitics." [26] By so doing they claimed an inherent continental unity for Europe, whose eastern boundary was defined as a line running from Lake Peipus to the lower course of the Dneister River. The U.S.S.R. was considered Asian

[26] Derwent Whittlesey, *German Strategy of World Conquest* (New York: Farrar and Rinehart, 1942), p. 170.

by Haushofer. Europe, including the Slavic lands of Eastern Europe, was to be unified under Germany as the prerequisite to achieving accommodation with the Russians over the fate of Eurasia.

Thus, Eastern Europe was to be the springboard for German ambitions in Eurasia. The German geopoliticians generally hoped to force the Russians into a voluntary agreement in the control of Eurasia. Military conquest of the Soviet Union was never wholeheartedly subscribed to by Haushofer, who doubted that blitzkrieg methods would succeed in conquering the vast Russian space.

A different form of continental setting was proposed by the geopoliticians in their pan-regional concepts. Alternately suggesting three or four regions (Pan-America, Pan-Eurafrica, Pan-East Asia and, when matters suited them, Pan-Russia), the geopoliticians suggested that the world be organized along north-south double-continent lines. This was to provide for complementary products and peoples. Within continental boundaries, they argued, lay the vast, contiguous space and the self-sufficiency of economy that would enable world power equilibrium to be attained.

In theory, however, Haushofer could never reconcile this pan-regional subdivision with an Old World-New World geopolitical division, which he frequently proposed. For he felt that Pan-Eurafrica, Pan-Russia, and Pan-East Asia would have to combine to stand on a par with Pan-America. In this last geographical setting, the Old World-New World equilibrium, we find a contradiction to the Mackinder view, which had also been espoused by Haushofer. This latter view considered the Americas as separate continental islands, destined to remain satellites of the World-Island. (See Map 3.)

The inadequacies of the pan-regional concept have been pointed out by many. Pan-regions could only be achieved by war. They did not offer the world a strategic equilibrium, for the southern half of each pan-region is not sufficiently remote from the opposing northern core region to be free of its pressures. South America is no closer to North America than it is to Africa or Europe; Africa is as close to the U.S.S.R. as it is to Germany;

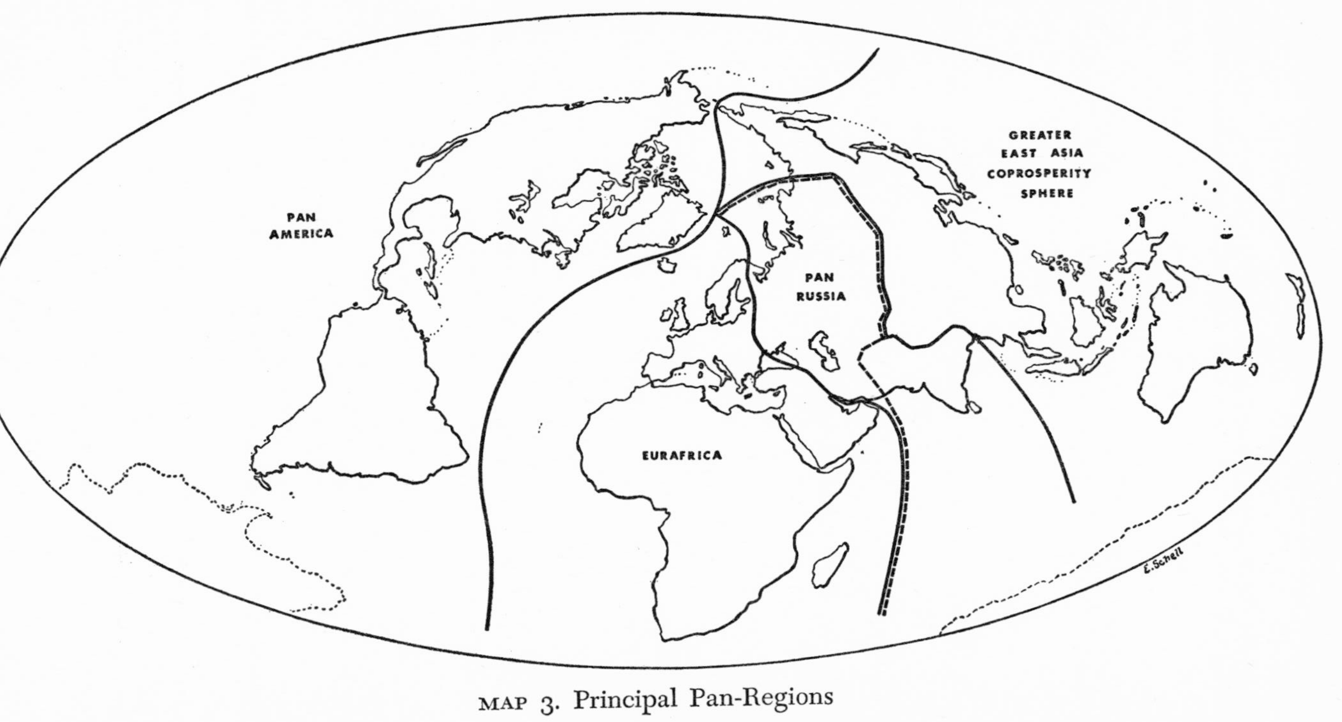

MAP 3. Principal Pan-Regions

and India is not much farther away from East Asia than it is from most of the U.S.S.R.

Nonetheless, it must be pointed out that since the Second World War there has been a closer drawing together of the world on north-south lines, at least for economic purposes. Europe's withdrawal from South and East Asia has stimulated much stronger European-African economic contacts. Japan has increased its economic involvement with many of the lands to its south, and Mainland China has made strong inroads in part of Southeast Asia. Most recently, renewed United States concern with Latin America has redirected the thinking of many of our people along north-south lines. Whether economic lines necessarily presume or justify strategic ties, as suggested by the pan-regionalists is, of course, an entirely different proposition.

That German geopoliticians expressed such contradictory views of the geographical setting can be understood. *Geopolitik* lacked scientific limits. It was a normative rather than an empirical study. As a nationalist-propagandist doctrine in the Germany of the 1930's, *Geopolitik* did not have to meet standards of objective criticism, and thus lacked the basic elements of scholarly self-discipline. Also, with the launching of the Nazi attack against the Soviet Union, the geopoliticians dared not publish opinions that ran counter to Hitler's strategy of the moment. In fact, Karl Haushofer was imprisoned in the Dachau concentration camp in 1944, and his son Albrecht, also a geopolitician, was executed for having become implicated in the army plot against Hitler of 1944.

The Seapower Setting

We have thus far followed the line of Ratzel-Mackinder-Haushofer, with their basic emphasis upon the advantages of landpower within the continental setting. Now it is time to return to the evolution of views of the geographical setting that were ocean-oriented.

Alfred T. Mahan was not a professional geographer. He was a naval historian and strategist, a journalist, and the second president of the United States Naval War College. However,

Mahan expressed a view of the geographical setting that was of pioneering geographical significance.

Admiral Mahan is best known for his analysis of the basis of seapower. When Mahan wrote of seapower, he was referring to sea-transported power. Control of the sea could only be achieved by controlling those land bases that had the advantages of strategic location, coastal shape, and defensive depth to their hinterlands.

It is Mahan's view of the world that makes his writings so significant to the geographer. This view, first expressed in *The Problem of Asia,*[27] was Eurasian-centered. Mahan felt that the northern land hemisphere was the key to world power, with Panama and Suez marking the southern limit of the most active commerce and politics. Within Eurasia, the most important component of the northern land hemisphere, he recognized Russia's position as the dominant Asian landpower, and felt that it was unassailable. Mahan pointed out, however, that this landlocked position presented certain disadvantages as well as advantages. He then described the zone between the thirty and forty degree parallels in Asia as the zone of conflict between Russian landpower and British seapower. Finally, he predicted that world dominance could be held by the Anglo-American alliance from key land bases surrounding Eurasia because of the inherent advantages of sea-movement over land-movement. Indeed, Mahan predicted that an alliance of the United States, the United Kingdom, Germany, and Japan would one day hold common cause against Russia and China.[28]

In a real sense, then, Mahan held a view of the world that anticipated Mackinder's World-Island view but culminated in diametrically opposed strategic conclusions.

Nicholas Spykman can be described as the direct heir of Mahan's strategic doctrines, in a geopolitical sense. However, Spykman's terminology, his detailed global geographical settings, and the political conclusions that he derived from his views of the world show that his basic inspiration came from Mackinder,

[27] Alfred T. Mahan, *The Problem of Asia and Its Effects upon International Policies* (Boston: Little, Brown, 1900).
[28] *Ibid.*

whose strategic conclusions he attempted to refute. Essentially, Spykman sought to arouse the United States against the danger of world domination by Germany. He felt that only a dedicated alliance of Anglo-American seapower and Soviet landpower could prevent Germany from seizing control of all the Eurasian shorelines and thereby gaining domination over World-Island.

What Spykman did was to suggest that the Eurasian coastal lands (Mackinder's "Marginal Crescent," including Maritime Europe, the Middle East, India, Southeast Asia, and China) were the key to world control because of their great populations, their rich resources, and their use of interior sea lines.

In essence, Spykman had the same global view as Mackinder, but he rejected the landpower doctrine to say: "Who controls the Rimland rules Eurasia; who rules Eurasia controls the destinies of the world." [29] To Spykman, the Rimland, Mackinder's Marginal Crescent, was the key to the struggle for the world. (See Map 4.) In the past, the fragmentation of the Western European portion of Rimland and the power of the United Kingdom and the United States made unitary control of the Rimland impossible. Spykman feared that one power, such as Germany, might seize control of European Rimland and then sweep onto the other portions through various combinations of conquests and alliances, using ship superiority and command of a network of naval and air bases around Eurasia. Certainly there is still much to be said in favor of sea communication as far as the movement of goods is concerned. Also, aircraft carriers and submarines have given a mobility in the use of aircraft and missiles to ocean basin powers that fixed land air bases lack.

The inadequacy of Spykman's doctrine is today most clearly apparent from the fact that no Rimland power is capable of organizing all of the Rimland because of the vulnerability of the Rimland to both the Heartland and the Offshore Powers. A united Maritime Europe would have to have complete control of the Mediterranean, North Africa, Middle East, Africa south of the Sahara, and Australia, before it could attempt to exert its strategic dominance upon the remainder of the Rimland. It could succeed only if the Heartland or the Continental American

[29] Nicholas Spykman, *The Geography of the Peace* (New York: Harcourt, Brace & Co., 1944), p. 43.

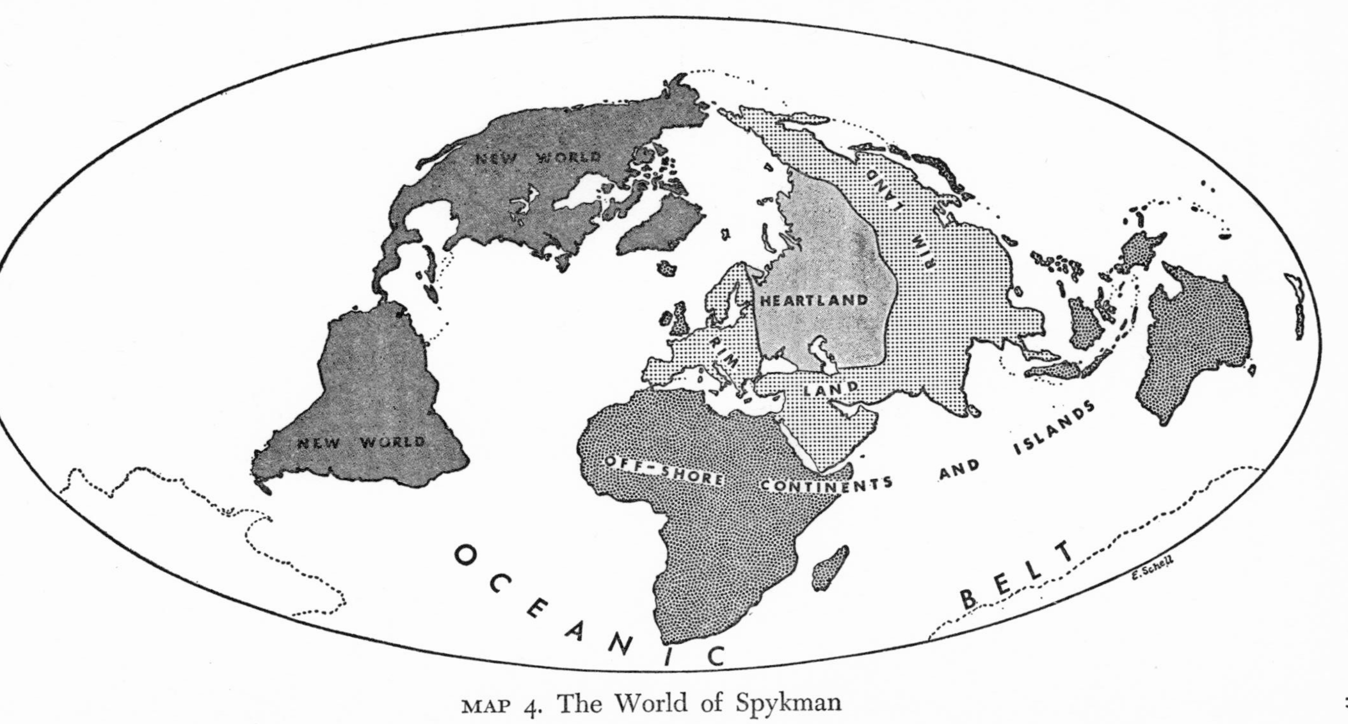

MAP 4. The World of Spykman

power did not intervene. By the same token, a Rimland China that swept into control of South Asia would be at a disadvantage in seeking to control the Middle East against Heartland, Western European, or African-based pressures.

Today's realities are that Mackinder's Outer Crescent, or continental islands like the Americas, Africa south of the Sahara, and Australia, and the large islands off the Eurasian shore, like the United Kingdom and Japan, are in competition with the Heartland for the lands and the minds of Rimland peoples. In this struggle, Africa's role is unique. While we may hesitate to call Africa the "Second Heartland" (as Mackinder did) it nevertheless need not be permanently tied to the other Outer Crescent lands in a political-strategic sense. Complete control of Rimland by either side would mean world domination. A Rimland divided or partly neutralized means a world more nearly in power balance. It is important to note that just as rule of the Heartland does not automatically mean command of World-Island, so rule of Rimland would not mean automatic command of World-Island.

The importance of interior lines of land communication, even between parts of the Rimland, looms greater today than it did in Spykman's considerations. Thus, the China land base was able to sustain North Korea and North Vietnam in spite of the control of the seas and the air by offshore powers. Communist development of networks of rails and modern highways, in South China and North Vietnam, as the sinews of politico-economic penetration have put Laos and South Vietnam in critical positions and threaten Northern Thailand. These are further examples of a Rimland power's use of land communications when denied access to connecting seas.

The development of railroads and highways in Sinkiang, Mongolia, and Tibet by the Chinese is an interesting example of a Rimland power penetrating parts of what Mackinder included in his 1919 Heartland. Indeed, as we have noted, he warned of a Chinese-dominated pivot area in his very first article. One might suggest that in the long run Sinkiang will be more easily controlled from the Heartland (Russian Turkestan) than from North China, by means of the railroad now being built from Lake Balkhash to Lanchow, but this is not the case for Tibet. China's vast space, population, and zeal to become a great power, and its bases in both Tibet and Vietminh, have for several years foreshadowed the use of land connections to threaten India and Nepal as well as southeastern Asia. The outbreak of conflict over the Sino-Indian frontier in October, 1962, is doubtlessly only the forerunner of continuing military and political pressure by the Chinese against India. The Tarim Desert, the Karakorum Range, the Kun Lun Mountains, and the Tibet Basin are formidable barriers to competition from China's northern ally, as China strengthens its position in southern Tibet. The remainder of the Rimland (the Middle East and Maritime Europe) is less susceptible to land-base conquest from adjoining Rimland areas, but it is of course more susceptible to Heartland's pressures.

The Airpower Setting

The impact of the air age upon geopolitical thought has produced a variety of views. In 1944, Renner suggested that the air lanes had united the Heartland of Eurasia with a second, somewhat smaller Heartland in Anglo-America, across Arctic ice fields, to form a new, expanded Heartland within the northern hemisphere.[30] A major attribute of this new pivot area would be the mutual vulnerability of its Eurasian and its Anglo-American portions across the Arctic. Such a pivotal area would not only be a great Heartland in the power sense of the word, it would also afford the advantages of interior air, sea, and land routes across the polar world, which as the arena of movement might well be the key to Heartland and therefore to world control.

Another opinion, that of Alexander de Seversky, has been described by Jones as the "airman's global view." [31] De Seversky's map of the world is an azimuthal equidistant projection centered on the North Pole.[32] The western hemisphere lies to the south of the pole, Eurasia and Africa to the north. Here again is an Old

[30] George T. Renner, "Peace by the Map," *Colliers,* CXIII (1944), pp. 44-47.

[31] Stephen Jones: "Global Strategic Views," *The Geographical Review,* XLV, No. 4 (July 1955), p. 501.

[32] Alexander P. de Seversky, *Air Power: Key to Survival* (New York: Simon and Schuster, 1950).

World-New World division. North America's area of "air dominance" is Latin America (our area of reserve for resources and manufacturing); the Soviet Union's area of air dominance is South and Southeast Asia and Africa south of the Sahara. Where North American and Soviet air dominance areas overlap (this includes Anglo-America, the Eurasian Heartland, Maritime Europe, North Africa, and the Middle East), de Seversky considers this the area of decision. Here, according to this view, air mastery and therefore global control can be gained.

In one sense, this view is an extension of that of Renner. In another, however, it has led to two different, and highly questionable, conclusions. The first stems from the distortion of the map projection, which suggests that Africa and South America are so widely separated that they are mutually defensible by their respective "senior" partners—the Soviet Union and the United States. In actuality, Africa and South America are closer to one another than to their "senior" partners. And for all practical purposes, Africa and South America are equidistant from the United States.

Secondly, de Seversky's view was that air supremacy, and with it control of the northern hemispheric area of decision, could be achieved by one power through all-out aerial warfare. While he spoke of only the United States, the U.S.S.R., and perhaps the United Kingdom as having the potentialities of Great Power, in theory any country with the necessary military hardware, recuperative strength, and will could achieve dominance. That country might be located within the northern hemispheric area of decision; but it might be located anywhere on earth, say Argentina or Australia, as the manned bomber and missile have become truly intercontinental. Thus de Seversky's views lead to two conclusions: 1) "air isolationism" that suggests a viable division of the world into two; and 2) "a unitary global view" that suggests that, in the event of all-out war, the power that leads in military hardware can dominate the world regardless of its location.

De Seversky's major work, written in 1950, did not anticipate that several powers might achieve the capabilities of mutual destruction. He felt that the strongest air fleet would be able to knock out its opponent's air fleet and thus achieve complete mastery of the world.[33] Today, we know that we may face a situation of mutual destruction in an all-out nuclear conflict, or of limited destruction in limited wars. However the case may be, comparative advantage of space owing to dispersal or time-distance re-emerges as a factor. While such advantage might be of small solace to the survivors of a nuclear war, it at least serves as a form of deterrent. In the case of limited wars and subversion, where air mastery in itself cannot play a decisive role unless coupled with land- and sea-based actions, comparative locational advantages certainly remain a key factor.

There are those who hold that air power has added, not a third dimension as such to land and sea movement, but simply a complementary dimension to each of these channels. Particularly if all-out warfare is eliminated, this view of what Jones calls the "air-first moderates"[34] suggests that air power can be decisive only as it lends a comparative advantage to land or sea powers.

Sir John Slessor is an exponent of air-borne nuclear weapons as "The Great Deterrent" against total war. Ruling out total war, Slessor concludes that air power's role is to supplement sea- or land-based forces. He holds that even an invasion of Western Europe could be countered by a limited type of air attack—land defense to arrest invasion without all-out nuclear war. To Slessor, whose strategic doctrine follows a Rimland-Heartland equilibrium theory, the likely arenas for limited war are the Middle East and Southeast Asia, with air power being the key supplement to sea-supported land actions.[35]

[33] In a more recent publication, *America: Too Young to Die* (New York: McGraw-Hill, 1961), de Seversky's views show little change. Thus he says: "One either controls the entire air ocean around the globe or one controls nothing (pp. 36, 37) . . . Unless we take leave of our strategic senses we are not going to fight limited wars (p. 113) . . . The fact is that in any territories contiguous to Communist Russia or China, the Communist forces cannot be stopped by limited war. The same thing in reverse applies to Africa and other continents (here is a change from his previous 'strategic assignment' of Africa to the U.S.S.R. (p. 118) . . . it would be wise to look to the nations of Central and South America, our neighbors in this hemisphere, before we scatter largess over Asia and Africa (p. 134) . . . Our only hope is to make of our own heartland an invincible base from which we can project our offensive against any part of the world."

[34] Jones, "Global Strategic Views, *The Geo. Rev.*, p. 500.

[35] John Slessor, *The Great Deterrent* (New York: Praeger, 1957), pp. 264-85.

Mackinder's World-War-Two World

We have described the flexibility of thought that was characteristic of Mackinder in his 1904-19 period. That he continued to be aware of the implications of geographical change is even more apparent from an article written by him in 1943, in which he both reassessed the nature of the Heartland and reviewed his global views. It is ironic that much of what has been written about Halford Mackinder's views pays scant heed to his last published work.

At that time, at the age of 83, Mackinder wrote an article entitled, "The Round World and the Winning of the Peace." [36] In this article he consigned to the ashes his famous 1919 dictum about rule of the Heartland meaning command of World-Island. Mackinder drew no map to accompany his article. Therefore, a map which cartographically expresses what Mackinder wrote is presented here, as well as one which shows the new boundary of Heartland. (See Map 5.) First, Lenaland (the Central Siberian Tableland) is detached from the Heartland. Thus, Heartland now consists largely of the cleared forest and steppe portions of Eurasia. More important, Mackinder's concept of the map of the world had changed. He now spoke of a North Atlantic unit (the Midland Ocean) as being as significant as the Heartland—its transpolar counterpart. He also referred to Monsoonal Asia and the South Atlantic Basin as important units of the future. A fifth unit, described as a "Mantle of Vacancies," is the barrier zone that separates the Heartland and the Midland Ocean units from the others.

The changing yardsticks that Mackinder used in drawing the boundaries for Heartland indicate that the original concept of the pivot area of the world had changed from that of an arena of movement (i.e., as a region of mobility for land forces) to one of a "power citadel," based upon people, resources, and interior lines. The three boundaries (see Map 6) that reflect his changing views of the earth indicate that he was well aware of technological developments including air power.

[36] Halford J. Mackinder, "The Round World and the Winning of the Peace," *Foreign Affairs*, XXI, No. 4 (July 1943).

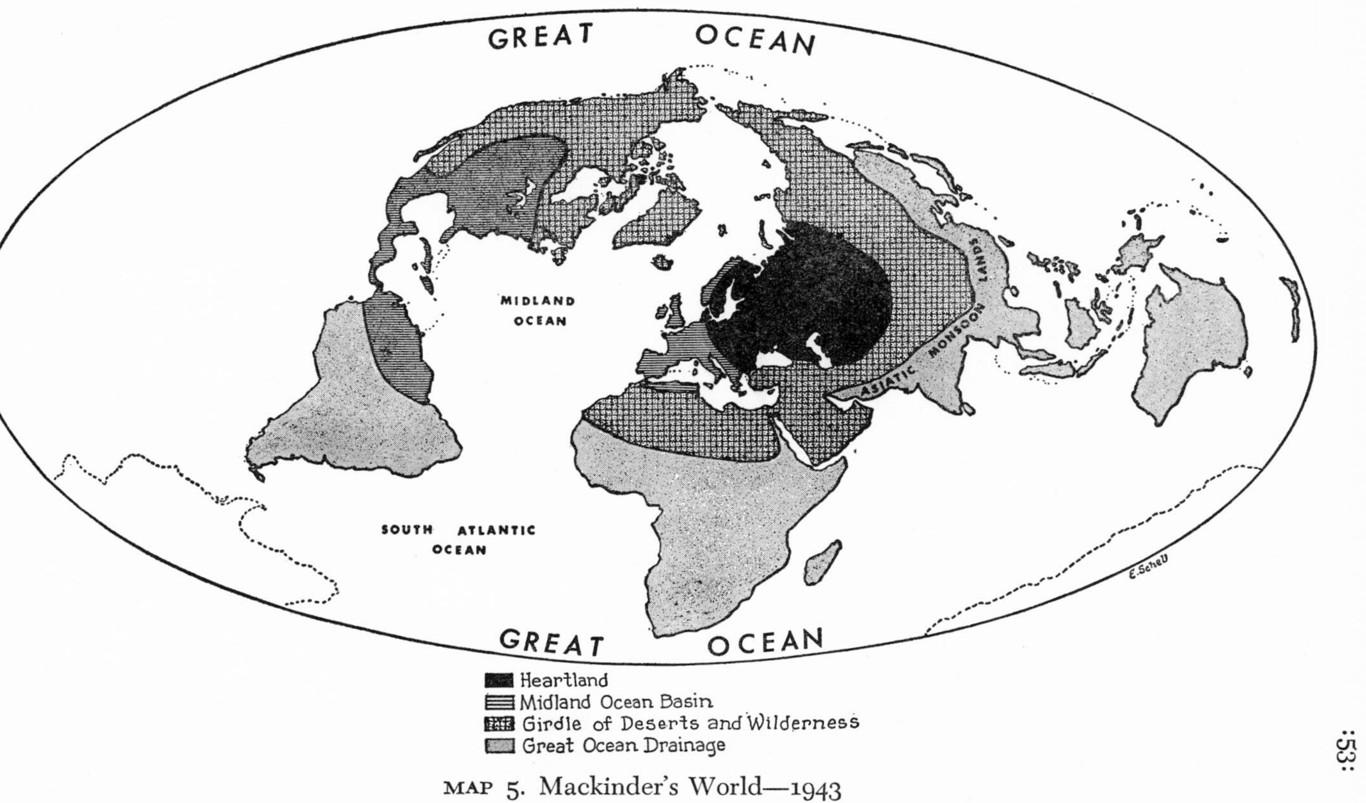

MAP 5. Mackinder's World—1943

It is futile to debate the merits of Mackinder's views today unless we take into account the changes he himself made during his lifetime. There are, of course, certain weaknesses in the Heartland theory. One is that Heartland's centrality is not necessarily an advantage, because of the concentration of targets in the event of air attack from peripheral lands. Another fact, unforeseen up to World War Two's end, is that the Soviet Union is today far better equipped to control Eastern Europe's tidal lands than is Germany. Thus, while we might rephrase part of the 1919 dictum to state that who rules the Heartland commands Eastern Europe, it is now clear that rule of the Heartland (and Eastern Europe) does not mean automatic command over Maritime Europe or other parts of the Rimland.

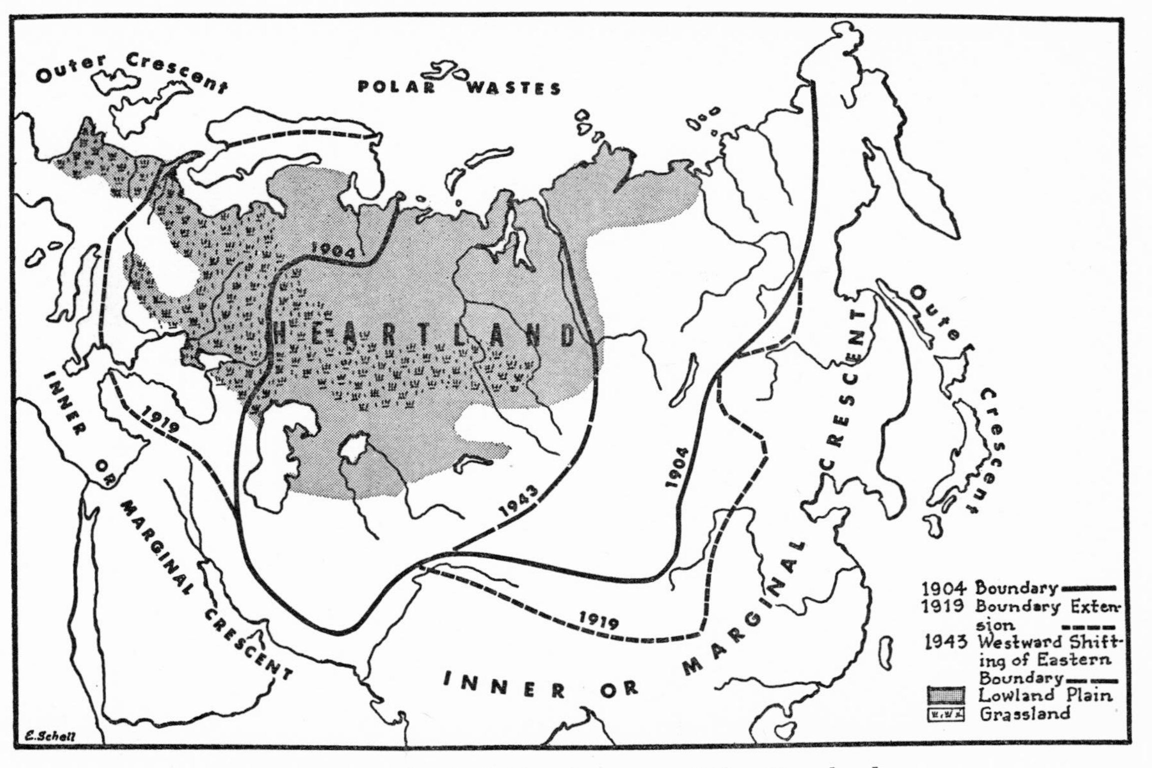

MAP 6. Mackinder's Development of the Heartland

·3·

GEOSTRATEGIC AND GEOPOLITICAL REGIONS

Alignments for Our Age

In the global strategic views that have been outlined, emphasis has been placed upon the strategic unity of space, organized through a single arena of movement. Unity of the land-mass through the channel of railroads and highways is the basis of the Heartland concept. Unity of the sea through the channel of ships is the basis of the Rimland and North Atlantic Basin concepts. Unity of the air through bombers and missiles is the basis of the North Polar concept, and of the concept that brushes aside the variable significance of land and sea masses to say that the dominant airpower can command the world, regardless of the location of that power's land base.

A basic premise of these global strategic concepts is that the unity of one arena of movement is indivisible—that the dominant fleet can rule the entirety of the open seas; the dominant land army can rule all of the land space; the dominant airpower can rule all of the air.

But today's realities suggest otherwise. Unity of arenas of movement cannot be complete, and power within such avenues is therefore divisible. This is because complete dominance of one avenue of movement cannot be attained unless one power completely destroys another through nuclear warfare. Sea-controlling powers cannot prevent the landpower from building up its air and sea forces and continuously attacking the sea lanes via the medium of aircraft, missiles, and nuclear-powered submarines. A landpower cannot be impervious to attack from the sea, because of the striking capability that seapowers can exercise through aircraft, missiles, air-borne troops, and submarines. The basic advantages that these arenas offer to their prime users are, therefore, coming more and more to be shared by the secondary users. For example, sea lanes are not fixed and are thus more difficult to block. However, the seas are open and enable opposing nuclear-powered submarines to position themselves anywhere with increasing ease as range, depth, and time cease to limit submarine operations. Or, land lanes lie within territorial boundaries and are thus somewhat screened by distance from prying, hostile eyes. However, the fact that land lanes are far less variable than sea routes exposes them to the increasing accuracy of long range "zeroing-in" devices, as intelligence techniques make it possible to pinpoint the location of these land lanes.

Many in the Free World regard the sea as the most important arena of movement because it binds our global components. They seek to attain total control of the sea through control of key land bases. However, it is fallacious to think of the indivisibility of the seas, and to continue to assume that it is absolutely vital that the Soviet landpower be denied contact with any part of the open sea. The U.S.S.R. does not need a foothold on the open sea to threaten Free World sea lanes. This it is doing with missiles and submarines. Containing the U.S.S.R. in a spatial sense—trying to prevent Soviet influence from breaking into parts of the Rimland—does not safeguard our sea lanes. Soviet use of bases on the Caribbean, Mediterranean, Red, or China Seas do not create new threats to our global security; they only intensify the basic threat. Whether or not the U.S.S.R. is denied further access to the Rimland, the shores of the United States will not be safe against Soviet nuclear submarine-based missiles.

In their uncritical acceptance of Heartland-Rimland views of the world, many American policy-makers have tried to maintain the *status quo* throughout the Eurasian Rimland, and drawn rigid political and economic battlelines everywhere, regardless of the specific territory, government, or people involved. In so doing they tend to accept obligations to compete everywhere and anywhere with the landpower, no matter how unfavorable the terms.

The Free World has become the victim of a myth—the myth of the inherent unity of World-Island, given the unity of Heartland in combination with part of the Rimland. An adjunct of the myth is that the sea-based powers cannot maintain their position unless complete command over all parts of the Eurasian littoral is maintained. This is the myth that stems from Mackinder's earlier writings and Spykman's rejoinders. It is especially ironic that so little attention was paid to Mackinder in 1943, when he suggested that the maritime world was ultimately divisible into three units.

This is not to question the thesis that control of the World-Island by one power would ultimately spell world control, but rather the assumption that the Free World cannot stand unless it rigidly contains the U.S.S.R. from spilling onto the Eurasian littoral—that if parts of this littoral are hostile or neutral, our over-all position as an alliance of nations that are interconnected by the sea is untenable. We question the assumed need to try to contain Communist power at every point on the fringe of Eurasia, regardless of whether or not such a containment is militarily or ideologically tenable. Above all, we question the concept that suggests it is strategically necessary to treat *all* of the ocean-rimming lands as part of one global strategic region, granted that the Free World must be in a position to maintain sea communications as effectively as possible.

We consider ourselves to be the Maritime World, and rightly so. Our difficulties stem, however, from a false image of the Maritime World. A maritime-oriented state must have more than a coastal location. It must have useful ports and harbors, access to the hinterland, sea-mindedness, and an economic structure that depends upon international trade, either because of the advantages of product specialization or because of the absence of a broad base for relative self-sufficiency. A maritime-oriented global strategic region can be globe-embracing without having to include all ocean-fronting countries and regions. It need include part, but not all, of the classical Rimland. Recognition of this would enable the Free World to choose its allies with more discrimination, to avoid international blackmail, and to select bases for their ideological as well as purely territorial significance.

Those who have accepted the Heartland-Rimland thesis have also accepted the "falling-domino" game as applied to the Rimland. They have driven themselves into a frenzy of effort to plug all possible leaks in the Rimland dike, regardless of the risks involved in making commitments or the chances of success.

Let us illustrate this uncritical acceptance of the myth. The following report appeared in *The Stars and Stripes,* Friday, August 19, 1960, datelined Tokyo—UPI:

> Although Laos is not strategically important for its manpower or natural resources, it shares a 620-mile border with Red China and Communist North Vietnam. Loss of Laos to the Bamboo Curtain bloc would "pull the plug" so to speak, opening Communist floodgates to Southeast Asia.

We should not dismiss this piece of prose as mere reporting for our foreign policy has guided itself along such lines. We were told that Southeast Asia would fall if France lost Indochina. We were told that Laos was necessary to safeguard Thailand, Cambodia, and Vietnam. But actually, Laos could have remained firmly in the Western camp and neutralist Cambodia could swing over to China—or a *coup d'état* in Thailand could change that country's foreign policy. Vietnam's fate depends essentially on its struggle with North Vietnam, and only secondarily on events in Laos. Indonesia came close to swinging into the Communist orbit in 1957 irrespective of events on the Southeast Asian mainland. And Malaya, the most important Free World link in Southeast Asia, ideologically as well as strategically and economically, will remain with us to the degree that its government succeeds in strengthening its central authority, improving living standards, and unifying its people. Having Thailand and Laos as screens between Malaya and China is a secondary consideration.

The same holds true for our ventures in the Middle East. We were told that Iraq was the cornerstone of METO because it was the land link (and basically the sea link) between Turkey and

Iran. We invoked the Eisenhower Doctrine to keep a pro-Western government from being toppled in Lebanon. In both cases our efforts were in vain, Iraq now holding a hostilely neutral and Lebanon a quietly neutral position towards the West. We were told, during the critical period of intervention in Lebanon, that King Hussein of Jordan would have to be kept in power at all costs, lest the West be driven from the Middle East. Consequently British support was tendered the monarch. More recently, to protect Kuwait against threatened Iraqi annexation, British troops entered that principality. But direct intervention to favor pro-Western Arab leadership elements does not guarantee the maintenance of lasting ties with the Western world. Jordan can easily veer toward Syria, or some day to Iraq, and British troops were quickly withdrawn from Kuwait in the face of Arab League pressure.

Does this mean that it is not important to maintain Western footholds in the Middle East or in other critical regions? Clearly not. However, it is entirely possible to maintain such footholds without having blanket control of the region. At present, the keys to our Middle Eastern position are Turkey, Iran, and Israel. Events in the Arab world need not and usually do not affect our ability to work out accommodations with these non-Arab states.

Regions

Geographers recognize two forms of subdivision, or regions. One is a single-feature region; the other is a multi-featured, or composite, region. The single-feature region may be an agricultural region, like the Commercial Crop and Livestock of the United States or Amazonia's Shifting Cultivation region. It may be a climatic, or a physiographic, or a trading region. The multi-featured region is what geographers call the geographical region, or the *compage*.

The geographical region is the organization of space, based on both quantitative and qualitative criteria, and expressing associations of various elements. Non-geographers tend to think of such areal units as "total" regions which, while difficult to define in apprehensible terms, are nevertheless objectively real. The geographer rejects the "total" region. He considers the region to be merely a device for separating areal features. It is "a community of physical, biotic, and societal features that depict, or are functionally associated with man's occupance of an area." [1] To constitute such a geographic region there must be sufficient heterogeneous elements present capable of blending into a unity, but this unity does not achieve totality.

The geographical region may be a more clear-cut example, but no region, including the single-feature one, is finite, so regional boundaries can scarcely lay claim to universal acceptance. Thus Hartshorne has said, "Any regional division is not a true picture of reality, but it is an arbitrary device of the student . . . depending on what elements appear to him as most significant." [2]

It is easier to define single-feature regions. Among these, the political region can lay claim to being the most tangible and to having its roots in "reality." Political divisions, either by states, or by groups of associated states, are clear-cut. Their boundaries can frequently be seen on the ground, or at least they are mapped with precision. Moreover, these boundaries act as walls behind which differences within the national state or the association of states can be blurred or eliminated, and beyond which differences with other states or groups of states can be accentuated.

But how tangible or close to reality is the political region if we compare the world political map of 1939 with that of 1962? Those who recall the school texts of the 1930's can scarcely forget the spread of the British and French Empires over approximately 35 per cent of the earth's surface. The political divisions

[1] "The region that is defined in terms of the entire content of the human occupance of the area, is an association of interrelated natural and societal features chosen from a still more complex totality because they are believed relevant to geographic study." Whittlesey terms this the "compage." Compages differ, in size or rank, from the small locality (like the Damascus oasis) which can be represented on a map on a scale of one inch to the mile, to the large realm (like the Middle East) which can be presented on a scale of one inch to 80 miles. From "The Regional Concept and the Regional Method," by Derwent S. Whittlesey, Chapter 2 of *American Geography—Inventory and Prospect,* P. E. James and C. F. Jones, pp. 19-70.

[2] Richard Hartshorne, *The Nature of Geography* (Lancaster, Pa.: Association of American Geographers, 1939), p. 285.

were real—yet they have proved ephemeral. This is indeed the difficulty with political regions. They are real and tangible for the moment, but if they lack firm groundings in broader political, social, economic, and physical "realities," then they are fleeting.

It is to geography that we turn for a true appreciation of political realities. The geographical setting, both that which is fixed and that which is dynamic, provides us with a basis for understanding today's political map and for anticipating change. Therefore the geopolitical map is more closely attuned to reality than is the political map.

Geostrategic and Geopolitical Regions

A framework for geopolitical analysis should distinguish between divisions that have global extent, and those that have regional extent. For this purpose, we shall employ the terms *geostrategic regions* and *geopolitical regions.*

The geostrategic region must be large enough to possess certain globe-influencing characteristics and functions, because today's strategy can only be expressed in global terms. The geostrategic region is the expression of the interrelationship of a large part of the world in terms of location, movement, trade orientation, and cultural or ideological bonds. While it is a single-feature region in the sense that its purpose is to embrace areas over which power can be applied, it is a multi-feature region in its composition. Control of strategic passageways on land and sea is frequently crucial to the unity of geostrategic regions.

The geopolitical region is a subdivision of the above. It expresses the unity of geographic features. Because it is derived directly from geographic regions, this unit can provide a framework for common political and economic actions. Contiguity of location and complementarity of resources are particularly distinguishing marks of the geopolitical region. Geopolitical regions are the basis for the emergence of multiple power nodes within a geostrategic region, as exemplified by the emergence of Mainland China as a second power center in the Communist world. Put another way, the geostrategic region has a strategic role to play and the geopolitical region has a tactical one.

It is important to keep clear the distinction between geostrate-

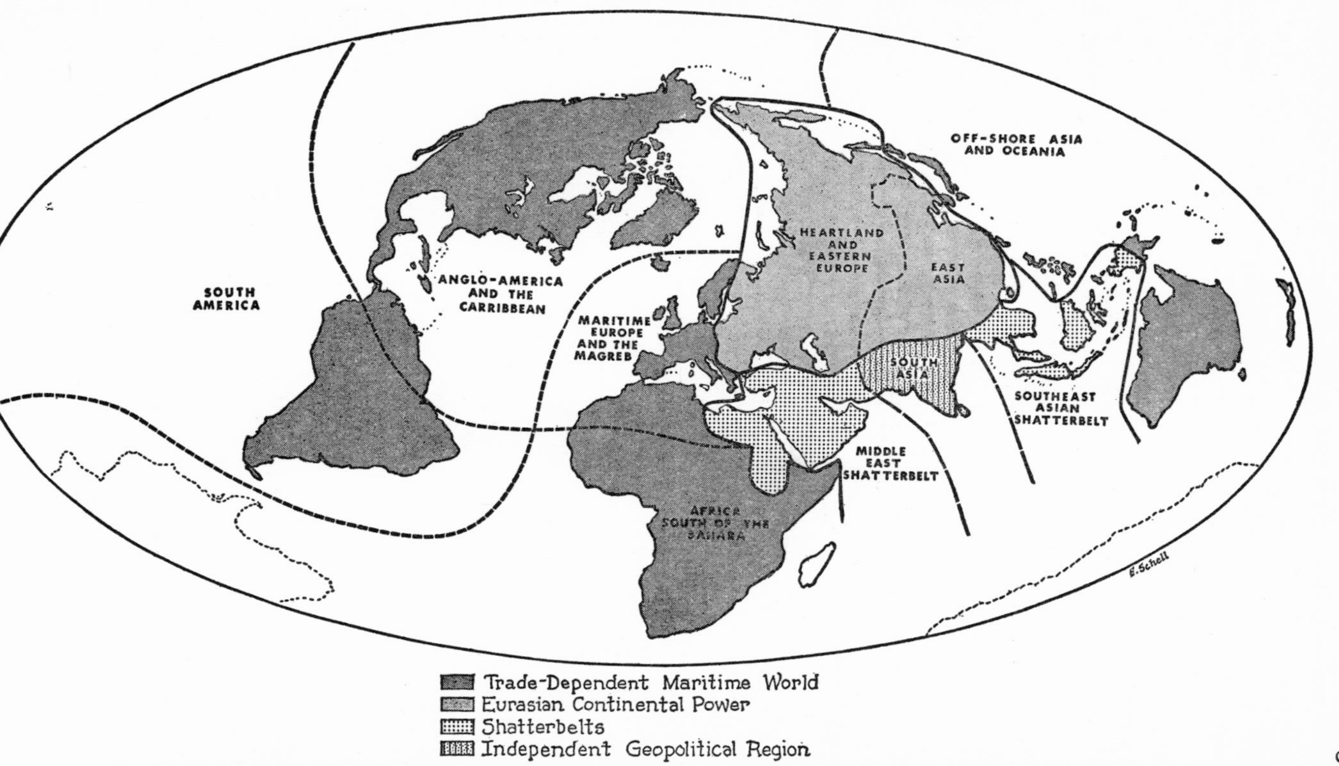

MAP 7. The World's Geostrategic Regions and Their Geopolitical Subdivisions

gic and geopolitical units. Confusing their characteristics and functions may result in an overestimation of the capacity of geostrategic regions for political and economic unity, or in an underestimation of the capacity for unity within geopolitical regions. The attempt to convert the global Free World military alliances into a tightly knit political and economic unit, or the assumption that the political differences between Maritime Europe and the Maghreb, where basic geographic unity exists, cannot be reconciled, are examples resulting from such confusion.

The emerging concepts of geostrategic and geopolitical regions were a product of the rise of Europe's colonial empires and the drives to acquire key islands and coastal enclaves as a means of uniting ocean basins. The strategy of building the Portuguese, Spanish, French, Dutch, and British Empires, of carving out spheres of influence in the "exploitable" world, began to take on global or geostrategic connotations. And drives to expand the frontiers of the United States and Russia or to gain unified control over Maritime Europe and the Mediterranean sought to fulfill goals of political unity within and among geographical regions, and therefore took on geopolitical overtones.

Our scheme for the geostrategic partitioning of the earth rests essentially upon the yardsticks of *place* and *movement*. Place includes the location of regional population and economic cores and great barrier zones; movement includes trade orientation and ideological-cultural bonds.

There are, strictly speaking, only two geostrategic regions today: 1) The Trade-Dependent Maritime World, and 2) The Eurasian Continental World. Projecting our views into the future, we anticipate the eventual emergence of a third geostrategic region—the Indian Ocean Plateau realm. Such a region, likely to arise from the ashes of the British Commonwealth and other formerly European colonial areas, may not possess all of the qualifications for playing a truly global power role. Yet this former colonial intertropical world is likely to attain second-rank geostrategic status under certain eventualities that we will discuss in a later chapter.

The core of the Trade-Dependent Maritime World is the Maritime Ring of the United States; that of the Eurasian Continental World is the Russian Industrialized Triangle. Thus both regions can be described as "nodal." Maritime Europe and Mainland China have emerged as second power nodes within these geostrategic regions.

The United States is thrusting its development energies toward its coastal rims, intensifying connections with other parts of the Maritime World. The Soviet Union's development thrust is landward, with its major direction into the Eurasian Heartland. The secondary thrust along the western and eastern frontiers is spearheaded by pipeline and railroad construction.

Geostrategic regions can be subdivided into various geopolitical regions. The Trade-Dependent Maritime World includes: a) Anglo-America and the Caribbean, b) Maritime Europe and the Maghreb, c) Offshore Asia and Oceania, and d) South America. The Eurasian Continental World includes: a) The Russian Heartland and Eastern Europe, and b) The East Asian Mainland. Between these two geostrategic regions lie Shatterbelts—the Middle East and Southeast Asia. (See Map 7.)

Unaccounted for in this scheme are Africa south of the Sahara and South Asia. South Asia does possess qualities of geopolitical unity that make it likely to be recognized, in the near future, as a unit separate from both geostrategic regions. Africa, on the other hand, shows little sign of being able to attain continental geopolitical unity. This does not mean that Africa is not important to the sphere of influence of the Trade-Dependent Maritime World, nor is it outside of it. What it does mean is that Africa south of the Sahara is not likely to find internal geopolitical unity within the framework that has been outlined. If, however, the European footholds in Central and South Africa should be lost, then the entire eastern half of the continent might gravitate geostrategically to South Asia.

Several criteria have been used to define the Trade-Dependent Maritime geostrategic region. These include: 1) orientation to the Atlantic and Pacific Ocean basins, 2) primacy of sea communications in interconnecting this region, 3) distribution of raw materials and people so as to call for regional specialization and interdependence, 4) a band of white settlement across the temperate lands of the southern hemisphere, 5) trade-dependence with the North Atlantic Basin, and 6) highest levels of technology. The major ecumene of this geostrategic region extends from the

Northeastern United States through Northwestern Europe. This may soon grow to include the Southeastern United States and Cuba. The secondary ecumene extends from Los Angeles-San Francisco through Southern Japan. This is in the process of being extended to Taiwan and the Central Philippines. Although sea lanes tie these two ecumenes together, it is the combination of overland and coastal United States routes that directs these ties.[3]

Ideological bonds, complicated by present or recent aspects of colonialism, are not as strong within the Trade-Dependent Maritime World as they are within the Eurasian Continental Communist World. In part, these bonds will be strengthened as the "have" parts of the Maritime World share more of their wealth with the "have-nots." To help to describe this Trade-Dependent Maritime World, the dependence of nations upon sea trade has been mapped according to the ratio of imports to national income. This map (See Map 8.) reflects a variety of factors, such as limitations of land bases, underdevelopment or absence of resources for manufacturing, colonialism, and alliances.

If we look at the world as seen on Map 8, we note that certain parts of the so-called Maritime World are far less dependent upon sea lanes than other parts. What we see are groupings of trade-oriented "islands," which we have called *Ocean Trade-Dependent.* A second grouping is trade-oriented, but to a lesser extent. This we have called *Ocean Trade-Oriented.* Lastly, we have the *Inwardly Oriented* countries, mostly within the northern hemisphere. The economic and the strategic interests of these groupings vary, but the trade "islands," above all, must be free to trade with one another and with the rest of the world. The global nature of the American commitment is readily apparent from this map. As long as its important allies are so heavily dependent upon overseas trade, the United States has to help them maintain their sea contacts. When this map is related to global location, contiguity, unity of arenas of movement, strategic

[3] *Ecumene* is used to describe the area of densest population in coincidence with rail, highway, ship or air networks or any combination of these. Variability and low costs for sea lanes and variability and speed for air lanes make it unnecessary for the ecumene to require the contiguity on sea that it must show on land.

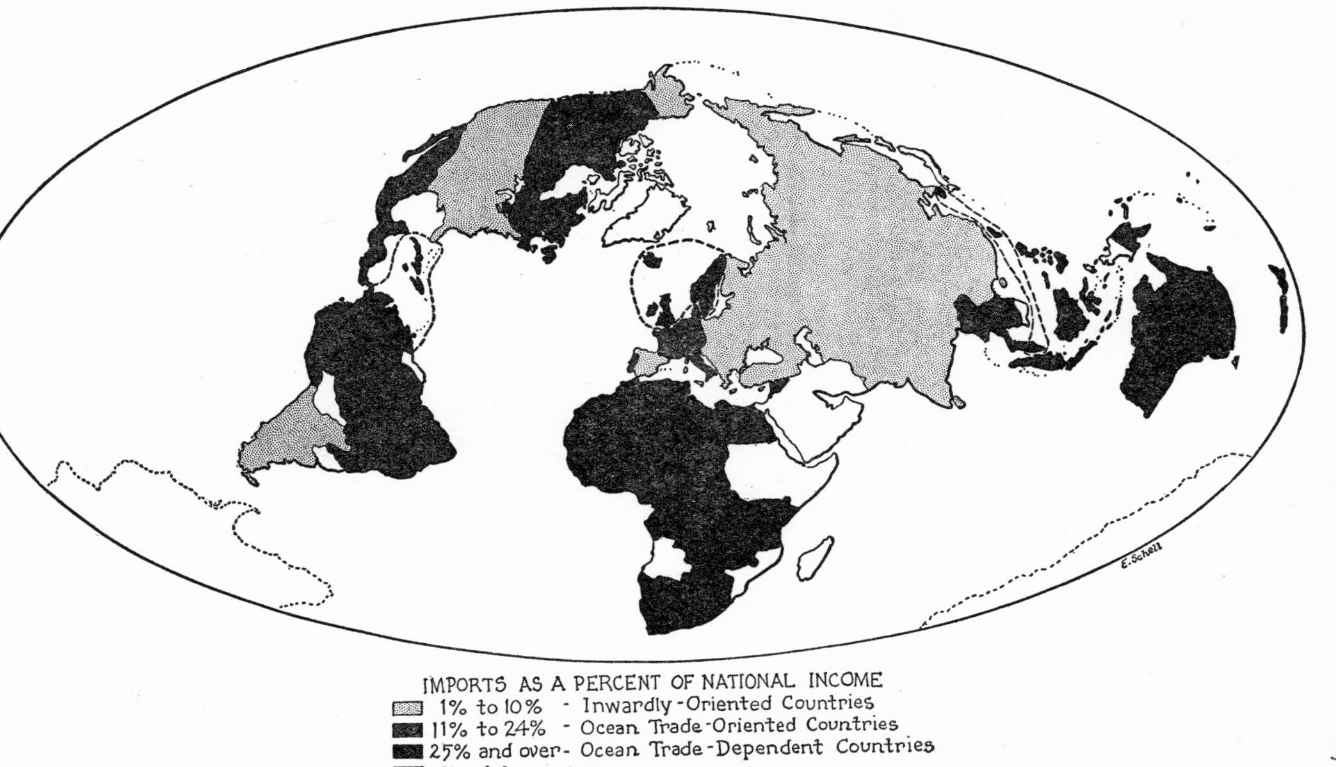

MAP 8. Geopolitics and Trade

raw material trade, population distribution, and ideology, we arrive at the Trade-Dependent Maritime geostrategic region.

The major ecumene of the Trade-Dependent Maritime Region consists of the Northeastern United States and Western Europe. This ecumene's components in Anglo-America and Maritime Europe are the cores of the two most richly endowed and strongest geopolitical regions within the Free World. Co-ordinated action between these two geopolitical units is imperative if the strategic unity of the Maritime World is to be maintained. Such action must be on a global scale, because the Maritime World's extent is global.

While warning Europeans against taking us for granted, we Americans tend to take our European partners for granted. However, in most important European countries there exist strong forces that favor neutrality and Cold War disengagement. These forces, in combination with active Communist party cadres in Italy, France, and Greece, make it imperative for us to recognize that partnership must walk a two-way street.

Much of Maritime Europe's disenchantment with American leadership stems from Washington's stand on the Suez Canal crisis of 1956, which effectively destroyed the Anglo-French position in the Middle East without offering adequate substitutes. Subsequently, such issues as the mishandling of the U-2 incident, the inability to formulate an effective NATO nuclear weapons policy, the *volte-faces* with respect to Laotian policy, the ineffectual stand on India's take-over of Goa, and the American-influenced solution to the West New Guinea dispute have shaken many Europeans' confidence in their transatlantic partner. The merits of the specific issues are less important than the background to their emergence. In most cases, United States action has been taken without consultation with European nations or consideration of their sensitivities and needs. One can cite many examples of the failure of Western European countries to foresee the handwriting on their colonial walls or, in their turn, to consult frankly and freely with the United States. But leadership of the Atlantic Alliance demands from us more than simply petulant reactions or playing to the galleries of world opinion. Our errors of omission are as serious as our errors of commission. The responsibility of leadership bears with it the responsibility for consultation with our partners.

The most significant geopolitical action taken by the United States since the Second World War was to take the initiative in supporting European economic recovery and in forging the North Atlantic Treaty Organization. If we should fail to follow up these accomplishments and lose our position as senior partner of the Atlantic Alliance, the Free World will become hopelessly divided through the shattering of its geostrategic framework. Moscow's road to victory lies, in the last analysis, not through Belgrade, Tirana, Saigon, or Delhi, but through Paris, London, Bonn, Rome, and, in the Pacific, through Tokyo.

To speak of the Eurasian Continental World as including Mainland East Asia may appear to some readers to be an overweighting of ideology—Communism—as the criterion. Mackinder felt that the belt of deserts and mountains separating China from the Soviet Union would be a sufficient barrier to separate the Heartland from what he called Monsoonal Asia. And some contemporary observers, like George Kennan, hold that: "If time was against him [Stalin] in 1927, so was space. He faced the fact that he was 5,000 miles from the scene of action, and a foreigner, whereas Chiang and Mao were Chinese, and were right there . . . there are geographic limits to the possibilities of military expansion"[4] (again with reference to Soviet relations with China). Kennan believes that the Sino-Soviet alliance is destined to break apart because of the cultural, racial, and physical differences that divide the two powers.

We may not be able to prove or to disprove the thesis that the gulf between a Westernized, Christianized Russia and Oriental China is too great to be bridged by Marxism. But we can challenge the thesis that China and the Soviet Union are too far part to be able to operate within a unified geostrategic framework. While the distance from Canton to Riga is about 5,000 air miles, and that from Shanghai to Moscow is about 3,700 miles, the gap between Lanchow, China's "Chicago of the West," and Alma Ata, Kazakhstan's scientific university center, is only 1,500 miles.

[4] George F. Kennan, *Russia and the West under Lenin and Stalin* (Boston: Little, Brown, 1960), p. 276.

Paotou, the new steel city of North China, is but 900 miles from Irkutsk.

Admittedly, there are vast empty areas between the two states. Semipalatinsk, a site of Soviet nuclear testing, lies exactly midway between Peiping and Moscow and is surrounded by empty reaches. However, the true test of proximity in space is the distance that separates the two national ecumenes and the channels of movement that bind them together. Novosibirsk, a city of nearly one million people, and now the eastern edge of the Soviet ecumene, is 1,800 miles from Peiping, the focus of the North-Northeast Chinese ecumene. Moreover, Sinkiang, China's "New Frontier" of the Northwest for mineral and industrial development, adjoins one of the Soviet "New Frontiers," Kazakhstan.

Deep ideological rifts, such as those over Stalinism, coexistence, and the communes, exist between the Soviet Union and China. Moreover, China has begun to challenge the position of preeminence hitherto held by the U.S.S.R. within the Communist bloc. The Chinese first issued this challenge in striving for regional hegemony over North Korean and Viet Minh Communist affairs. Then they broadened this challenge through support of Albania and a show of diplomatic strength in such countries as Cuba and Egypt. What is probably involved is not a permanent splitting of the Communist World, but rather the emergence of multiple power cores within it. Such a course is to be expected within any geostrategic region, because of the cohesion and uniqueness of its geopolitical subdivisions. As serious as Sino-Soviet divergencies are, they are no greater than, and in many ways resemble quite closely, the divisions that exist among the geopolitical regions of the Maritime World.

In viewing the ties of the East Asia Mainland geopolitical region to that of the Soviet Heartland-East European region, we can draw some useful parallels from the relations between two comparable units—Maritime Europe and the Maghreb, and Anglo-America and the Caribbean Basin.

First, the gap between the respective ecumenes is not substantially different. About 2,000 miles separate the Chinese and Soviet ecumenes, and 3,000 miles are needed to span the North Atlantic. In time-distance terms, the overland gap is shorter (three to four days as compared with five to six days). On the other hand, if we weight time-distance by cost of freight movement, we find that the advantage shifts to the North Atlantic sailing route and that, economically, the ecumenes that are the termini of this route are closer together. Sea routes also exist as links between China and the U.S.S.R. However, these (the 6,000-mile Northern Sea route and the 9,000-mile Indian Ocean route) are longer, slower, and less reliable, and should not enter this process of comparison.

Second, the mutual relations of these geopolitical regions are comparable in terms of size, population, and gross national product. Omitting from consideration all North American lands north of the Arctic Circle, we find the following:

TABLE 3

Selected Data—Major Geopolitical Regions

Geopolitical Region	Land Area (Sq. Mi.)	Population	Annual Gross National Product
East Asia Mainland	3,750,000	650,000,000	$35,000,000,000
Soviet Heartland and Eastern Europe	9,000,000	325,000,000	$190,000,000,000
Maritime Europe and the Maghreb	2,500,000	325,000,000	$215,000,000,000
Anglo-America and the Caribbean	8,000,000	260,000,000	$430,000,000,000

The land area ratios are quite similar: 1 to 2.5 for China and its neighboring Heartland unit, and 1 to 3 for Maritime Europe and Anglo-America. The population ratios are somewhat wider apart, 2 to 1 and 1¼ to 1 respectively, but maintain the same order. Gross national product ratios, again in the same order, show a wider disparity, 1 to 5 as against 1 to 2. However, if we give combined weight to population and gross national product, we find China's ratio to the Soviet Heartland to be 1 to 2.5, while Maritime Europe's ratio to Anglo-America is 1 to 1.6.

Third, just as the North Atlantic regions have become increasingly interdependent strategically and economically, so have the two Eurasian Continental geopolitical units. Traditionally, the U.S.S.R. has feared the pressures upon its Siberian lands that might be exerted from Chinese Turkestan, Outer Mongolia, and Manchuria. In recent decades these pressures originated from Japan and more distant Pacific-held bases of the Western world. In the future, such pressures will emanate from Mainland Chinese areas that are within the strategic reach of Soviet landpower.

As Soviet agriculture and industry continue to spread into Russian Central Asia, Central Siberia, and the Far Eastern provinces, the U.S.S.R. will surely become more vulnerable to Chinese pressures. At the same time, the greater Soviet stake in Asia and increased Siberian self-sufficiency will both force and enable the U.S.S.R. to find a modus vivendi with its neighbor. Extension of the Chinese frontier northeastward (Manchuria) and northwestward (Chinese Mongolia and Sinkiang) is likely to have the same effect upon Chinese relations with the Soviet Union. The result, in our opinion, will lead to greater interdependence between the two, from the conditions of mutual vulnerability.

China has always had two faces—the Continental North and the Monsoonal South. It is our belief that Chinese industrial progress and agricultural developments will give primacy to the continental face. Therefore, in our geopolitical scheme, we have departed from Mackinder and Spykman, who considered China to be one of Eurasia's marginal regions—a monsoonal land, turned towards the Pacific, open to sea power and permitting the exercise of sea power from it.

In our opinion, China's ocean frontage is not first-class.[5] Without control of Offshore Asia, China will not be able to live apart from, let alone dominate, the Eurasian Heartland. And Offshore Asia, the combination of a populous string of island-nations and Australasia, buttressed by the North American landmass to the

[5] Fairgrieve, on this point, observed: "the position of China fronting the open ocean, on the road to nowhere by sea, and the absence of any Mediterranean Sea, are great, silent, negative controls which have . . . tended to confirm the Chinese . . . as landsmen, and to prevent them from becoming seamen." *Geography and World Power,* p. 242. A similar view of China as a Heartland-orientated power is presented by W. A. Douglas Jackson in his penetrating interpretation of the Russo-Chinese borderlands. *The Russo-Chinese Borderlands* (Princeton: Van Nostrand, 1962).

north, is not easy strategic game for Mainland China. On the contrary, it constitutes a region that appears to be quite capable of shaping a unique geopolitical consciousness.

Boundaries of the Geostrategic Regions

The boundaries that separate the Trade-Dependent Maritime and the Eurasian Continental worlds next tempt our geographical appetites.

While Arctic wastes and mountains-deserts serve as broad boundary zones to the north and south, only thin lines separate the two geostrategic regions along the east-west axis. The boundary in Asia runs through the Sea of Japan, the East China Sea, and the South China Sea. It divides Mainland Asia from the great string of insular states from Japan to Maritime South Korea to Taiwan to the Philippines. Anchoring this offshore string is Alaska on the north and Australia on the south.

That such a boundary can be claimed for Mainland and Offshore Asia is more than simply an expression of current political realities and wishful thinking for the future. Mainland China is not maritime-oriented. Its most important and most rapidly expanding industrial areas lie in North China—a region that lacks good water communications. Even in South China, where fine ports are to be found, these ports are blocked from the interior by jumbled masses of hills and mountains. Moreover, South China's industrial potential is more limited than North China's.

On the other hand, Japan, South Korea, Taiwan, and the Philippines are part of the Trade-Dependent Maritime world. Their faces are to the sea, both in a commercial-technological sense and in a strategic sense. Japan is the core of Offshore Asia. Without Japan there can be no broad geopolitical region such as we have outlined. The fact that most of Japan's population, ports, and resources face the open Pacific and not the Sea of Japan is a further reflection of its maritime orientation. Korea, historically the buffer between continental Asia and the offshore islands, retains this function today. Its southern half serves to enclose the Yellow Sea and at the same time to bar Mainland China from Southern Japan.

Some geographers have held that Japan's location with respect to the East Asia Mainland is similar to the location of the British Isles with respect to Western Europe. If this were true, then the geopolitical relationships of each to its mainland would have to be similar. In fact, however, the parallel is a poor one. The British Isles are a single group of islands, 120,000 square miles in area, with 60 million people, and only 26 miles from the continent. They have no association with other offshore islands. In terms of culture and trade, Britain's fate is inextricably bound with that of the continent. Japan, with 142,000 square miles in area and 95 million people, is, at its closest, 210 miles from the continent and 450 miles from Mainland China. Japan has close associations with other, large offshore islands. Highly industrialized, westernized, and ocean-oriented, Japan has demonstrated in the past decade and a half an ability to turn its back economically on the mainland. Indeed, even at the height of Japan's involvement with Mainland Asia, its trade with the mainland was proportionally only half that of Britain's with Western Europe.

As we look at Japan's associates in Offshore Asia, we find a similar picture of aloofness from the mainland. Taiwan is 100 miles distant from the continent, and the Philippines, 450 miles. With their trade interconnections and their general cultural-ideological orientation, these islands are closer to one another than they are to the mainland. If we extend the region to include Australian New Guinea and Australia-Oceania, there unfolds the concept of a Western Pacific geopolitical region that has moved rapidly in the direction of interdependence, both internally and with the rest of the Trade-Dependent Maritime World.

In looking at the Western Pacific boundary between the Trade-Dependent Maritime World and the Eurasian Landpower, we see that it has become a line within a rather narrow water zone. South Korea plays a most vital role in the establishment of this line. While Dean Acheson may once have felt that "Korea is of no strategic importance to the security of the United States," events that have occurred in the last decade emphasize that the contrary is true. The security of Japan requires that South Korea remain within the Maritime sphere of influence and Japan's inclusion within the Trade-Dependent Maritime World is vital to the security of the United States. Korea is the only portion of the mainland that we have included within our Offshore Asian geopolitical region. Shannon McCune has pointed out Korea's historic and current role as contact zone between the Asian continent and seapower.[6] In modern times isolationism proved impossible for the "hermit kingdom." Japanese rule of Korea took place at a time of weakness for China and Russia. But the recent conflict has occurred at a time of balance between Sino-Soviet and Western forces. Political partition was probably the inevitable result of this stalemate. From a Korean standpoint this partition is most assuredly unhappy because the two Koreas have not found economic orientation to the Great Powers to be a substitute for prewar unity. On the other hand, the mutual needs of the major powers require either bufferdom or division, and bufferdom proved unfeasible. Under such circumstances Korea has become a pawn in the global power struggle. Extraordinary American financial aid to the South Korean economy is therefore not only strategically vital and praiseworthy from a humane point of view; it is a moral obligation that we must continue to honor. Many critics of the Korean War of 1950-53 have described this as the "wrong war at the wrong time and in the wrong place." There can be no right war. But the Korean War had to be fought where it was and when it was to affix a Western Pacific boundary to the interests of the world's two geostrategic regions. The boundary in Europe had been fixed by the disposition of victorious allied forces in the wake of World War Two, but the one in Asia was still fluid. When the Bamboo Curtain was drawn on Mainland China, the Korean War became inevitable and the resulting stalemate can be said to have met Maritime World security objectives. Under the pressures of the Korean War, both the peace treaty with Japan and the ANZUS Pact were signed. Then, in 1954, SEATO was established. Thus was Offshore Asia's role within the Trade-Dependent Maritime World geostrategically recognized in a formal sense.

Turning to the European boundary that separates these two geostrategic regions, we find ourselves confronted with a clear, hard line—the Iron Curtain. This is the boundary that divides Maritime from Continental Europe.

Mackinder was, as we have noted, the first modern geographi-

[6] Norton Ginsburg, editor, *The Pattern of Asia* (Englewood Cliffs, N.J.: Prentice-Hall, 1958), p. 130.

cal strategist to look at the world and its history from the "seaman's" and the "landsman's" points of view. In recalling the various boundaries employed by Mackinder to divide the Continental from the Maritime portions of Western Eurasia, we note three changes. In 1904, the boundary was delineated by a line running from the Caspian Sea to the White Sea. In 1919, it was shifted westward to include an area bounded by a line cutting through the Anatolian plateau, the Pindus Mountains, the Dinaric Alps, the middle Danube, central Germany, Denmark, and the Scandinavian peninsula. In 1943, Mackinder emphasized the difficulty of laying down a western boundary line. He spoke, rather, of a border zone, extending in general from the Baltic to the Black seas. Thus, in seeking a yardstick for the Heartland's western border, Mackinder finally fell back upon a broad strategic zone where Eurasian land power met European sea power supported from overseas. The delineation of a line within the zone was to be subject to revision in accordance with technological change and other developments.

The importance of this zone was not lost to the German geopoliticians who aspired to world domination. They viewed Germany's position as central, or intermediate, between Eurasian land power and Western sea power. Most, like Banse,[7] conceived of Germany as the European spearhead against the Russian landpower of the east. They preferred that Germany play this role, not through direct military conquest of the U.S.S.R., but through conquest of Eastern Europe and then through political and economic pressure upon the Soviet Union. To this way of thinking Germany's two wars in the west were "civil wars"; those in the east were considered ill-timed, but nonetheless these wars did express the fundamental clash between European civilization and the Slavic world. A contrary view that was voiced in the West during the Second World War was that German history, from the Teutonic struggle against Rome, through Luther's revolt against the Church, to Nazism, was fundamentally a revolt against Western civilization.[8] This was translated geopolitically

[7] Ewald Banse, *Germany Prepares for War,* translated by Alan Harris from the German edition of 1932 (New York: Harcourt Brace, 1941).

[8] Raoul de Roussy de Sales, *The Making of Tomorrow* (New York: Reynal & Hitchcock, 1942).

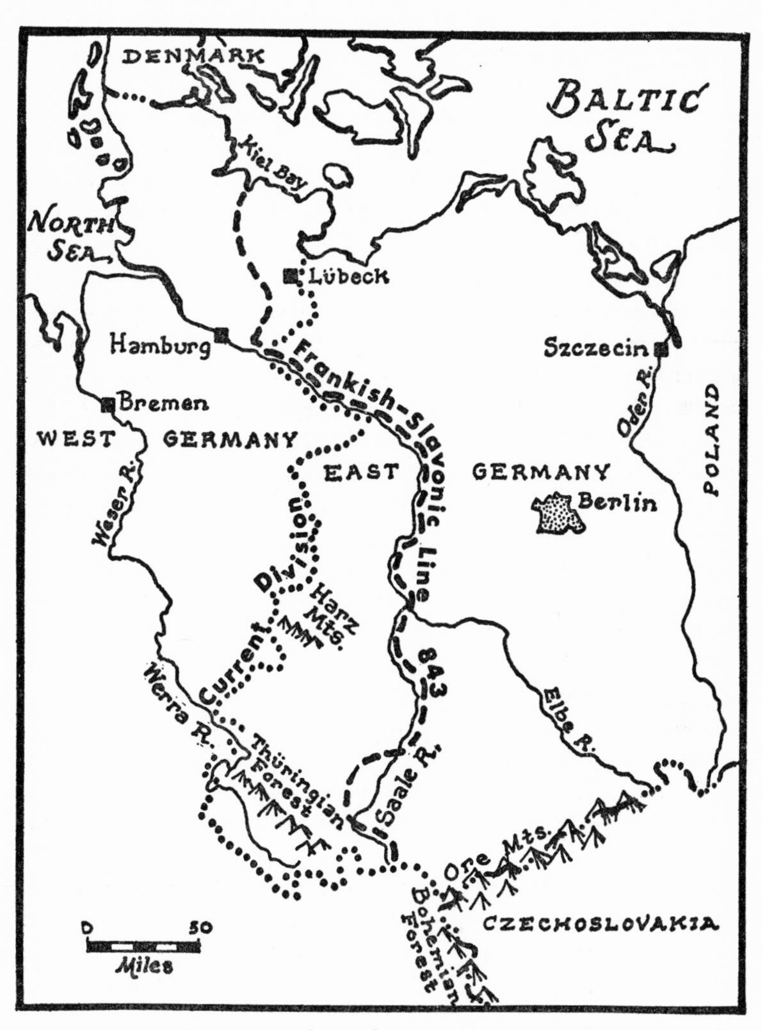

MAP 9. Ancient and Modern Divisions of Germany

into the thesis that Germany, with her historic strivings eastward, was essentially part of the Eurasian landmass. Appeasers of Hitler could see in this thesis a means of satisfying Germany's ambitions at the expense of the U.S.S.R. Opponents of Hitler who adopted this thesis saw Germany's invasion of Russia as Germany's major step towards world conquest.

Regardless of how we feel about such speculations, we can assert that Germany has been the land of geopolitical doubt. It has had two components: 1) the Industrial West, with its urban concentrations, its dependence upon European and world trade, and its physical connections with the Rhine, the North Sea, and the English Channel as outlets for its commerce; and 2) the Agricultural-Industrial East—home of the *Junkers,* the peasant farmers, Prussian militarism, and German *Kulture.* It is in the East that German aggression and dreams of world domination have traditionally flourished. The 1,100-year-old *Drang nach Osten,* and the more recent secondary pulls towards Western Europe can perhaps be said to characterize "landward" Germany. This eastern area has been the symbol of a landpower that has striven to add more and more space to its political bounds, but failed in its attempts to unite Eurasia because of its cardinal error of seeking to unify the Heartland by force while simultaneously striking out at the Western sea power area.

Germany remains the question mark of Europe. Today it is divided along the Elbe. Eastern "landward" Germany is within the landpower orbit of the U.S.S.R.; western "seaward" Germany is highly dependent upon the rest of Maritime Europe and Anglo-America.

The boundary zone that divides the East from West Germany today is one of the oldest in European history. The eastern boundary of the Germanic tribes, as affixed at the Treaty of Verdun in 843, lay along the Elbe. The boundary between the East Frankish Kingdom of Louis and the Slavonic tribes included Holstein and ran along the Elbe and Saale line to Erfurt, and from there southeastward along the Bohemian Forest. (See Map 9.) The Slavonic lands east of the Elbe were overrun by Germanic peoples in the following two centuries, and the subsequent unification of East Prussia with Brandenburg led to the eventual unification of all Germany.

The present political line between East Germany and West Germany runs from Lübeck south to the most northerly part of Bavaria, and eastward along the Ore Mountains to Czechoslovakia. This roughly follows the old Slav border line, although it includes portions of Thuringia that were never held by the Slavs.

The division of Germany into two, coming as it has with the reduction of the combined German territory by 24 per cent and the repatriation of twelve million Germans from Eastern Europe, has altered the Eurasian geopolitical map in a most fundamental manner. Prewar Germany was a balanced entity, which had a central location within Europe and possessed qualities of both a seapower and a landpower. It was, in this sense, a frontier state between the Eurasian coast and the interior. Today, the German Federal Republic is a remarkable reflection of Maritime Europe as a whole. It is the prime example of the seaward-oriented state, vying with the United Kingdom for second place in the international trade world. West Germany's manufacturing base has made unprecedented strides in the past decade in steel, chemicals, textiles, automobiles, machinery, and ships. This has been accomplished through ever increasing dependence upon foreign raw materials like fuels, fibres, and iron ore; foreign labor; and foreign markets. Population density for West Germany is 580 persons per square mile (that of Prewar Germany was 355 per square mile)—certainly an indication of the highly urbanized state of the economy. In area, population and manufacturing, West Germany and the United Kingdom are now remarkably similar.

What has changed the face of West Germany even more is that agriculture has lost ground. Prewar united Germany produced, on an average, 80 per cent of its total food needs and was as close to being a balanced industrial-agricultural state as could have been expected. Today, only about half of the lands and crops that were available to Germany's 1937 population of 70,000,000 are available to West Germany's 55,000,000 people. The varied landscape of the country—plain, plateau, and mountain—makes possible the cultivation of only about one-third of the total land area. The attendant land pressure results in smaller farms, smaller cultivated acreage to agricultural population ratios (three-quarters that of East Germany), and high dependence upon imported foodstuffs, Germany's largest import item.

The increased dependence of West Germany upon international trade is reflected in its booming ports. Hamburg, Bremen, and Lübeck have become almost completely dependent upon the North Atlantic region, which accounts for about 70 per cent of all West German foreign trade. Where once Hamburg handled a good deal of Czech as well as East German trade, it now turns mainly to the Atlantic for markets and raw materials. Bremen has lost the Central European hinterland to which it once sent cotton, rice, and jute and from which it received textiles and chemicals. Lübeck, formerly a Baltic trading *entrepôt,* has seen its eastward trade in timber, fish, coal, and cattle shrink.

West Germany is today an integral part of the Maritime World. There is little reason to suspect that the prosperity that has been won from this new-found association, as well as the political freedoms currently enjoyed, would be given up in return for unification with the East if this were the sole alternative laid before the West German people.

Meanwhile, Germany east of the Elbe has become even more inextricably part of the Continental Landpower Realm. Physically, politically, economically, and strategically East Germany has passed into the East European orbit.

While East Germany also is an urbanized, industrialized society, it is far more closely identified with the heavily agricultural East European plain than with the West European landscape. East Germany is an exporter of foodstuffs. Nearly half of the country's total land area is under cultivation, a figure that is the average for Hungary, Poland, Romania, and Czechoslovakia. With grain production at two-thirds, livestock at one-half, and cultivated land per capita at one-and-one-half times that of West Germany, the role of East German agriculture within its national economy is far more important than that of West Germany's agriculture relative to the West German economy.

Another mark of East Germany's mixed industrial-agricultural character is its population density of 390 persons per square mile. This is two-thirds the population density of West Germany. On the other hand, such a density is higher than that of the other East European countries, where agriculture has still greater prominence.

East German economic integration within the Soviet bloc began in 1949 with the formation of the Council for Mutual Economic Aid. Fully 80 per cent of its trade today is with the Soviet bloc (and only 11 per cent with West Germany). Almost all of the raw materials needed by its industry—such as rolled steel, iron ore, and oil—come from the Soviet Union. Communications, too, have been directed eastward through such devices as linking the television system to that of Poland, Czechoslovakia, and Hungary.

For our generation, at least, it would appear that the geopolitical dualism of Germany has been established. Mackinder's boundary that divided the Heartland from Maritime Europe was given political status shortly after World War Two. Within a decade and a half, ideological and economic forces have given political reality to the distinction between landpower- and seapower-orientation in Central Europe.

We feel that the current division of Germany is geopolitically sound and strategically necessary. From the standpoint of Eastern Europe and the Soviet Union, the loss of East Germany to a united, Western-oriented Germany would represent a security threat that could not be accepted and doubtless would bring on war. Not only would the U.S.S.R. be exposed once again to the Maritime World, but more important, such a step could only be brought about through the destruction of the unified Eastern European political and economic system, a system that the U.S.S.R. has shown it will maintain at the risk of war. But the other side of the coin is equally important. A unified Germany within the landpower orbit would destroy the economic and strategic being of Maritime Europe, whose current integration is dependent upon West German participation. Certainly the West would go to war to prevent this. What then of the prospects for a united "neutral" Germany? Uneasy would lie the heads of statesmen of both West and East if such a land were to re-emerge. Size, wealth, regained central position, and claims to the "lost provinces" would probably put Germany into the position of playing off both sides. To encourage ideas of a reunited, neutralized Germany would indeed be to play a game of "Russian Roulette" with all-out East-West war as the likely outcome.

Postwar German geopoliticians have not been so naïve as to

suggest that a united Germany, by itself, can act as a third power to balance the scales between East and West. They have, instead, emphasized the role that a German-led, united Europe might play as a balancer or stabilizer, to act as a brake on the United States and the Soviet Union.[9] Germany in control of Western Europe, and in a position to throw its weight with either side, would be the logical outcome of the creation of a unified, neutral state.

United, and dominating Western Europe, Germany might be able to hold the balance of power between East and West. Divided, Germany remains an important element within both the Maritime and Continental realms, without the ability to disturb the security of either realm. It is through partition that Germany can best separate the Great Powers.

What is particularly disturbing to this viewer is the espousal of German unity as formal United States foreign policy. The Communist World has, during the months of the Berlin crisis, brought the issue to the forefront. Growing sentiment for Germany's division is to be found within the non-aligned states and the Maritime European World, as well as in the Soviet Union. The United States, by adhering to a policy that is geopolitically unsound, runs the risk of political isolation and strategic "brinkmanship." Granted that our foreign policy decisions should not be made as concessions to Soviet threats, are we prepared to accept a divided Germany once the Berlin crisis eases? To date, the American record of post-crisis foreign policy soul-searching is a dismal one. We have not wanted to negotiate on the Offshore Chinese Islands during periods of Communist Chinese attacks, and rightfully so. But as the crises have died down, so has our desire to consider the problem of these islands in a cold, dispassionate light. The same holds true for our attitudes towards Berlin and German reunification. In times of crisis we cannot negotiate for fear of giving in to Soviet pressures; in times of quiet we do not feel pressed to negotiate.

To date few clear voices in this country have challenged the German reunification policy of the United States. The fact that the division of Germany is favored by the Soviet Union need not

[9] E. W. Schnitzer: *German Geopolitics Revived: A Survey of Geopolitical Writing in Germany Today,* The Rand Corporation, 1954, pp. 34-37.

mean that the West must favor unification. On the contrary, to continue to favor unification would be to fall into the gravest strategic trap of the twentieth century. For there will be no peace in Europe, and therefore in the world, unless we recognize the need to establish a clear boundary between Western sea power and Eurasian land power in Europe. Here we speak for the moment of *de facto* recognition, not *de jure*, for West Berlin must be kept free, and *de jure* recognition of East Germany by the United States is likely to make West Berlin more of a pawn in East German-West German politics. A realistic solution would be one by which both the division of Germany and the freedom of West Berlin were recognized and guaranteed by the Great Power blocs, perhaps through the mechanism of NATO and the Warsaw Pact countries.

Shatterbelts

Two Shatterbelts divide the Trade-Department Maritime from the Eurasian Continental geostrategic regions. These are the Middle East and Southeast Asia. A Shatterbelt is here defined as a large, strategically located region that is occupied by a number of conflicting states and is caught between the conflicting interests of adjoining Great Powers.

In his volume *Geography and World Power,* James Fairgrieve called attention to a "Crush Zone" of small states that had gradually come into existence between the Eurasian Heartland and the seapowers (essentially European, such as Britain, France, Portugal, Spain, and Italy, but also Japan). He spoke of these states as "largely survivals from earlier time, when political and economic organizations were on a smaller scale . . . each [with] characteristics partly acquired in that earlier time and partly natural . . . [each] with sufficient individuality to withstand absorptions, but unable or unwilling to unite with others to form any larger whole." [10]

Fairgrieve viewed these states as buffers, "precariously independent politically, and more surely dependent economically." He listed within this "Crush Zone" such states as "Finland,

[10] Fairgrieve, op. cit., p. 329.

Sweden, Norway, Denmark, Holland, Belgium, Luxemburg, Switzerland, Poland, the Balkans, Iran, Afghanistan, Siam, and Korea."[11] He conceded that in a certain sense Germany, China, and even India might be expected to belong to this belt. However, their uniqueness, Fairgrieve recognized, lay in size, resources, and historic relationship to the encircling land and sea worlds. Above all their uniqueness lay in their roles as possible centers from which the Heartland might be organized.

Much has happened to this "Crush Zone" in the military, political, and economic sense since Fairgrieve described it in 1915. In Central and Eastern Europe, the "Crush Zone" has disappeared, replaced by political and economic blocs, clearly allied with the contending geostrategic regions. Buffers like Finland, Austria, and Yugoslavia exist. However, they do not form part of a continuous zone and are in the process of strengthening economic ties with larger, neighboring units.

Reflecting the elimination of the European "Crush Zone" are World War II-inspired changes in boundary lines, political and economic consolidation of national states, integration of transportation along the North European and Danubian plains, and merging of economic core areas on a broad regional basis.

Mainland China is no longer even a possible part of the "Crush Zone" and Korea lies outside it. For Korea, as we have seen, is too small to provide elbowroom for bufferdom. Its partition serves as the line of contact btween the two geostrategic regions. But elsewhere the zone described by Fairgrieve has retained its essential character. Indeed, the post-World War Two attainment of independence by many colonial peoples has tended to strengthen fragmentation in the "Crush Zone."

As we survey politically fragmentized areas of contact between the world's seaward-oriented powers and the Soviet bloc, we find, not a continuous zone, but two distinct belts. These are the *Shatterbelts* of the Middle East and Southeast Asia. Because they command strategic narrow seas and because of their specialized agricultural and mineral products, the political and economic fate of the Shatterbelts is of vital concern to the Trade-Dependent Maritime World. Because their land avenues project towards

[11] *Ibid.*, p. 330.

important parts of the Eurasian Continental World, their fate is of equal concern to this geostrategic region.

What is peculiar to the Shatterbelt is its fragmented political and economic character. Owing to physical, environmental, historical, cultural, and political differences, the Shatterbelt appears to be incapable of attaining political and/or economic unity of action. Parts of the Shatterbelts tend to seek neutrality and to lead the entire region into this path, but other portions are committed to external ties, either because of their self-interest or because of military and economic pressures from the external power centers.

Since the Second World War, both geostrategic regions have shown that they regard retention or establishment of spheres of influence within the two Shatterbelts to be strategically vital. In various discussions of the possibilities of reducing tensions within the Middle East and Southeast Asia through restriction of armament sales, the Great Powers have not been willing to restrict sale of arms to these regions in their entirety. Each of the Great Powers has allies which it insists upon strengthening.

A locational characteristic of these belts is that they do not adjoin the core areas of opposing Great Powers. Instead, they are physically removed and are not subject to the same rigid pressures that exist between the opposing sides in Central Europe or along Asia's inner seas. On the other hand, because these Shatterbelts are easily accessible to adjoining regions, they exhibit many extra-regional cultural and economic features.

Complete control of the Shatterbelts is no longer possible for either side, nor is it theoretically desirable, since this would mean an expenditure of energies in blanket fashion over an area of variable internal significance.

Each Shatterbelt offers footholds to the contending Great Powers. Footholds perform a variety of functions. First, these footholds can serve as bases in "cold" and "hot" war situations, checkmating adjoining areas which might be used as springboards for attack. Second, they maintain the buffer qualities of the Shatterbelt, insuring that one force will not swallow it up. If, for example, the Middle East were to lose its current Shatterbelt characteristics and fall completely under Moscow domination, the arena of contention would shift directly to Africa, thereby placing Maritime Europe in mortal strategic danger. Third, the maintaining of Free World footholds within Shatterbelts clearly indicates, to Communist, neutral, and allied states alike, that we have no intention of withdrawing to positions that are so rigid and crucial as to leave no alternative but to wage nuclear wars. In other words, Shatterbelts offer the elbowroom for various forms of contention that other areas do not. Finally, footholds can better enable Great Powers to encourage "friendly" neutrals and to discourage "hostile" neutrals. But, for the Free World, these footholds would best be based upon stable alliances with internally popular governments. Otherwise, they become nothing but minority-controlled puppets and a constant source of weakness.

Conclusion

A policy of containment that views the world according to the Heartland-Rimland pattern draws us into grave strategic errors, for all parts of the Eurasian littoral are not of equal strategic significance to the Trade-Dependent Maritime World. Nor does a policy of complete disengagement from overseas areas meet the strategic needs of the United States and its major allies. We should, therefore, in our global approach distinguish between those parts of the world that: 1) warrant Free World support at the risk of total war; 2) warrant Free World support at the risk of limited wars, and therefore limited objectives; 3) warrant indirect military and diplomatic support; 4) warrant no Free World military involvement. The same applies to our economic activities in our economic war with the Soviet bloc. Only if we do this can we form alliances that will carry out the objectives of our strategy, rather than dictate our strategy.

Broadly speaking, the lands that border the Atlantic and those that overlook the open Pacific are the lands that must be rigidly protected. Within the Shatterbelt areas, the Free World has the ability to choose its allies—and should not continue to try to involve countries or peoples whose motives are basically anti-Western or whose genuine aim is to achieve a position of neutrality in the world. There is a place in this world for neutrals, particularly in South Asia, Africa, and within the Shatterbelts. But at the same time we regard as critical the need to maintain Free World footholds within the Shatterbelts and Africa. In North Africa, in the Middle East, in Africa south of the Sahara, and in Southeast Asia stable and long-lasting links must be forged with like-minded and interested nations. We cannot regard as suitable partners areas of limited space—such as small offshore islands, weak enclaves surrounded by stronger powers, or countries whose populations are basically opposed to Free World alliances.

In certain instances political partitioning along ethnic (or national) lines may be unavoidable if Free World links are to be assured. In this vein, racial separation along territorial lines and the setting up of independent White and African national states, rather than the apartheid policy, which seeks communal partition at the expense of the Africans, might offer the most realistic long-range solution in South Africa. Plans to partition Palestine and India were regarded by many as naïve and impractical, but they have been carried out and are, at a minimum, short-term solutions to "insoluble" problems.

Implicit in these observations is the fact that all geographic areas need not and should not be treated as strategic "wholes." In this respect, it is unsound to issue blanket invitations to countries of certain areas to enter defense pacts, or to ally ourselves with governments that are totally divorced from their people, when there is the possibility of our becoming committed to countries whose defense is not strategically vital to Free World survival.

These views are some of the results that we have obtained from relating our knowledge of geography to strategy. Since geography, in its broadest sense, is constantly changing, and since movement mirrors these changes, we dare not rely upon concepts of the past, but must be continuously on the alert to examine the changing geographic scene, and to interpret the impact of this change in the formulation of strategy. This is the approach through which we can genuinely understand geography's influences upon strategy—an influence that we may try to ignore, but that will not ignore us.

Part Two

POWER CORES IN A DIVIDED WORLD

·4·

THE UNITED STATES

Change and Interdependence

This study of the world's geostrategic regions and their geopolitical subdivisions will focus upon the cores of the three major geopolitical regions: Anglo-America and the Caribbean; Maritime Europe and the Maghreb; and the U.S.S.R. and Eastern Europe.

The first of the divided world's power cores to be discussed is the United States. This selection was not made on the premise that a volume written by an American author for an essentially American audience should begin with the home front. It was based, instead, on the fact that the United States occupies the primary and central position within the Trade-Dependent Maritime geostrategic region. Further, the United States is the world's leading power, when the combination of economic and military strength within a unified central political framework is considered. Finally, much of what is happening within the Soviet Union and Maritime Europe is based upon attempts to copy or to improve upon the American power position, and can therefore be better understood if the American geopolitical scene is first examined.

How we Americans occupy our landscape has much to do with the geopolitical role that we project for our country in world affairs. Three different orientations have characterized the changing landscape of the United States: 1) the Maritime, 2) the Continental, and 3) the Continental-Maritime. We have now entered the fourth stage: the Maritime-Continental.

The Maritime pattern prevailed from Colonial times to the War of 1812. Whether acting in concert with or in isolation from Europe, we regarded ourselves as an Atlantic-seaboard people, deriving our sustenance from and, exposed to the political fortunes of, an Atlantic coastal location.

From 1812 to the Spanish-American War we were continentally oriented. The Louisiana Purchase heralded the beginning of this era, and the results of the War of 1812 assured our Atlantic, Gulf, and Great Lakes frontiers. A few years after the war, the Red River of the North was ceded by Britain, and Florida by Spain, to complete our ownership of the coast up to Texas. For nearly a century we concerned ourselves with continental expansion and political consolidation. By 1893 Frederick Jackson Turner was able to call attention to the passing of the American frontier. Statehood had been granted to the northwest and, on the continent, only Utah, Oklahoma, New Mexico, and Arizona remained to be admitted to the Union.

Outbreak of the war with Spain in 1898 heralded the era of involvement in both the Caribbean and the Pacific, and the beginning of the Continental-Maritime period. Hawaii, Guam, the Philippines, and Puerto Rico were annexed, and extensive political and military commitments were made elsewhere in Pacific and Caribbean waters. But the intensive development of the interior continued. These were some of the internal developments that occurred between 1900 and 1920: 50,000 miles of railroad trackage were constructed; 14,500,000 immigrants were admitted to the country; total population growth was 30 million; the majority of our national parks were established; farm acreage was expanded by nearly 100 million acres; and manufacturing increased substantially in the Middle West and the Pacific Coast, partly at the expense of the Northeast. Because of factors such as these, the Continental was dominant over the Maritime orientation. The period between the two World Wars was transitional. Its end marked the beginning of our present era—the Maritime-Continental. The geopolitical consequences of this shift in orientation have fundamentally affected our lives and those of generations to come.

When we view the map of the United States today, we see, in effect, a Maritime Outer Ring and a Continental Inner Ring. The Maritime Ring faces the open water. Our ports and their dependent industries, our heavily urbanized population, our overseas political and trade involvements radiate outward from the Maritime Ring. The Continental Inner Ring, with a smaller population but with a surplus of material resources, helps both to support the Maritime Ring and to interconnect it via land lanes. Continental expansion is far from over. Growth is particularly rapid in the western parts of the Continental Interior. However, the focus of human occupance in the United States lies within the Maritime Ring.

The United States in its World Setting

The geographical setting of a state and its global outlook are interrelated. As settings change, so must these outlooks. When Arnold Guyot took a geographer's look at continental United States in 1849,[1] he regarded it as one of the three northern continental cores destined to control the world. Europe and Asia were considered as partners with North America in Guyot's three double-continent global view. Of the three cores, he felt that the United States would take the leading role because of two basic advantages over the others: 1) centrality within the northern hemispheric setting, behind a screen of ocean which possessed both isolating and interacting qualities, and 2) size and interconnectibility of the well-watered interior that was the challenge and the fulfillment of the United States.

Alfred Mahan had a different view of the geographical setting of the United States. He espoused a Maritime-Continental view, within a twofold global framework: the Western and the Oriental halves. To Mahan, the United States was an outpost of European power and civilization. Its Pacific shorelands and islands were simply extensions of the Atlantic-oriented European realm.

Half a century later, Nicholas Spykman saw the United States

[1] Guyot, *op. cit.*

in still a different setting. He divided the world into two:[2] 1) the Eurasian Rimland, and 2) the combination of Eurasian Heartland and Continental Islands. The latter, essentially, represented the circum-North Polar lands of Anglo-America, Britain, and the Soviet Union. Within this framework a Maritime United States held a central location, with sea lanes to Britain and air-sea lanes to the U.S.S.R. While bordering the Eurasian Rimland from the circum-polar northern position, the Heartland-Continental Island group also surrounded the Rimland from positions along the southern continents. From such a view, Spykman concluded that the United States should maintain Trans-Atlantic and Trans-Pacific bases within striking distance of Eurasia to control the balance of power along the Rimlands. This would have to be done in partnership with the Soviet Union and Britain, not in competition with them.

As opposed to Spykman's doctrines, Continentalist views during and after the Second World War presented a totally different case. James Malin, for example, took a "quarterspheric" approach to the world. He felt that the United States was a landmass state that should not extend its commitments across the Pacific and the Atlantic, or south of the Amazon.[3] He felt that there would be room in the postwar world for seven or more major powers (North America, Japan, China, Russia, Germany, Latin Europe, and the British Empire). Malin derived much of his inspiration from his studies of the American frontier and from his readings of de Seversky. His view was an amalgam of continentalism, northern hemispheric supremacy, and circum-North Polarism.

Following the war, George Cressey suggested that North America had become the real Heartland of the world. Cressey redefined Mackinder's Heartland as a "World Citadel." He suggested that North America, not Eurasia, contained this citadel because the core of North America was the one area in the world that possessed all the advantages of interior space, size and resources, and access to the sea.[4] Lest Cressey be regarded as a

[2] Spykman, *op. cit.*, pp. 51-61.

[3] James Malin, "Space and History," Part 2, *Agricultural History*, 18 (July 1944), pp. 107-26.

[4] George Cressey, *The Basis of Soviet Strength* (New York: McGraw-Hill, 1945), pp. 245-46.

pure Continentalist, we should add that in other writings he presents the Continental-Maritime view. He links the United States to the Atlantic, suggesting that our Trans-Pacific commitments be limited to the Northeast Pacific,[5] and states that "the permanent assets of the Atlantic powers should always exceed the limitations of continental Eurasia." [6] Earlier American geographers like Semple held similar views: "The preëminence which the Atlantic has gained will long dominate the Pacific, and geographical conditions make it doubtful whether this supremacy will pass to the larger basin." [7]

Our view of the Maritime-Continental setting of the United States does not draw any geopolitical doctrinal conclusions from the fact that the center of gravity of the country's maritime orientation faces the Atlantic. However, we must look to all of the elements that unify a state if we are to project that state's world geopolitical position. The Pacific coastlands of the United States are today fast-growing, mature components of the Union. The conferring of statehood upon Alaska and Hawaii is an act whose geopolitical consequences must not be underestimated. The United States is now a Pacific power, no less than an Atlantic power. Alaska not only neighbors Siberia; its borders are a short 1,400 miles from Hokkaido. To talk of dividing the Pacific down its middle (the 180th meridian) as the westward boundary of American power[8] makes no sense politically or strategically today. The Northwest Pacific is as important to Alaska as is the Caribbean to Florida. Events in either sea affect the security of the United States as a whole.

As we picture the Maritime United States then, it is as an Outer Ring which surrounds and dominates the Continental Interior. (See Map 10.) Specialization increases the complementary nature of the various portions of the Maritime Ring. It is this Ring that gives to the United States both a central and an interconnecting position in relation to the rest of the Trade-Depend-

[5] George Cressey, *Asia's Lands and Peoples* (New York: McGraw-Hill, 1951, rev. ed.), p. 17.

[6] George Cressey, *How Strong Is Russia* (Syracuse: Syracuse University Press, 1954), p. 133.

[7] E. Semple and C. Jones, *American History and Its Geographic Conditions* (Boston: Houghton, Mifflin, 1933), p. 422.

[8] Cressey, *Asia's Lands and Peoples*, p. 17.

end Maritime World. This geostrategic region, as outlined in Chapter 3, includes two-thirds of the earth's water and land surface and one-third of its population. The center of the region's surface area lies midway between the Hawaiian Islands and California. The center of its population (and land) area lies along the southeastern tip of the United States. Clearly, if any one part of the Maritime United States is at the center of the population and land area of the Trade-Dependent Maritime Region it is the Gulf-Atlantic coast. But without the unity of the Maritime United States, including its Pacific borderlands, the concept of American centrality within its broader geostrategic setting would become meaningless.

The Maritime Ring

America's experience with the development of the West set geographers to speculating on the relationship between Continentality and Seapower. Ratzel saw the two elements as complementary. To him and to his disciple Semple the conquest of the interior was made possible by the unifying qualities of the Mississippi drainage system, which had oceanic outlets. The vast North American Continental Interior could be viewed, not in land-oriented isolation, but in a maritime-connected framework. During this period, however, others tended to draw distinctions between the "closed space" of the coastlands and the "open space" of the expanding Continental Interior. When Turner called attention to the passing of the frontier, he wrote of the beginning of the era of "closed space" for the country as a whole. In a "closed space" era, new uses of and adjustments to the land would be necessary, both economically and politically. Malin, however, dissented, asserting that the "closed space" doctrine was related to the continental agricultural realm of the nineteenth-century United States, with little relevance to the urban industrial scene of this century.[9] He then proceeded to suggest that the Continental Interior holds the same wealth of raw materials for industry today that it held for agriculture in the past. In Malin's analysis, the "open space" of the interior can

[9] James Malin, "Mobility and History," *Agricultural History*, 17 (October 1943), p. 177.

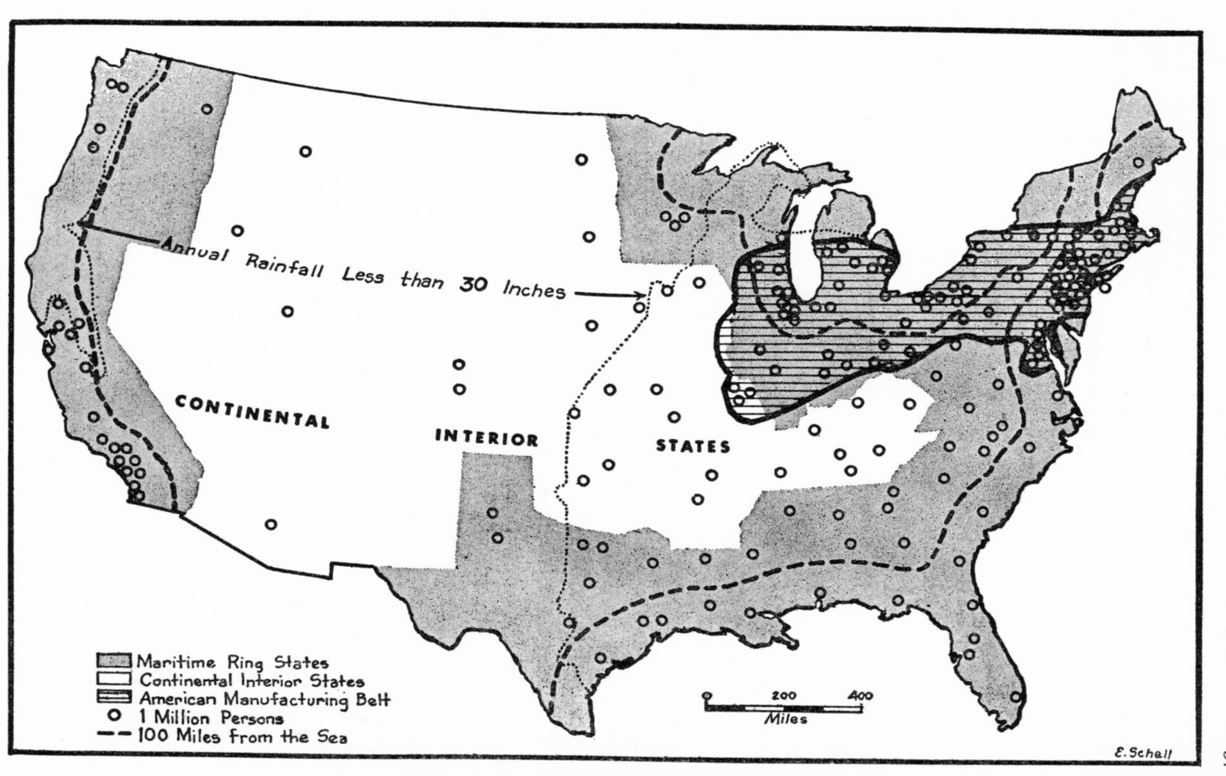

MAP 10. The Maritime Ring of the United States

still be the dominant factor in American life. He drew the picture of a central power axis running north-south from Winnipeg to Dallas-Fort Worth, with "power potential distributed along the length of the axis with the effective center shifting to fit changing requirements."[10] Writing in 1944, Malin predicted that industry would migrate into the interior and that population distribution would accompany the shift. In this scheme, population would move towards the supply of food and towards light-weight metals, alloys, plastics, and hydro-power, to find in the interior its most logical locational setting. Also, greater north-south mobility than now exists would be provided along the central axis by major air commercial centers.

Such a view of the interior is a synthesis of Continentalist-Isolation and Air Age views. Malin is not the only one to project a great future for the Great Plain states as the center of an industrialized continental interior. De Seversky placed his center of United States power in Kansas.

Events of the past decade, however, belie the claims of the prophets of continental supremacy. Those states that lie along the central axis of the interior remain lightly populated and only moderately industrialized. Their population growth pattern of the past decade has been below that of the entire country. The rate of growth for all states between the Mississippi and the Rockies was 17 per cent over the past decade and, if maritime Texas, Louisiana, and Minnesota are omitted, it was only 13 per cent. This compares with 18.5 per cent for the country as a whole. An indication of the political weakening of this Mississippi-Rockies Continental Interior is its 1960 loss of seven seats in the House of Representatives. The taking-over of the Continental Interior by large-scale, mechanized farming has been accompanied by a drop in rural population, for which population loss manufacturing has not compensated.

The unlocking of the mineral riches of the Continental Interior, the intensification of its agriculture, the populating of the great cities—in other words, the inward-turning of America—has not come to pass. Instead the coal of the Great Plains remains locked beneath the black earth, agriculture has become mechanized and increasingly extensive, market villages and towns have

[10] James Malin, "Space and History," Part 2, *op. cit.* p. 110.

lost their traditional functions, and manufacturing cities have not grown as rapidly as their Maritime Ring counterparts. The cost and difficulty of developing broad manufacturing bases from which to urbanize the Continental Interior is proving substantially greater than is the case within the Maritime Ring, and the dreams of the Continental supremacists are far from realization.

To debate whether our Continental Interior is "open" or "closed" space today seems fruitless, for these terms are no longer expressions of what is meaningful in our land use patterns. Instead, the concept of the changing use of space must be substituted. Change is occurring in areas where land is in surplus as well as scarce, for change is as evident in the rural Continental Interior as it is in the urbanized Maritime Ring. Change in the use of space results from new uses of local resources or from the movement factor that allows distant resources to be brought to the scene.

In the Continental Interior, millions of acres may be involved in change. An example is the 25 million acres of grasslands that were converted to crop acreage in the 1920's and 1930's, or the similar amount of land that was recently taken out of production to be put into the conservation reserve soil bank. In urban areas change may involve only a handful of acres, but the impact upon society, economically and socially, is profound. When, for example, the Delaware-Lower Schuylkill became developed as the newest and second largest oil refining area of our country, only about 15,000 acres of land were involved. But the Delaware Oil Refinery District represents an investment of over $1 billion, and gives direct employment to 20,000 workers and indirect employment to twice that number in associated chemical industries. A far smaller tract of land, 80 acres, was involved when a regional planned shopping center was constructed in Metropolitan Boston. However, this center has one-fifth of the total retail space of the Boston central business district; its appearance on the scene has drastically changed suburban shopping and residential patterns. In Baltimore, architects and planners who are working towards the revitalization of a great city, are fixing their attention on a mere 22-acre plot. This civic and office center is projected as of sufficient size and scope to change the form of the central business district by its presence and influence. Downtown Cleveland's revitalization plan includes the settlement of 12,000 new residents on an 80-acre tract. Clearly, then, the considerations of vast space *versus* limited space are secondary when it comes to change in a modern society.

Since the Second World War, change in space has been most marked along our Maritime Ring, not within the Continental Interior. This Ring might well be described as the *United States of the Four Seas*—the Great Lakes, the Atlantic, the Gulf, and the Pacific. These coastlands vary in many ways: climate, elevation, landforms, natural vegetation, agriculture, and minerals. But they are unified in more important features: dense populations, high degrees of urbanization, large numbers of usable ports, and strong concentrations of manufacturing. Among the important physical elements of unity are humidity, natural harbors, and the barrier effects of the Appalachians and the Western ranges. Average annual rainfall for the Maritime Ring is over 30 inches (save in southeast Texas and along the southwest California coast). In most instances the rainfall is over 40 inches. Such precipitation is adequate for the water needs of both urban centers and productive agricultural hinterlands. The best natural harbors occur along the highland-framed Northeast and Pacific coasts, and where the Coastal Plains Interior Lowland (the low-lying, eroded portions of the inner coastal plain) has been joined to the ocean through submergence—from Buzzards Bay to the James River. The South Atlantic, Gulf Coast, and Great Lakes have poorer natural harbors, which have required dredging, and, in many cases, upstream locations. Nonetheless, as we consider the Ring in its entirety we find that no single maritime state except Mississippi lacks a good deep-water port, be it natural or artificial.

While the mountains have not served as complete barriers between the sea and the interior, they have directed the alignment of land transportation lines along specific avenues. The Southeast Atlantic coast has poor overland connections with the Midwest. This has, in turn, given stronger impetus to north-south movement along the Atlantic Seaboard. Where the Great Lakes and the Atlantic come closest together (the New York, New England, Pennsylvania, and Maryland corridors), east-west land links are best. Because of the north-south trend of the West's mountain-desert-plateau reaches, land links between the Gulf and the Pacific Northwest coasts have been weak.

Complementary resources and products also help to unify the Maritime Ring. Petroleum, coal, forest products, sulphur, cotton, phosphates, iron and steel products, and canned fruits and vegetables are the sort of materials that are interchanged.

Some of the larger cities and population concentrations that are oriented to the Maritime Ring are as much as from 150 to 250 miles from the sea (the Inner Lowland cities of Texas and the "central place cities" of the farm belt of the Great Lakes states). The majority of the population, however, lives within three hours' automobile drive of open water. Indeed, the 100-mile contour from the coast includes 60 per cent of the entire population of the United States.

On Map 10 (p. 97) we have noted the states that are within the Maritime Ring. They total 30 of the 50 states, but include 82 per cent of the population (as against 80 per cent in 1950). The ten states to achieve the largest absolute population growth within the decade were maritime states. Nine of the country's ten largest cities and 28 of the 50 largest are Maritime Ring ports. In percentage of urbanized population and manufacturing output, the Maritime Ring accounts for even more than its total share of the population, with 90 per cent and 89 per cent, respectively.

This same measure of preponderance does not quite hold true for agriculture and mining, where the Maritime Ring accounts for 63 per cent and 73 per cent of our total national output. If the Maritime Ring were to balance its agricultural and mining outputs with its population, it would have to produce an additional $6.7 billion worth of agricultural products (over current output of $22.1 billion) and $1.3 billion worth of minerals (over current production of $11 billion). These figures emphasize the importance of the Continental Interior as the support base for the Maritime Ring. On the other hand, the fact that we import $4 billion worth of agricultural products and over $1 billion worth of minerals suggests that the role of international trade as a supporter of the Maritime Ring is substantial, if not actually comparable with that of the Continental Interior.

The earmark of the Maritime Ring is intensive movement of goods by sea. This movement is threefold: local, intercoastal, and foreign. Ship movements to and within the Ring account for about 40 per cent of all United States goods movement in ton-mileage, and for about 30 per cent in tonnage.

Trade among the states of the Maritime Ring is considerably heavier than trade between these states and the Continental Interior. This fact is illustrated by data mapped by Ullman in his *American Commodity Flow*.[11] Analysis of selected maps dealing with rail commodity flows for three states (Connecticut, Washington, and Iowa) indicates that the two maritime states, Connecticut and Washington, do their overland rail trading overwhelmingly (96 per cent and 72 per cent, respectively) with other states of the Maritime Ring. Even Iowa, a part of the Continental Interior, does 67 per cent of its trade with the Ring.[12] Thus, the complementary nature of the highly specialized portions of the American Seaboard is a stronger inducement for land trade than the lower transport costs to the interior.

National political power in the United States resides within the Maritime Ring. In the 1960 presidential elections, the Democratic Party prevailed by winning 18 of the 30 Maritime states, even though it won in only five of the 20 Continental states. The gubernatorial elections revealed the same incidence of Democratic Party mastery within the Maritime Ring: ten of 14 Maritime state contests were won by Democrats, but only five of 13 in the Continental states.

Political power; economic strength; urbanization; dense and well-integrated land, sea, and air links; foreign-trade contacts—these are all characteristics of the Maritime Ring. The Seaboard is the American frontier; it is the frontier of change and of diversity. The emptying out of the rural countryside, the decline of the central city, and the patterns of suburbanization are changing the face of the Maritime Ring. Human diversity, the feature of most borderlands because of their proximity to other areas, is also a feature of the Maritime Ring. The French-Canadian of the

[11] Edward Ullman, *American Commodity Flow* (Seattle: University of Washington Press, 1957).

[12] The commodities that were analyzed were agriculture, manufacturing, and minerals (exclusive of petroleum).

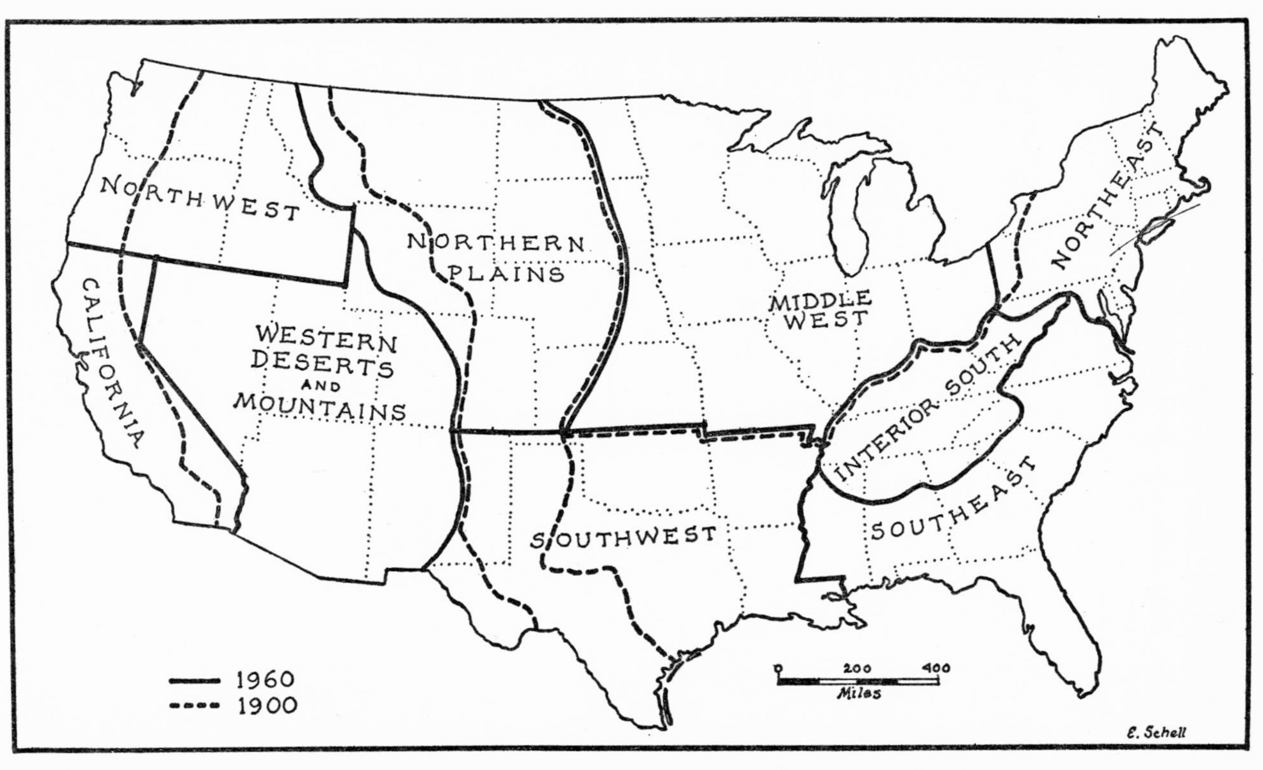

MAP 11. Changing Geographical Regions of the United States

Northeast, the Puerto Rican of New York, the Latin American of Florida, the Cajun of Louisiana, the Mexican-American of the Southwest and California, the Negro of the Great Lakes, the Atlantic, and the Gulf, and the Japanese- and Chinese-Americans of the Pacific, give to the Maritime Ring a highly diverse racial and ethnic flavor. To this may be added the diversities of religion that characterize the region. Of 14 states with estimated Catholic populations of over 20 per cent, only one—Montana—is non-Maritime. These diversities, with their attendant contrasts in standard of living, educational level, and socio-political outlook, form the American "melting pot" of the mid-twentieth century. Since change is the most striking characteristic of a frontier, and since the Maritime Ring is the most significant area of change, then surely the "New Frontier" of the United States is the Maritime Ring. Here is the arena where our greatest challenges and fulfillments lie.

Geographical Regions

While we have divided the United States in two realms—the Maritime and the Continental—these realms are so vast that they need, in turn, to be subdivided into geographical regions. Ours is a country composed of smaller "countries" that differ from one another physiographically, climatically, agriculturally, culturally, and in degree of self-containment. These smaller "countries" and their differences can be described through the process of regionalism.

Often we equate geographic regions with the apparently rigid framework that characterizes the physical landscape. In fact, however, the geographic regions of the United States constantly change in their character and extent, because the geographic region is a combination of various physical, biotic, and cultural regions. As these latter change in relation to one another, the geographic region—which is something more than a simple sum total of a number of single-feature physical and cultural regions—also changes.

We can go back to Colonial times to find examples of regional change. In the early Colonial period, there were three geographical regions in the East: the Southern, Middle, and Northeastern.

But while Maryland was regarded as a Middle Colony at the beginning of this era, it had become part of the Southern region by the end of Colonial times. This was because tobacco and slave culture gained a firm position, while manufacturing failed to entrench itself. The physical environment had not altered, but man's emphasis in the use of the environment had.

At the end of the nineteenth century, there was a radically different regional map. (See Map 11.) The Middle and Northeastern regions had merged. The Middle West—which had had such close ties to the Northeast during and before the Civil War—was now quite distinct; the old links of history, settlement, and land-use patterns that had tied the interior plains to northern New York and New England had lost much of their meaning. Perhaps the most important conflicting set of interests among all of these regions stemmed from the dryness and land policies of the West as compared to the humidity and manufacturing interests of the East. The geographic regions of 1900 were closely framed by either landform or climatic features. But they were also framed by the limited use of the land. Thus, the Pacific coast was regarded as one region because man had not yet begun to develop his diversified activities to the point where the differences between the Northwest and the Southwest coasts had become geographically meaningful.

Today's regional map is the product of several factors, the more important of which are the physical environment, population growth, urbanization, agricultural shifts, and dispersal of manufacturing. The Northeast is the land of commerce, manufacturing, and recreation; the Southeast, of specialized agriculture, lumbering, and light industry; the Interior South, of specialized crops and manufacturing; the Southwest, of chemicals, light metals, and grazing. Many of these are activities that date back only a decade or two. The Middle West, while continuing to show strength in commercial agriculture, is increasing its manufacturing and commerce. But even agriculture is changing. Sorghum and soybeans are now as important as corn, and "Corn Belt" is a misnomer.

The Northern Plains, the lands of wheat and cattle, are still sparsely settled and have yet to solve their water deficit problems. But some of the commercial cities have become manufacturers also, as in farm implements and aircraft production. The Western Deserts and Mountains, traditionally a region of mineral production, are making extremely important advances in irrigated agriculture—fruits, vegetables, and cotton. In the Far West, the distinction between the Pacific North West and the California regions has become more marked, with lumbering, manufacturing, fishing, and interior dry farming in the north, and manufacturing, horticulture, and recreation in California.

An example of how regional change is brought about can be drawn from a study of cotton. The old cotton belt, from the Atlantic through Texas, with the Mississippi Valley as the center of gravity, has disappeared. Today nearly 60 per cent of all cotton is being grown from the East Texas borders to California. As cotton has declined in the South, the South has lost its common denominator and has become divided into three distinct regions: the Southeast, the Southwest, and the Interior South. The Mississippi, formerly the focal point for the South as a whole, is becoming a contact zone between Southeast, Southwest, and Middle West (as it was prior to the Civil War). In this valley, general agriculture and manufacturing are replacing cotton. South of Memphis, for example, depleted loessal soils are being scraped down and seeded with grass to sustain a new livestock industry. The Polled Hereford and the Black Angus are moving down from their cool Midwestern habitat to take up an "air-conditioned" life in the South (including ventilated barns and summer night grazings). Meanwhile, lacking the jobs formerly supplied by cotton, Negroes continue to move northward—to St. Louis, the Ohio River, the Great Lakes, and the Northeast.

Another element that has reshaped the South has been Drainage Basin development activities in the valley of the Tennessee. A third has been the growth of mining and manufacturing along the Gulf Coast. All of this has contributed to create three geographical regions where formerly there was one. The change in California is equally marked. Whereas in the past the region was limited to the California Mediterranean, today's region embraces desert and range areas as well. This is because recreation and manufacturing have developed as arid-land outliers of the southern California population and economic core.

What regional changes may we anticipate in the next half-century? The Northeast and the Great Lakes regions will probably come to be considered one region. Factors contributing to this will be the development of larger ocean ports along the St. Lawrence Seaway and filling in with population of empty or rural areas in New York State and Pennsylvania.

The Ohio, Tennessee, Mississippi, and Missouri basins may emerge in a single mixed agricultural and manufacturing region, embracing the present Northern Plains, western Middle West, and Interior South regions. This would, in effect, make a regional unit of the more populous half of the Continental Interior.

The improvement of highways, waterways, and air routes should cut down the current advantages that our long-haul East-West railroad system possesses and give more of a North-South axial characteristic to our interior. The Southwest and the Southeast we foresee as mature, distinct regions, with increased contacts with the rest of the Maritime Ring. The Western Deserts and Mountains Province will become more important as a support base for California. But distance and barriers to the West, as well as population orientation and accessibility to the Continental Interior, should allow this region to maintain separate identity. As Alaska matures, it will become more firmly embraced within the regional confines of the older Pacific Northwest.

Population Distribution

Several Western nations have experienced psychological shocks and fear the loss of national dynamism with the slowdown of their population growth. The near-cessation of immigration and the decline in family size during the 1930's and early 1940's pointed to population decline as an element of American life. However, post-World War II demographic history has shown an unexpected reverse of the declining population growth curve. Population is on the increase once more. Greater prosperity, better housing, improved transportation, social attitudes toward larger families, health and educational benefits, earlier family formations—all account for our population increase. For 1950 to 1960, the increase was 18.5 per cent—the highest increase for a decade since 1900-10 (which was 21 per cent). To the geographer, a major question is, Where is this population distributed and what are the trends in changes in distribution? First, the Northeast and North Central regions (as defined by the United States Bureau of the Census) are losing their overwhelming dominance as population regions. In 1930, they accounted for 64 per cent of the total population; in 1960, they accounted for only 54 per cent. The South and the West not only experienced far greater rates of population increase over the past ten years; they had greater absolute growth (15.6 million, against 12.3 million). By 1985, at current growth rates, the South and the West are likely to be as populous as the North Central and the Northeast regions.

Recasting these national population growth figures, in our broader division, we find that the Maritime Ring grew by 25 million, or 20 per cent during the past decade, while the Continental Interior grew by only three million, or 10 per cent. Population is spreading over the national map. This would seem, in a small measure, to be reducing our vulnerability to nuclear attack. However, two forces serve to concentrate this population spread: the Maritime Ring and urbanization. Actually, they are interlocking forces, for the Maritime Ring intensifies urbanized-industrial developments. Population density in the Maritime Ring has increased to the point of being four and one-fifth times that of the

TABLE 4

United States Population Density by Rings

	Sq. Miles Area (exc. Alaska)	1960 Pop. Density/Sq. Mi.	1950 Pop. Density/Sq. Mi.
Maritime Ring	1,609,000	92	76
Continental Interior	1,473,000	22	19
U.S.A. Total	3,082,000	58	50

Continental Interior. Within the Maritime Ring, urban, and particularly metropolitan, populace dominates. Seventy-three per cent of the ring is urban, and two-thirds is metropolitan. Most of the population growth of the United States (85 per cent) occurred in standard metropolitan statistical areas—that is, in cities of 50,000 or more and the areas surrounding them; of this metropolitan growth about 85 per cent took place within the Maritime Ring.

What is of strategic importance is the measure of concentration of our metropolitan population within a few metropolitan areas. First, over 50 million people live in only 16 metropolitan areas (each of which has a population of 1,250,000 or more). This is about 45 per cent of the total metropolitan population of 112 million. Second, central cities within the metropolitan areas account for 58 million people, or about half the total metropolitan populace. These cities are densely populated, many of the houses are old, and streets are narrow. Plans for successful evacuations of such areas in event of war are highly illusory. By far the greatest concentration of our big central cities is in the North Atlantic-Great Lakes districts. Of 60 central cities of 200,000 population and over, 27 are in this region. The two other major clusters of central cities occur in the California and the Texas-Gulf areas, each with seven central cities.

Finally, let us consider population concentration within the American Manufacturing Belt. This belt of 400,000 square miles, which extends as a modified rectangle from the Eastern Seaboard to Milwaukee to St. Louis, contains two-thirds of our manufacturing output (and one-third of Canada's). Here are 61 central cities with populations of 100,000 and over, totalling over 30 million people. If we go beyond the central cities to consider standard metropolitan statistical areas with populations of over 100,000, within the belt, there are 80 such areas with a combined population of about 50 million. Another 20 million people, in smaller urban cities and places and in rural areas, fill out the belt. Population density for the American Manufacturing Belt is 175 persons per square mile. By contrast, the Soviet Manufacturing Belt is two and one-half times the size of ours, and contains within it 111 cities with populations of 100,000 and over. Their combined population is about 50 million. Evenly spread over the Soviet belt are another 100 million rural folk. Population density for the Soviet Manufacturing belt is therefore broadly comparable to ours, with 150 persons per square mile. But when we consider that we have as many people in urban areas of 100,000 and over in two-thirds as many cities, and in two-fifths as big an area, the greater dispersal of the Soviet population becomes readily apparent.

Suburbanization

Were the urban populace of the United States to continue to concentrate in central cities, the strategic outlook would indeed be bleak with respect to the vulnerability that comes from overconcentration of people, manufacturing, and distribution facilities. However, suburbanization is the major feature of our modern urban life; and suburbanization means population dispersal. By 1960, 47 per cent of the total metropolitan population was suburban, the great majority living in small, scattered towns, villages, and subdivisions, rather than in suburban cities of 50,000 and over. The 1960 suburban population represents almost a 50 per cent increase over the 1950 population and a rate of growth that is five times that of our large central cities. By 1962, suburban population will exceed central city population.

With our suburbs accounting for two-thirds of the country's entire population increase, the effects upon the landscape have become marked. Dispersal is the essential feature of the new population distribution pattern. Attendant upon this dispersal is the multiple-core character of such aspects of urban life as manufacturing, retailing, transportation, and government. There are those who criticize suburbanization as being wasteful of land, materials, transportation, and human energies. They advocate, as an alternative, the renewal of the central city. But renewal can no longer be seriously posed as the alternative to suburbanization. Renewal can only preserve part of the functions that have been left to the central city in the wake of the unprecedented suburbanization movement. Rather than bemoan suburbanization because of its imperfections, it is time to maximize its potential. If our country can find the financial and administrative resources to initiate vast central city renewal programs, then we can certainly allocate part of those resources to guide suburban growth.

Where suburban dispersal is carried out within limited forms of self-containment, we make the most efficient use of our space and of the transportation channels that link this space. In this context, the role of industrial parks and planned shopping centers assumes crucial importance, insofar as they, along with highways and residences, mold the shape of our urban areas. Up to now, American cities have been star-shaped, with major arteries radiating from the single central core. The urbanized area of today is assuming a multiple-core form. The cores are set within a form that resembles a series of concentric wheels, connected by spokes. These cores are located at strategic intersections of the wheels and spokes. The rims of the wheels are the highway belt systems, many of which are part of our new national Interstate Highway program. The spokes are the older radial arteries, developed initially as railroad and streetcar lines. Duplicatory public transport facilities along these radial arteries are gradually being eliminated, to be replaced, probably, by rapid transit lines.

This new pattern of urban areas is molding and being molded by the location of industrial parks and planned shopping centers. Seeking cheaper land, parking space, and intersecting circumferential-radial highway routes, such centers have stimulated residential building and feeder highways in their vicinities.

Suburban industrial park and shopping center growth is taking place most rapidly in the Middle West, Southwest, and California. Where flat terrain is encountered, as along the Great Lakes' outwash plain or the Texas prairies, suburbs tend to adjoin one another. The fact that relatively few unplanned secondary business and industrial districts exist in these areas, as compared to the Northeast, is due to the ease of public and private transit connections to the downtown area in the 1920's and 1930's that concentrated retailing and manufacturing there. Now, with the great surge of suburban growth, new industrial and shopping centers find that they can tap virgin territory because of lack of competition. In the Northeast, on the other hand, older outlying towns still represent formidable competition to various new planned enterprises.

If dispersal is in keeping with national security needs, the location of centers on the periphery of urbanized areas is desirable. On the other hand, transportation costs and the convenience of labor force or of customers frequently dictates that these centers be located on the more heavily populated side of the suburbs in the direction of the central city. To reconcile these two forces—peripheral strategic dispersal and "inboard" orientation—is not easy. But planning agencies might well pay greater attention to the need for such a resolution, and federal, state, and city groups might employ the power of tax inducement more widely than they have heretofore.

The channeling of people between their places of residence and the new industrial and shopping centers has increased the strain upon our highways, necessitating the creation of a new highway system. At the same time, however, these patterns of work and shopping trips continue to decrease the strain on arteries leading into town. In the burst of highway building that is scheduled to last until 1975, it is as important that we avoid overbuilding as underbuilding. It would seem to us, from observing the highway programs of several large metropolitan areas, that there is likely to be an overbuilding of radial highways leading into the central city downtowns and an excess of downtown parking capacity.

Urbanization and the American Negro

To prevent sprawling suburbs from atomizing, intermediate centers and efficient means of transportation are being forged. But another form of atomization is on the horizon, which is social and political in nature. It threatens to split central cities away from their suburbs. This is the fact that northern cities are becoming Negro, as the growing suburbs remain White. Such a phenomenon weakens the socio-economic strength and cohesiveness of the United States. It may also have an important impact upon our relations with other parts of the world, especially the non-White sectors.

The South is no longer the exclusive habitat of the Negro. On the contrary, about half of the 19 million Negroes of the United States now live outside the South. With an annual migration northward of 200,000, and a rate of increase that is one and one-half times that of the White population, the American Negro, who was a rural Southerner two generations ago, is rapidly becoming an urban Northerner or Westerner." [13] So dramatic has

[13] J. F. Hart, "Changing Distribution of the American Negro," *Annals of Association of American Geographers,* 50, No. 3, September 1960, p. 260.

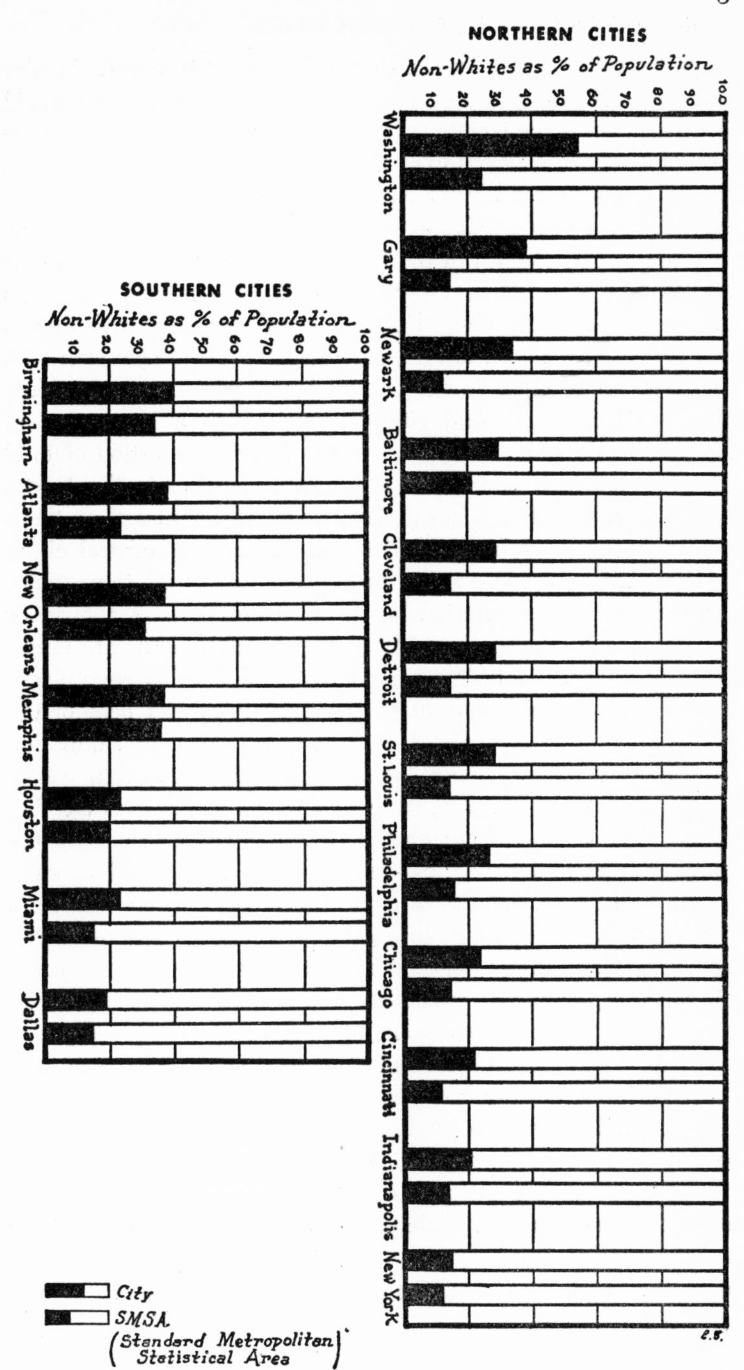

FIGURE 12. Negroes and Other Non-Whites, as Percent of Urban Population in the United States

been the change-over for the Negro from farm to city that today a higher percentage of the non-White population (72 per cent) is urban than is the country as a whole (70 per cent). The migration of southern Negroes to southern cities is negligible. Houston, the largest southern city of Negro immigration, attracts as many Negroes in a year as Chicago does in two months. Segregation, as practiced by Whites in the North, coupled with the economic and cultural status of the Negro migrants, has confined the Negro of the North to the central city. The suburbs are, with only a few exceptions, closed to him. Mapping the racial characteristics of large central cities in the United States presents the problem vividly. Northern central cities have as high a proportion of Negroes as do southern cities, but the Negro proportion of total metropolitan area population is relatively smaller in the North. (See Figure 12.) This is because of two characteristics of southern urbanized areas: suburbs tend to be annexed by central cities, and suburbs are more open to Negroes. Most of these cities continue to lose population but to gain hundreds of thousands of Negroes in the process. Washington, Baltimore, St. Louis, Gary, Cleveland, Detroit, Chicago, and Philadelphia have Negro populations that range from 50 per cent to 20 per cent of the entire population. Cleveland, for example, which had only 87,000 Negroes in 1940, now has 250,000. Within 12 to 24 years, Cleveland could have a Negro majority. As the central city becomes "black" and the suburbs remain "white," there is the grave danger that a political-cultural iron curtain will be rung down between the two. Are we to renew our central cities physically without taking into account the implications of the demographic pattern? If Negro migration can be channeled into the suburbs, then this new form of spatial segregation can be broken. But if not, we are going to have to devise radically new political and administrative frameworks to prevent racial walls from dividing our metropolitan areas to the detriment of all concerned. The forces behind metropolitan government will have to act more vigorously and with greater federal support if maintenance of the central city is to be shared by the entire metropolitan populace. Unless action is swift we may not be able to avoid a new and ugly political phenomenon—the division of the metropolitan area along racial lines.

What has been said about the Negro can be said, too, for the Puerto Rican. Indeed, the problem is more complex because it is regional as well as metropolitan. About 80 per cent of all mainland Puerto Ricans live in New York City. This places an overwhelming burden upon one city's economic-cultural absorption capacities, as well as adding to the plight of the Puerto Ricans themselves. A major national effort is required to encourage the dispersal of Puerto Rican immigrants throughout the country. Federal planning to stimulate the creation of job opportunities in urban areas of various sizes and functions, and the offer of travel, housing, and social inducements to the immigrant, appear necessary to resolve the problem. Our country will be poorly served if the present trend continues. Indeed, the economic, moral, and social climate of New York City is a national, not a local, problem, and the measure of success that we meet in absorbing our Puerto Rican citizens on the mainland has great repercussions throughout Latin America.

The Urbanized Region

A final aspect of this discussion of population distribution is the urbanized region. Metropolitan areas have begun to overlap one another, leapfrogging and bypassing rural areas to form continuous regions. We have eighteen such urbanized regions today, containing a combined total of about 70 million people.

The largest of these regions is the Eastern Seaboard, or Megalopolis. It extends from north of Boston to Fairfax County, Virginia, with a population of over 30 million. Megalopolis arose as a grouping of the country's major seaports, commercial centers, and manufacturing activities. Its future growth is uncertain—some feel that it will continue to grow, but only along the coast, north to Portland and south to Norfolk; others feel that the region will expand westward along the New York and Pennsylvania corridors, to include the Great Lakes areas; still others feel that the New York corridor will become so heavily filled with transportation lines that it will lack the room for sufficient people to warrant the area's inclusion within Megalopolis.

A major significance of Megalopolis lies in its impact upon population distribution. Megalopolis, today, expresses a relatively even distribution of our increasing population, with densities of 100 to 250 persons per square mile. If Megalopolis were to expand across the New York and Pennsylvania corridors to the Great Lakes, adjoining areas in upper New York, central Pennsylvania, and eastern Ohio would probably become emptier. In the face of this possibility, there is need to plan for an even distribution of the incoming people. This will call for the development of well-spaced, medium-sized central cities, with their surrounding rings of suburbs and agricultural areas—all tied together by an adequate land and air transportational net. By dispersing the population within the urbanized region, we shall enhance our national security. On the other hand, poor planning that permits an imbalance of population within such regions will heighten our vulnerability.

Manufacturing and Resources

The map of American manufacturing is undergoing change, although this change has not yet produced the dispersal of facilities that strategic planners would like to see. As of today, the American Manufacturing Belt shows only slightly less relative strength than it did two decades ago. Sixty-eight per cent of the value added by manufacturing is generated by factories located within the Belt. A major reason for this continued dominance is the industrial strength of the Pittsburgh-Cleveland-Detroit, Chicago, and Miami Valley districts. Government-financed industry was heavily built up in these areas during the Second World War, and the momentum of this industry in attracting all forms of supplementary and by-product industries has been maintained —accelerated during the Korean War.

However, outside manufacturing districts are on the upswing, and are gaining an increasing share of national manufacturing. The bulk of this activity is taking place in other parts of the Maritime Ring. Some examples are: 1) aircraft, electronics, shipbuilding, petroleum, and chemicals in California; 2) aluminum, chemicals, petroleum, metallurgy, shipbuilding, electronics, and aircraft in the Gulf Southwest; 3) textiles, paper and pulp, fertilizers, and food processing in the Southeast. Outside the Maritime Ring, aircraft and petrochemicals are on an increase in the Great

Plains, and steel and electronics in the Western Deserts and Mountains.

To appreciate trends, we can note that expenditures for new plants and equipment in the Southeast, Southwest, and Far West regions are now 36 per cent of total capital expenditure for the country as a whole. However, the current manufacturing output in these regions is only 30 per cent of the national output. In other words, rate of growth based upon capital investment is 20 per cent higher in these regions than in the country as a whole.

Why is manufacturing spreading over the United States landscape, and what are the prospects for the eventual creation of a new and larger American Manufacturing Belt? Growing population, improved transportation and communications, and discoveries and new uses of raw materials are responsible for the growth and dispersal of our manufacturing plants. As examples of new sources of domestic raw materials we can cite magnesium along the Gulf Coast; wood pulp in Tennessee; open-pit coal mines in eastern Ohio; coal in Utah; petroleum in California, Wyoming, and offshore Louisiana; phosphates in Tennessee and Idaho; and even deposits of iron ore in Colorado and southern California. These minerals have stimulated local manufacturing and, at the same time, have attracted allied industries that require raw materials from other parts of the country.

Another reason for manufacturing dispersal lies in the greater use of imported raw materials. One such resource, which is reshaping the map of the American iron and steel industry, is iron ore. As we look back we recall how the industry developed in Pittsburgh, and then followed the Ohio River-Youngstown corridor to Cleveland, Lorain, Detroit, Chicago, and Buffalo. In shifting towards the Great Lakes, the steel industry took up a position intermediate between Appalachian coal and upper Great Lakes iron ore and limestone. Today the southern shores of the Great Lakes account for 35 per cent of United States steel capacity. Pittsburgh accounts for only 13 per cent.

Despite impressive supplies of domestic iron ore and taconite, we have had to begin to exploit new deposits of foreign iron ores. Moderate resources were first tapped in Chile, Cuba, Sweden, North Africa, and Liberia. Then vast deposits were uncovered in the Guiana Highlands of Venezuela, and along Canada's Quebec-Labrador border. We now import over 25 per cent of our iron ore from foreign areas. By 1970, it is estimated that over 35 per cent of our ore will be imported.

Over the past ten years steel mills with coastal locations have had high growth rates. The continuing emphasis upon iron ore imports should maintain this growth in the years ahead. The Great Lakes steel centers, including the Canadian one at Hamilton, are likely to continue to increase their capacity faster than the national rate of increase. Two major companies, for example, have recently acquired sites for new plants in the Chicago area. The Atlantic Seaboard should also continue to grow more rapidly than the national capacity. Sparrow's Point and Morrisville have plants that can now produce over 11,000,000 tons of steel, and a site for a new plant at Camden has been acquired by a major company.

Birmingham is using more and more Venezuelan ores because of the low iron content of its local ores. Rate of growth for Birmingham steel over the past decade has not matched the national rate. This can be attributed, not to location factors, but to company policy. The Birmingham steel industry is owned by the United States Steel Corporation, whose general rate of expansion has been relatively low because of its already high share of the market. Nonetheless, the rate of expansion at Birmingham was considerably higher than U. S. Steel's total rate of expansion.[14]

Improvement of the waterways to allow shipment of Southern Appalachian coal to Mobile might stimulate the creation of a steel industry there. Plants along the lower Mississippi using Ohio River coal may also be anticipated. Finally, the small plants along the Gulf, such as those at Houston and in California at Fontana, can be expected to increase their capacity. These, incidentally, experienced the fastest rate of growth in the past decade. While the center of gravity of the steel industry will remain along the Great Lakes, the increase of capacity along the entire Maritime Ring will be economically—as well as strategically—beneficial to the nation as a whole, for a dispersed steel industry means greater dispersal in the transportation, construc-

[14] Gunnar Alexandersson, "Changes in the Location Pattern of the Anglo-American Steel Industry: 1948-1959," *Economic Geography,* Vol. 37, No. 2 (April 1961), pp. 95-114.

tion, machinery, fuel and mining equipment, and non-durable consumer goods industries.

Aluminum manufacturing is another example of a change in an industry's location that is dependent in great measure upon foreign raw materials. In the last few years, this industry's location concentration has shifted from the Northwest to the Texas-Louisiana-Arkansas area. It is also growing along the St. Lawrence and Ohio rivers. The major sources for our bauxite are in Surinam, Jamaica, British Guiana, Ghana, Brazil, and Hispaniola. As Pacific Northwest hydroelectric power has become scarcer, the Gulf's natural gas has taken on new importance in aluminum reduction. In this context we should note that the cost of fuel, in making aluminum metal, is 20 per cent of the total cost—higher than the fuel cost involved in extracting alumina from bauxite. We should also note that the growth of the industry in Canada, first at Arvida on the Saguenay and most recently at Kitimat, British Columbia, is largely aimed at the United States market, and is located accordingly.

Many other industries are taking a coastal location because of their dependence upon such imported materials as wood pulp from New Brunswick, petroleum from Venezuela and the Middle East, and natural gas from the Peace River in British Columbia. We could add food, wool, hides, cement, manganese, cobalt, uranium, abrasives, mica, chrome, copper, tungsten, and tin to this list of raw materials that affect plant location. It adds up to the fact that today's rapid industrial growth and dispersal is in part a product of our interdependence with other portions of the Free World, especially the Atlantic Basin through which pass over 75 per cent of our imports. The changing significance of areas from which our imports are obtained is shown in Table 5.

Over the past quarter of a century, Maritime Europe has become increasingly important as a source of United States imports. So has Canada. Maritime Europe, Canada, and Latin America together furnish over three-quarters of our imports. South and East Asia are far less important as suppliers than they were in 1937; Africa, the Middle East, Australia, and Eastern Europe show little change.

In examining the role of individual countries, however, we find some deviations from the regional import trends. While

TABLE 5

United States Imports by Region

Region	Per Cent of United States Imports, by value		
	1960	1955	1937
American Republics	26%	32%	24%
Canada	20%	23%	13%
Western Europe	30%	20%	26% (Western Europe, Eastern Europe, Middle East combined)
Eastern Europe	—	1%	
Middle East	2%	3%	
South and East Asia	16%	14%	32%
Australia and Oceania	2%	2%	2%
Africa	4%	5%	3%

Canada is by far our most important source of imports (three times the value of the next supplier), Japan now ranks second, having slightly outstripped the United Kingdom. Venezuela and West Germany follow closely upon the United Kingdom. Within the various import regions we find that the United States is overly dependent upon one country in some regions, but has a more balanced number of suppliers in others. In Latin America, one country, Venezuela, supplies us with a fourth of our imports from that region—twice as much as we normally receive from Brazil, Cuba, and Mexico. In South and East Asia, Japan is even more dominant, supplying us with about half of all of our imports from the region, or over three times that supplied to us by the next ranking country, the Philippines. On the other hand, while the United Kingdom sells us 25 per cent of the imports received from Maritime Europe, West Germany accounts for another 20 per cent, and France, Belgium, and Italy combined account for another 33 per cent. With generally competitive economies, therefore, no single Maritime European country can achieve a position of monopoly within its region as a seller of goods to the United States. This is not true in the case of Venezuela or Japan. With Venezuela's oil and Japan's manufactures, these two countries lack regional competitors for the sale of commodities to the United States. If Britain should join with the Common Market, then this trade bloc would dominate Europe's export trade to the United States. This would be comparable to the positions of Japan and Venezuela within their respective regions.

Another measure of association is the degree to which other regions are dependent upon the United States for their exports. This is shown in Table 6.

TABLE 6

Regional Exports to the United States

Region	Per Cent of Exports to the United States, by value (1960)
Latin America Republics	42%
Canada	70%
Western Europe	12%
Middle East	12%
South and East Asia	24%
Australia and Oceania	10%
Africa	10%

It can be seen that the trade dependence of Canada and Latin America upon the United States is very heavy, and that of South and East Asia moderately so. If, however, we look into the details of this regional dependence, we find some highly revealing national relationships. In the Western Hemisphere, countries like Canada, Colombia, the Dominican Republic, Ecuador, Guatemala, Mexico, and Panama send at least half of their exports to the United States, and Brazil, Bolivia, Chile, Costa Rica, El Salvador, Haiti, Honduras, Peru, and Venezuela, a minimum of one-third. Elsewhere, other closely associated traders are the Philippines, which sends us over 50 per cent of its exports, and Japan, with about one-third of its exports. On the other hand, countries like the United Kingdom, West Germany, and India ship 10 per cent or less of their exports to us.

While the political association that stems from trade dependence can change almost overnight for any single country, it is far less likely that such associations could change quickly with regions as a whole. It is in this context, therefore, that the trade ties of the United States with Canada, Latin America, Maritime

Europe, and Offshore Asia take on such mutual long-range strategic importance.

We have thus far dealt in general with imports to the United States. The import of specific commodities that are crucial to the workings of our manufacturing economy and the sources of these imports further amplify the picture. Table 7 lists a few of the more critical materials and their chief suppliers.

TABLE 7

United States—Selected Imports and Major Countries of Origin

Materials That Are Mainly Imported	
Materials	Suppliers
Abrasives	Canada
Bauxite	Jamaica, Surinam
Chrome ores	Turkey, Southern Rhodesia
Cobalt	Congo, Canada
Columbium ores	Nigeria, Congo
Jute	India, Pakistan
Manganese	Brazil, India
Mercury	Italy, Spain
Mica	India, Brazil
Nickel	Canada, New Caledonia
Tin	Malaya, Bolivia
Tungsten	Bolivia, South Korea
Rubber	Indonesia, Malaya
Supplementary Imports	
Iron ore	Canada, Venezuela
Copper	Chile, Canada
Lead	Mexico, Canada
Zinc	Canada, Mexico
Petroleum	Venezuela, The Middle East
Potash	Germany, France
Sawmill products	Canada
Uranium	Canada, Union of South Africa
Wool	Australia, Argentina

Some of our supplementary imports are added to the output of materials in which we rank as the world's number one producer, such as iron ore, copper, lead, zinc, petroleum, and uranium. Nevertheless, we have become such hungry consumers that we still must import up to one-third of our production of these commodities to fulfill our needs. As we continue to consume more than we produce, our dependence upon foreign imports mounts. Since most of these imports enter by sea, the continued development of manufacturing within our Maritime Ring seems assured. In the long run, we believe that the new American Manufacturing Belt will extend from the Great Lakes-Northeast Region through the South Atlantic and Gulf (both the coastal strip and the inner strip from the Southeast Piedmont to the Texas prairies). Of this area, only the Carolinas and Georgia will not be strongly influenced by direct access to the sea. California, from San Francisco to San Diego, will be a separate, but closely interrelated, part of this belt. A second district—the combined Ohio, Missouri (up to Omaha), Tennessee (up to Knoxville), and Mississippi (north of Memphis) rivers—is likely to emerge as the river-oriented manufacturing belt of the Interior. The latter, however, will be partly dependent upon the open ocean, as its components are today, because of the advantages in using barges to move bulk products.

The creation of a global network of military and political alliances stimulated the United States to increase international trade, strategic materials stockpiling, and capital investment, as a means of strengthening this network. In turn, the greater role of international trade and foreign investment within the United States economy has made the maintenance of these alliances more vital. The net effect of these causally related forces has been to increase the measure of interrelationship between the United States and the rest of the Trade-Dependent Maritime world. This represents a fundamental change in the U.S. global position—a change which is most clearly expressed in America's role as the central and leading component of a thoroughly interdependent geostrategic region.

The United States and Canada

We have, in Chapter III, represented Anglo-America and the Caribbean Basin as one geopolitical unit. The ties between the United States and Canada are such that the geopolitical destiny of the two can hardly be separated. Neither Commonwealth status nor French-Canadian culture are sufficient bars to this common destiny.

Five elements combine to unify Anglo-America geopolitically: 1) the distributional pattern of Canada's population; 2) the United States-orientation of Canada's major geographical regions; 3) the extractive and primary-producing nature of Canada's economy; 4) Canada's position along the Arctic, facing the Soviet Heartland; and 5) the overwhelming dominance of the United States within this Anglo-American partnership.

Arctic and subarctic climates and soils confine Canada's 18 million people to a narrow population band that faces the United States border. Most of this band is within 50 miles of the international boundary; almost none of it is beyond 300 miles. The population band is not continuous. It is interrupted in its east-west extent by barrier areas that break across the border into the United States. These are the Rockies and two prongs of the Laurentian Uplands—the poorly drained Upper Great Lakes-Superior Highlands and the Algonquin Park-Adirondacks districts—and the Appalachians. The result is a fivefold clustering of Canada's population—along the Pacific Coast, in the Prairie Provinces, in the Ontario Peninsula, the Middle St. Lawrence, and the Maritime provinces. Each of these clusters is more remote from its Canadian neighbor than from its counterpart in the United States.

The association of Canada's population clusters with areas across the border is not exclusively due to east-west distances and north-south breaks. It is also due to the fact that Canada's geographical regions are northern extensions of United States regions. That the Canadian sections are generally complementary, not competitive, with their United States counterparts is due to the abundance and supplementary function of Canada's raw materials, the extractive nature of the Canadian economy, and the differences in age and rate of economic development between the two countries. Rail, highway, air, water, and telecommunication ties show marked north-south trends reflecting the movement of goods, men, and ideas across the border.

Save in Quebec, Canada's manufacturing centers are contiguous with those of the United States. They are strongly tied to American manufacturing in that they depend upon United States factory-made machinery and other goods. Many of these factories are United States branch plants. Also, Canadian consumer products tends to follow the style and trends set by United States products. Mining, too, shows strong orientation to the south. Since the annual output of Canada's manufacturing and mining is over four times that of agriculture in value, the first two industries are the keys to Canadian–United States economic associations. Such leading Canadian manufactures as pulp and paper, nonferrous metal smelting and refining, and sawmills are largely noncompetitive with United States industry. Petroleum refining and natural gas can serve those areas of the United States that lack petroleum, like the Pacific Northwest and the Northern Plains. Canada's mineral production is therefore either complementary or supplementary. Occasionally, however, temporary gluts in production create financial distress for Canadian suppliers of such minerals as petroleum, uranium, or gold.

It is only in agriculture that the two national economies are competitive. When we consider that farm products account for only 10 per cent of Canada's exports we can understand how competing farm export policies can irritate but cannot fundamentally alter the economic associations of the two countries. The same can be said for divergent farm policies which motivate Canada to sell vast amounts of wheat and barley to Communist China in the face of United States refusal to do so.

The location of Canada athwart the Arctic, facing the Soviet Heartland and separating Alaska from the United States, has made joint defense an absolute necessity. Much has been written about American bases on foreign soils peripheral to Eurasia. But we seem to take for granted the fact that some of our most crucial bases, both defensive and offensive, are on Canadian soil. There is no alternative to NORAD (the Canadian–United States North American Air Defense Command).

The size, wealth, and general nature of United States life tends to shape Canada's economic and cultural patterns. Frequently Canadians resent the various forms of pressure that result from their associations with Americans. But this resentment is tempered by the realization that the alternative would be economic disaster and military helplessness. Over 60 per cent of Canadian foreign trade moves across the border; $15 billion of United States investments are in Canada (one-third of total United States private investment abroad); such industries as petroleum and natural gas, aluminum, iron mining, and pulp and paper have been developed by United States market needs.

It is argued by some Canadians that the runaway exploitation of Canada's resources, owing to United States financial pressures, will one day bankrupt Canada. Their call is, therefore, for a form of economic nationalism that will conserve these resources. This fear of overexploitation is a valid one. The answer, however, does not lie in restraints on United States trade and investment. For the Canadian citizen does not live in isolation from life to the south—he lives in close proximity with it. He seeks the same living standards and consumer comforts that Americans seek. Choking off the output of Canada's raw materials would cause a radical, and politically unthinkable, drop in living standards.

In fact, the danger of the depletion of raw materials is common to both the United States and Canada. It can best be averted through joint economic planning. It is this type of planning that is so necessary in other fields as well. A smoother flow of raw materials to United States factories is needed to prevent sudden dips in Canadian employment opportunities, as is joint action on agricultural surpluses, to convert the farm economies from that of national problem to national asset.

United States–Canadian relations can proceed in only one direction—towards greater interdependence. If the United Kingdom must one day choose Continental Europe over the Commonwealth from an economic standpoint, then even greater economic unity between the United States and Canada may be the consequence. Even if this should not be the case, joint agencies for economic and military activities will require continued strengthening. The freest possible use of each other's territory should be encouraged to spearhead the closest relationships between the two countries. Such links as the St. Lawrence Seaway and the Portland-Montreal pipeline already exist. In 1961, the way was cleared to build natural gas pipelines from fields in British Columbia and Alberta to the United States Pacific Coast and the northern Continental Interior. The future may see the construction of a modern water route from Montreal to New York City, via the Richelieu River and Canal, Lake Champlain, and the Hudson; or it may see the development of a submarine tanker route across the Canadian Arctic to connect the east and west coasts of North America.

Mutuality of interests means, above all, mutuality of understanding. Because northern British Columbia and the Yukon Territory lack Canadian access to the Pacific, some Canadians have called for the granting of a corridor across Alaskan Panhandle territory. We may pass this off as being neither economically nor strategically important to Canada. However, the decision of 1903, which confirmed the landward boundaries of Canada so as to deny access to the sea, "is still a sore point in certain Canadian circles." [15]

Canadian interest has centered on the Chilkoot and White Passes, which link Whitehorse in the Yukon to the Lynn Canal and the sea via the Skagway. The latter is American territory. The granting of a corridor to Canada would not affect the strategic or economic position of the United States, because our major land link, the Alaskan Highway, passes through British Columbia for 634 miles before even entering the Yukon Territory. A far-sighted American policy that respected Canadian political-psychological yearnings in this particular instance would be a minor, but significant, expression of mutual understanding.

Nowhere else in the world should the United States be as sensitive to political developments as in Canada. Were political neutralism to take over in that country, it would represent our most serious international political setback. Strengthening the geopolitical unity between the United States and Canada is crucial to the well-being of both peoples. To this end, the closest economic and political planning is both necessary and possible.

The United States and the Caribbean

The Gulf of Mexico–Caribbean basins have often been described as the "American Mediterranean." Ratzel and Semple were among the early ones to note geographical similarities between the interior seas of the Old and the New worlds, and Spykman used the term in a geopolitical sense, describing the

[15] Norman Nicholson, *The Boundaries of Canada, Its Provinces and Territories* (Ottawa: Department of Mines and Technical Surveys, 1954) pp. 40-41.

American Mediterranean as the area over which the United States held absolute hegemony. He defined it as a tropical raw material zone lying between the continental masses of North and South America, and providing a transit zone between them and between the Atlantic and the Pacific.[16]

The "American Mediterranean" is indeed a useful term for geopolitical analysis, but its geographical setting must be clearly understood if the term is to be validly applied. (See Map 13.) Examination of the maps of landforms, demographic characteristics, and movement tells us that the Old World Mediterranean Sea is situated between North Africa and Europe, *not* between Africa and Europe. The sea is the intermediate that links two northern hemispheric territories—temperate Europe and subtropical North Africa. It does not link the two continents, for the Sahara bars the way. Most of Africa has an Atlantic orientation to Europe that bypasses the Mediterranean altogether.

Similarly, the New World Mediterranean is not situated between North and South America. It lies between, and connects, temperate Anglo-America with subtropical Middle America—both the islands and the Central American Mainland. The Amazon bars continental South America from the Caribbean, and most of South America has an Atlantic orientation to Europe or to eastern Anglo-America. Thus, both southern continents are removed from the Mediterraneans and lack close geopolitical associations with them.

Such a view places the Mediterraneans in their proper geographical settings—those of inland seas, surrounded by littorals whose northern reaches are disproportionately larger, more populous, more favorably endowed with varieties of raw materials, and more technologically developed. The ecumenes of both Maritime Europe and Anglo-America are being extended southward toward their Mediterraneans. These ecumenes obtain supplementary, as well as complementary, resources from their southern, neighboring lands. Thus, Caribbean petroleum and iron ore supplement the Anglo-American resource scene, while sugar, bananas, and bauxite complement it. North African grains, vines, iron ore, and phosphates supplement Maritime Europe's re-

[16] Spykman, *America's Strategy in World Politics,* New York: Harcourt, Brace, 1942, pp. 48, 49.

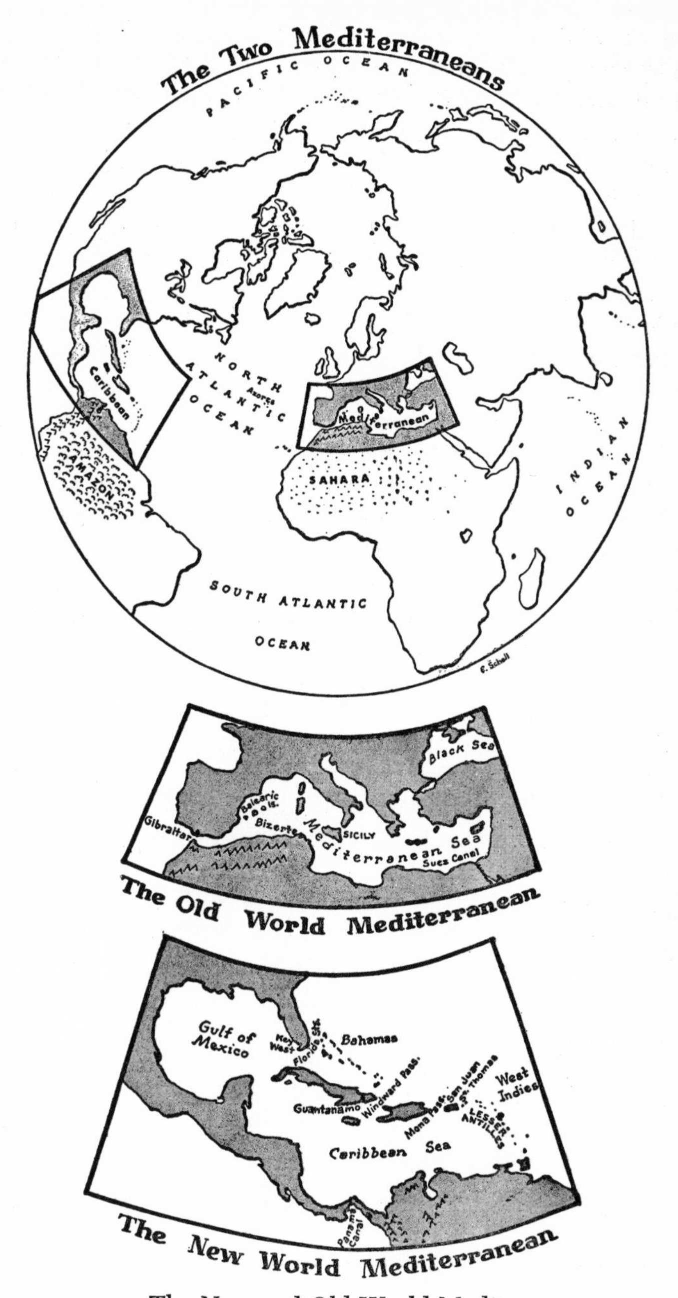

MAP 13. The New and Old World Mediterraneans

sources, while citrus, cotton, and petroleum complement them.

Physiographically, the two regions are subdivided—the Old World Mediterranean into two basin-rimming shorelands; the New World Mediterranean into Mainland and Island groupings. In this, and in a general location sense, lie subtle differences, of course, between the two regions. The open North African coast, devoid of water or forest barriers, can be more easily unified by a dominant power. Moreover, the Old World Mediterranean's western reaches lie under the influence of Maritime Europe, while its eastern reaches are subject to pressure from Asia (specifically, the U.S.S.R.). The New World is bordered by only one power core—Anglo-America. Finally, the Suez Canal is an extra-regional link for its Mediterranean. While performing a similar extra-regional function, the Panama Canal also serves as an internal link between and within American Mediterranean countries.

These differences notwithstanding, the analogies between the two regions are the more important elements of comparison. Geopolitical associations within the basins depend, essentially, upon the course of events along their northern shores. When most of Europe was unified by Rome, North Africa, too, was brought within the framework. When Europe became split and totally disorganized during medieval times, the Arab corelands to the east seized the opportunity to unify North Africa. Eventually, the revival of European power that began with the Discoveries returned North Africa to the European-oriented fold, but not within a unified framework, because Europe itself lacked unity.

The New World Mediterranean's history shows some striking parallels as well as obvious differences. As long as the North American Mainland remained underdeveloped and disorganized, unity of Middle America was supplied by an extraregional core—Spain. The emergence of European competitors to Spain brought those states into the American Mediterranean also. From the end of the seventeenth to the nineteenth centuries, Middle America lay divided, strategically and politically, because Europe was divided and because North America was geopolitically immature. Finally came the rise of the United States as the unified, mature overlord of the northern littoral. For over sixty years, command of the American Mediterranean has been held by the

United States. The European footholds that remained after the displacement of Spain are only "relicts." Strategic unity of Middle America has been enforced by the power from the north.

United States hegemony over the Caribbean lands did not follow the course of modern European hegemony over its southern Mediterranean littoral. For the United States has fostered the development of formally independent states within a unified strategic framework. North Africa, on the other hand, was developed through a colonial-imperialist process and independence has come in the face of European opposition.

We have used the term *hegemony* to describe North-South power relations in the two Mediterraneans. In the past, military and economic preponderance was equated with political and social attraction, and strategic dominance forced geopolitical cohesiveness. Today this is not necessarily the case. Strategic dominance can assure geopolitical cohesiveness only if the stronger power is prepared to apply naked force in the formation and control of political and economic processes. This European powers have done in North Africa and the United States has done in Middle America for most of the first half of the twentieth century. This, too, is the path that the U.S.S.R. has taken to create conditions for geopolitical unity with Eastern Europe. But if the use of direct and unremitting force is renounced, if continuous intervention in foreign political and economic processes is repudiated, then something in addition to strategic dominance is needed to assure geopolitical unity.

We have elsewhere described Anglo-America and the Caribbean, and Maritime Europe and the Maghreb, as geopolitical regions. This they have been in the recent past, this they are today, and this they are most likely to be in the future. But such regions will only stand as meaningful cohesive units if their northern littorals succeed in finding a new political and social modus vivendi with the lands to the south. The exercise of strategic power in finding this modus vivendi certainly cannot be renounced; it is a fact of political life! But its direct application will have to be in consonance with political and social objectives that are mutually desirable, not as a substitute for such objectives.

Since the Second World War many Americans have sat back

and viewed France's agonizing entanglements in the Maghreb as the just deserts of a colonial power. The inevitability of the fall of colonialism has been trumpeted and the rights of colonial peoples to independence has been championed. But we have not really felt morally and politically bound to concern ourselves with the future of European-North African relationships. We have buttressed France's position in Maritime Europe, but have considered that locale as totally separate from the North African scene. What we have failed to recognize is that just as it is inevitable that colonialism-imperialism must end, so is it absolutely essential that a new form of geopolitical association should emerge in its place within the Old World Mediterranean. Much of our lack of understanding of the problem stems from our complacency about our own stake in the American Mediterranean.

This complacency has been rudely shattered by Cuba's defection to the Soviet camp, and by gathering storms in the Dominican Republic, Guatemala, Haiti, Nicaragua, and Panama. Our leaders are seeking to reappraise past attitudes and to develop new forms of political and economic accommodation with the Caribbean. A by-product of this reappraisal will be to make the American public more conscious of Maritime Europe's analogous position in North Africa. The latter is as much a part of the European Inner Security Zone as is the Caribbean part of the United States' Inner Security Zone. Bizerte is France's Guantanamo Bay, and Algeria is France's Cuba. So long as Maritime Europe remains dependent upon Middle Eastern petroleum the Suez Canal is Europe's Panama Canal. The problems that the northern powers face in their relations with their southern Mediterranean littorals are analogous; the stake in their resolution is equally great.

The involvement of the United States in Caribbean Basin affairs can be divided into three phases of geopolitical association:

1) *The Period of Defensive Posture.* Americans had a legitimate fear of European states using their Caribbean island bases and Mexico to dominate the Gulf and the Mississippi, thereby confining the United States to the eastern seaboard. Moreover, Americans were attracted by the wealth of the Indies—sugar,

rum, and slaves—to which the subsistence Colonial economy stood in marked contrast.

2) *The Period of Emotional Aggressiveness.* With the slavery issue resolved by the Civil War, northern as well as southern voices could now be raised in favor of United States expansion in the Caribbean. The interests were commercial, humanitarian, and strategic. By the turn of this century, military and economic considerations had become sufficiently forceful to inspire a series of interventions in Cuba, Haiti, the Dominican Republic, Nicaragua, and Panama. With the growth of population and industry in the Gulf states and in California, the extension of United States interests into the open Pacific, and the cutting of the Panama Canal, strategic considerations became especially pressing. The Good Neighbor Policy represented a less emotional and more sympathetic approach to our relations with Latin America, but without any essential change in our aggressiveness toward the rest of the hemisphere.

3) *The Fear of Counter-Encirclement.* Today, while continuing to recognize the significance of the Caribbean Basin to the United States in a strategic-economic sense, we have also begun to consider the implications of our being cut off from Middle America in a political-social sense. While we continue to encircle the Soviet Heartland, we fear counter-encirclement from the Soviet Arctic and from the south for the first time in almost a century. The actual military threat posed by one hostile country like Cuba is negligible, but the success of its pro-Soviet policies could tap widespread anti-United States sentiment in Mexico, Panama, Venezuela, Hispaniola, and even Puerto Rico. The emergence of political systems radically opposed to United States political and social ideals, coupled with Soviet bases in Middle America, is not entirely inconceivable. The fears that we in the United States have of the implications of the Cuban situation are, in this sense, not unlike the fears of the Soviet Union at the time of the Hungarian revolt. In both cases the major powers feel compelled to resist political and military encirclement. The Soviet Union's solution to the problem was, and remains, continuous force exercised directly and through puppet regimes. The United States, as yet, has found no clear-cut answer to the ques-

tion of how it will maintain its primacy of influence in the Caribbean.

FORCES OF ATTRACTION AND DISRUPTION

Assessment of Middle America's geopolitical features shows that, while the majority of them serve as forces of attraction toward Anglo-America, some are disruptive forces.

Location is the most compelling force of attraction. Location has two faces: strategic and economic-demographic. Strategically, the Caribbean islands can be viewed as the northern and eastern sides of a frame that encloses the interior sea. The northern side is of particular significance to the United States. It consists of two "walls"—the Bahamas, which are the outer one, and the Greater Antilles, which are the inner one. Through this part of the frame, traffic is channeled in two major passageways: the Florida Straits and the Windward Passage. These passageways route the shipping of the Maritime Ring of the United States—Atlantic-Gulf movement via the Florida Straits, and Atlantic-Pacific movement via the Windward Passage and the Panama Canal. Venezuelan-United States traffic can use the Mona Passage, between Puerto Rico and Hispaniola. The eastern edge of the frame consists of the Lesser Antilles. These smaller and less populous portions of the Caribbean are mostly European dependencies, although American bases are spotted throughout. Shipping to Europe moves via St. Thomas at the northern end, and Trinidad at the southern end, of this island string. From such bases as Key West, Florida; Guantanamo, Cuba; San Juan, Puerto Rico; and Chaguaramas, Trinidad, the United States navy has traditionally guarded the waters of the American Mediterranean. There are those who today suggest that such a guardian role is unrealistic, in the face of the threat of intercontinental nuclear war. If we were to abandon our Caribbean naval-air defenses, however, and to ignore the threat of submarine attack upon the southern shores of United States territory with either nuclear or conventional warheads, would we be more realistic? Should we leave interior sea lanes, including the Panama Canal, unprotected from petty harassments during times of local flare-ups? Should we abandon bases from which we supervise South Atlantic missile-testing shoots and rocket launches, and rely upon more remote Mainland staging points? The Caribbean defense system may not have much strategic value in the face of all-out war, but in terms of limited arms engagements, and of economic and political warfare, its significance to the United States can scarcely be questioned.

Another aspect of location is the proximity of the major part of the insular Caribbean's population and resources to the southward-expanding United States ecumene. This population proximity is a relatively recent geopolitical phenomenon. To explain why Cuba had been able to remain politically free of the United States, despite very early interest in the acquisition of the island on the part of Thomas Jefferson and John Quincy Adams, Semple cited its physical isolation from the mainland during the eighteenth and nineteenth centuries:

> The peninsula of Florida . . . was in fact almost wholly inoperative as a connecting link because of its extensive swamp lands, which render the lower third of the peninsula almost uninhabitable. There was here, therefore, no chance of an increasing population which should outgrow the narrow limits of a peninsula and overflow into adjacent islands, as exemplified everywhere else by peninsula history.[17]

But the unprecedented growth of Florida in the last three decades has removed this element of isolation. The normal spillover from Florida and the steady flow of tourists and businessmen from all points of the east coast to Havana, and the large Cuban and Puerto Rican populations of Miami and Tampa, attest to this new proximity.

As we view the unprecedented strides made by manufacturing, mining, and diversified agriculture from Florida through the lower Mississippi to Texas, we are reminded of Semple's statement that "the United States has a greater claim to strength as a Gulf power than as a Pacific,"[18] and that Ratzel long ago stressed the leaning of the United States toward the Gulf.

The change-over of the United States Plantation South to a modern, urbanized, industrial-agricultural region can have great

[17] E. Semple and C. Jones, *American History and Its Geographic Conditions, op. cit.*, p. 441.

[18] *Ibid.*, p. 403.

impact upon Middle America's economy. The availability to the Caribbean lands of raw materials like phosphates, sulphur, cotton, refined petroleum, of a variety of manufactured items, and of a large consumer market from the United States Gulf region, could stimulate Caribbean economic developments.

Certainly the fact that half of Middle America's trade is with the United States, and Middle America ranks second only to Canada in United States foreign investments per capita, is a force for unity. In the past, the complementary resources of the temperate and tropical parts of the world were regarded as a major element in geographical attraction. Today, however, this is not necessarily the case. The traditional pattern of tropical raw materials and finished United States goods exchange is a geopolitically disruptive force. This is because the price of raw materials has failed to keep pace with those of manufactured articles, and "the rich have gotten richer, while the poor have gotten poorer." Moreover, national pride impels underdeveloped states to become manufacturers, whether or not they can financially justify such a position. What this means with respect to the Caribbean is clear. The people of this region will not be content to exchange their sugar, tobacco, cacao, henequen, bananas, iron ore, bauxite, nickel, lead, zinc, and petroleum for United States finished goods. And they will not accept their present status of one-crop or one-mineral countries, dependent upon political and market conditions that they cannot control. Instead, they desire diversified agriculture and consumer industries to supplement their extractive economies. Puerto Rico, with its cement, textiles, shoes, plastics, and glass is an example of the sort of economic diversification for which the others yearn. If the United States can spread the concept of "Operation Bootstrap" through all of insular and mainland Middle America, broadening the economic base without undercutting the present specialized economic resources that the Caribbean possesses, then economics will again become a force of attraction, rather than a disruptive force.

Two other major disruptive elements are political and social. The United States position in the Caribbean cannot be based upon dictatorships of the Right or of the Left. For if United States-style political and social democracy is to have any influence upon the Caribbean scene, it must be able to influence day-to-day events there. Until now we have depended upon small elites, backed by our economic and military force, to maintain our hegemony. The wave of today in the Caribbean calls for reform and our mission is to encourage this reform openly and wholeheartedly—to lead, not to follow. While this, too, would be a form of intervention in Caribbean affairs, intervention is likely to occur in whatever relations we possess with the American Mediterranean.

Another highly disruptive force in United States-Caribbean relations is racial discrimination in the United States. The Caribbean is a region that is Negro, White, Indian, East Indian, and mixed. Islands like Cuba, Haiti, Jamaica, Puerto Rico, and many of the eight smaller West Indies are heavily Negro. So are sections of the mainland, like British Honduras, the Nicaraguan coast, and Panama. The historic impact of plantation agriculture made much of the American Mediterranean (including the United States South) a "Negro Lake." While we have become aware of the complications that racial discrimination within the United States creates for our foreign relations with Africa and Asia, we overlook its effects upon the Caribbean. So long as we dealt with small, white oligarchies in most Middle American countries, we could be oblivious to the sensitivities of their non-White inhabitants. Now we will have to deal with "the people," and unless we can do so with clean hands, our hopes of leading the reform wave in the Caribbean may well founder on the rocks of domestic racial discrimination. One of the keys to our Caribbean policy, then, lies in the rapidity with which the American Negro is able to take his place as a full and equal member of our society.

Finally, the stark contrast in living standards between the United States and the Caribbean is a disruptive force to geopolitical unity. Rapid population growth, limitations of water and arable land, dependence upon a few commodities, and absence of manufacturing are all responsible for the Caribbean's plight. The region's current population of 65 million is more than double the 1920 population, and growth is 2.7 per cent annually. Fresh water has to be shipped to some West Indies islands because storage facilities are so limited. In Haiti, for example, land redistribution is no solution because most of the land is not arable. Haiti, a nation of small landholders, is one of the most poverty-stricken countries in the world. Urbanization within the essentially rural Caribbean has solved few economic problems and created many new ones. One single city in each of the following countries holds one-fifth of that country's population: Cuba, Venezuela, Panama, and Costa Rica. However, urbanization has not alleviated poverty. Instead, hundreds of thousands have crowded into urban centers that lack manufacturing bases. The result is a declassed urban people with little to do but to respond to revolutionary slogans.

Under such economic conditions, the contact that we make with Middle Americans through such forces of attraction as tourism, trade, baseball, and widespread use of the English language, are often turned against us.

Geopolitical unity between Anglo-America and the Caribbean is a logical, but not an inevitable, consequence of the geographical relations between the two regions. Forces of attraction are greater than the forces of disruption. And United States strategic needs are not among the least important of these attraction forces. Certainly the Caribbean is as vital to the military and psychological security of the United States as is Eastern Europe to the Soviet Union or the Maghreb to Maritime Europe. What we cannot afford to do, however, is to take the American Mediterranean for granted. Geography proposes; man disposes. Only a vigorous response to the challenges presented by the various disruptive elements that have been noted can provide the geopolitical unity that is so logical and so necessary.

The process of change and interdependence is the most striking characteristic of the geopolitical landscape of the United States and the rest of the Maritime World. Perhaps we are too close to the scene to appreciate the full implications of this process. Domestically, political and economic power is being reconcentrated within different portions of the Maritime Ring. Internationally, dependence upon foreign raw materials and foreign markets may necessitate sweeping changes in the production and marketing of American goods. For example, the subsidization of American manufactures for export may be no more far-fetched a proposal than were agricultural subsidies half a century ago. Also, on the international plane, a genuine partnership with Maritime Europe would have far-reaching effects upon our global foreign policy and our current controls over nuclear weapons.

·5·

MARITIME EUROPE

The Emergence of a New Type of Superstate

Today's superpowers, the United States and the Soviet Union, have in common the fact that they are political unions of diverse physical and cultural landscapes. Because of historical circumstances, racial and ethnic groups in the United States are not the basis for separate, internal, political components as they are in the Soviet Union. However, as we have noted, America's minority groups are concentrated in specific areas, and this concentration does have political and economic consequences. In addition, the superpowers have the following in common: 1) large, well-knit, and densely populated ecumenes; 2) vast areas of moderately populated, exploitable national territory in which extensive farming is carried on or extractive industries are pursued—such lands we will call "effective national territory"; and 3) huge tracts of unpopulated, barren land, both frozen and desert wastes —the empty spaces.

Both the effective national territories and the empty spaces provide abundant sources of raw materials and the bases within which to conduct many of the scientific activities of the nuclear age. They also offer in their subhumid-continental and subtropical-arid sectors a long-range outlet for expanding populations.

These vast tracts of land situated outside of the ecumene are national morale boosters; their environment provides continuous challenge to the national spirit and genius.

Maritime Europe is the third major power region of the globe. But Maritime Europe is different from the other two. It is not a superpower because it lacks political unity. It is also not a superpower because it lacks the vast effective national territories and the empty spaces of the United States and the Soviet Union.

Is it too late for Maritime Europe to copy the geopolitical structure of the superpowers? A unity of Maritime Europe, western North Africa, and the Sahara would present a diversified political landscape that would have much in common with that of the other two. Until the end of the Second World War, suggestions for the creation of such a structure would have been regarded as sheer fantasy. This was because of: 1) the stalemate stemming from the nearly balanced strength of Maritime Europe's separate core areas; 2) the interests of Germany in Eastern Europe; 3) the extra-regional associations of the United Kingdom and France. Today none of these three factors is of sufficient objective validity to deter Maritime Europe's geopolitical unity. The biggest obstacle is the problem of achieving geopolitical union with the Maghreb. Had such a federation been proposed forty years ago, its realization would have been relatively simple. At that time the ratio of Europeans to the Muslims of the Maghreb was 15 to 1. In contrast, the ratio of Slavs to non-Russians in 1917 Russia was only 3 to 1. Replacing European colonial rule with a genuine federation would, in all probability, have met with enthusiastic Muslim response. At worst, no greater force and pressure would have had to be applied than was applied by the Russians against native peoples in the conversion of the Czarist Empire to the Union of Republics.

It is pointless to bemoan what might have been. Today's problems will not be solved with yesterday's methods. European-North African geopolitical unity must now be achieved by subtle economic and political persuasion—not naked force; by appeal to the self-interest of each side—not one-way economic exploitation. Such a unity remains a practical possibility, if only because it is so sorely needed by both Europeans and North Africans. Realization of the union hinges, first, upon a speedy unification of the West European core without interim loss of the Maghreb to the Communist World. If unity of the European core is too long in coming, then the opportunity for the broader geopolitical structure will probably be lost.

In this chapter we shall discuss the prerequisites for a European superstate. Such a state would have, in common with the other superpowers, a large, well-developed middle latitude ecumene of 480,000 square miles, compared with 500,000 square miles for the United States core and 600,000 square miles for the Soviet Union. It would also have vast empty space—the Sahara. (See Map 14.)

However, the geopolitical structure of this European-North African state would differ in comparison with the others in five ways: 1) its ecumene would be far more densely populated; 2) it would lack extensive effective national territory outside the core area; 3) it would continue to suffer from its locational-strategic position of being caught between the other two superpowers; 4) it would maintain intimate ties with other parts of Asia and Africa that could not be altogether discarded in any superstate-building process; 5) its empty space would be considerably less accessible to the rest of the country than is the case with the American desert or Soviet Central Asia.

Maritime Europe's ecumene has a population of about 200 million and consequently a population density of 430 persons per square mile. This is more than twice the densities of the ecumenes of the two superpowers, the United States ecumene having a population of 90 million and a population density of 185 persons per square mile, and the Soviet ecumene having a population of 120 million and a density of 200 persons per square mile.

Contrasts in effective national territories are vivid. For Maritime Europe, only the Mediterranean shorelands are effective national territory—i.e., the "exploitable" lands outside the ecumene, which possess raw materials and offer favorable milieu for settlement. But these shorelands are not highly mineralized and agriculture suffers from absence of level land and lack of summer rainfall. Also, most important, these areas are already densely populated relative to their resource base. Spain alone might be described as lightly populated (150 persons per square mile),

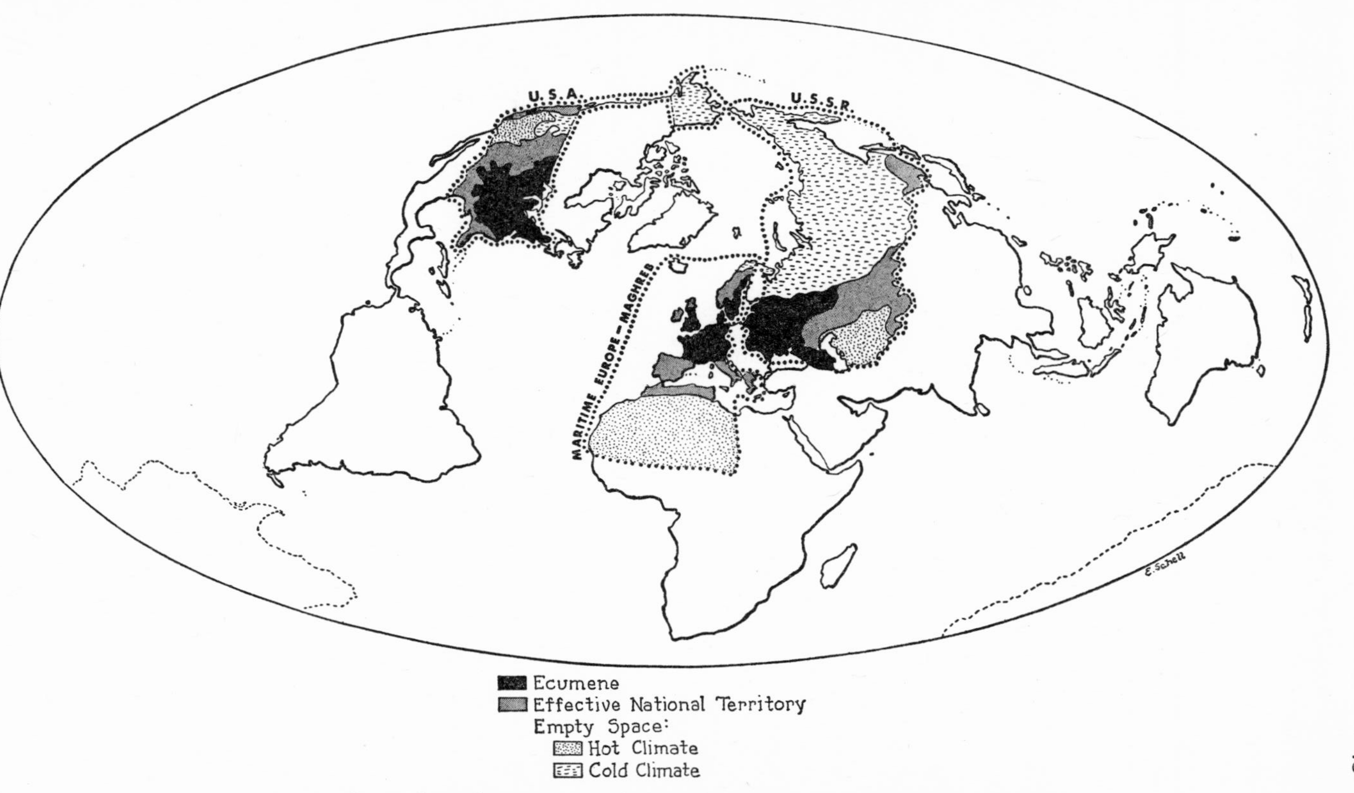

MAP 14. Geopolitical Features of the Three Major Geopolitical Regions

though its lack of water limits population growth potential. Thus, Maritime Europe and North Africa do not possess the effective national territory with limited populations that the U.S.S.R. possesses in Siberia or the United States has in its central and western interior reaches.

The geologic fates have not been kind to this part of the Old World. The land that might have been Europe's exploitable national territory lies covered by the Mediterranean's waters. In the Soviet Union and the United States, such lands were covered by inland seas in the geologic past, but they have since emerged in their present dry-land form.

With respect to its locational strategic position, the ecumene of Maritime Europe is open to the Soviet core via the North European plain and to the American ecumene via the North Atlantic. Thus the Maritime European core lies wedged in between those of its neighboring superpowers. Their ecumenes, in turn, however, lie adjacent to only one superpower core.

Another measure of difference is extra-regional links. The associations that European countries have in Sub-Saharan Africa, Asia, and Oceania help to mold the position of European uniqueness. Both the United States and Russia evolved in relative isolation. Their maturing economies rested on self-sufficiency. A European superstate will have to emerge from an already mature core. Consequently, existing extra-regional ties such as those held by the Commonwealth or French Community cannot be snapped, but will have to be reshaped to accommodate changes brought on by the political unity of the core area.

Finally, inaccessibility of the Sahara is a handicap to Maritime Europe that neither the United States nor the Soviet Union has to face with respect to its desert area. Like the Sahara, the deserts of the latter two superpowers can be approached directly from the ecumene and the effective national territories. Unlike the Sahara, however, these deserts can also be approached from their far side. The Pacific coast and its bordering mountains constitute a forward point of population and surface water supply which has enabled Americans to support desert developments from an adjoining base. In the same manner, the peoples, resources, and surface waters of the Soviet Central Asian mountains and the industrialized centers of the Caspian Sea adjoin the

Soviet Central Asian deserts, affording greater ease of development. South of the Sahara lies no modern European outlier, but Black Africa.

In consideration of all the above factors, we must conclude that a unified Maritime European-North African union would lack the completeness of geopolitical structure possessed by the other superpowers. Conceivably, a unified Maritime Europe might try to take up a third and balancing position in the East-West struggle. Such a position has, as we have pointed out earlier, been projected by contemporary German geopoliticians, and it has been suggested by Charles de Gaulle. But, without unity with Eastern Europe as well, the "balancer" would not be powerful enough to remain truly independent. Once committed to casting its weight with one superpower against the other, Maritime Europe would probably not be able to reverse its position. Most logically from a political-strategic and economic standpoint, and most probably from an historic-cultural orientation, Maritime Europe will continue to maintain its close ties with the rest of the Atlantic Basin. Continued external pressure from the Soviet Union and internal pressure from national Communist parties, as well as the counterweight of Mainland China as a global force, suggest that a unified Free Europe would not take up a posture of third force isolation. Far more likely, such a geopolitical region would play a reinvigorated role as a full partner in the Atlantic Alliance.

The Locational Perspective

Europe is not a clearly defined continent; it is a part of the Eurasian landmass. Moreover, its links southward via the Mediterranean Sea have brought it into close association with the North African littoral. To delimit Europe precisely is a matter of some difficulty, because Europe is not only a piece of land; it is a cultural concept. Europe is a place, but it is also civilization, history, land-use, urban patterns, trade, and above all, people. When European culture spills over into areas that are physically contiguous to what was traditionally known as Europe, the boundaries of Europe tend to change. Europe has expanded beyond its Urals boundary into Siberia, and across the Mediterranean into the Maghreb and the Levant. The English geographer Lyde aptly expressed this by saying, "The separation of Europe from Asia is, therefore, historic rather than geographical, political rather than physical . . . the weakness of any politico-historic influences is shown by the fact that the nominal frontier in the east runs neither along the Urals . . . nor along the Caucasus." [1]

In this chapter our concern is not with Continental Europe's eastern boundaries, but rather with the eastern borders of Maritime Europe. It is the separation of seaward from landward Europe that is the crucial geopolitical problem of the continent. For hundreds of years this boundary has lain along a belt of political instability, extending from Finland to Greece. North-south trade lines united the belt, but they were more than offset by clashes along the east-west axis. Lyde called that portion of the belt from the mouth of the Danube to the mouth of the Vistula "Isthmian" Europe.[2] The belt, in its entirety, has been called the Eastern Marchlands of Europe.[3] Mackinder described it as the "middle tier of states between Germany and Russia." [4] Now this belt of instability has shifted westward, from the Aegean and Black seas to the western end of the Baltic, to include the area known as *Mitteleuropa,* or Central Europe. Gottmann calls these central and eastern European lands, combined, the Tidal Lands of Europe.[5] We have, in Chapter 3, discussed the problem of drawing a boundary line through the Tidal Lands of Europe. Whereas in the past the balanced strength of Germany and Russia made it necessary to draw the boundary somewhere within Isthmian Europe, today's realities place all of the European Black Sea littoral and the Baltic within the orbit of Soviet land-power. Soviet-dominated Communism in Isthmian Europe represents a radical departure from older forms of extra-regional controls, because it involves large cadres of national elements

[1] Lionel W. Lyde, *The Continent of Europe* (London: Macmillan & Co., 1926), p. 7.

[2] *Ibid.*, p. 394.

[3] H. G. Wanklyn, *The Eastern Marchlands of Europe* (London: Philip, 1941.)

[4] Mackinder, *Democratic Ideals and Reality*, p. 161.

[5] Jean Gottmann, *A Geography of Europe* (New York: Holt, 1954), p. 333.

together with foreign Soviet forces in an enterprise of joint control.

In this chapter we shall focus our attention on Maritime Europe—that part of Europe that includes its western reaches, most of its northern reaches, part of its central reaches, and the Mediterranean reaches: all oriented toward the sea.

To Americans, the future without a free maritime Europe can scarcely be contemplated. Maritime Europe is more than simply part of our past. Our association with it is an essential ingredient of our present and future. It was in Maritime Europe that the modern national state arose and industrial and agricultural specialization evolved. The cultural-political mold of the United States was Western European-inspired. With the maturing of our national state has come the desire to strengthen our bonds with Europe, not to weaken them. For along with the recognition of the significance of past ties has come an appreciation that our fate is inseparably linked with Maritime Europe's security. From its end of the North Atlantic Basin, Europe faces the heart of North America, and is as near to most of South America as is the United States. Of equal locational significance is Europe's position at the center of the Old World Parallelogram. From there, it is the staging area that overlooks much of Asia and Africa. Finally, we can note Europe's central location in a global sense. Most of the world's landmasses lie within one hemisphere, called the "land hemisphere," and the center of this hemisphere lies in France.

When we view this strategic location along with the size and quality of Maritime Europe's population, its productive capacity and political and economic links to the rest of the world, then we can only conclude that it is destined to remain the most important extra-regional associate of the United States.

Background to Maritime Europe's Integration

If Asia is the most senior of the continents historically and culturally, then Maritime Europe is the most senior politically and technologically. From the Atlantic to the Elbe, little in the physical environment has been unaffected by this technology, whether applied through agriculture, manufacturing, or transportation.

And little of this technological application has been unaffected by political boundaries.

Nowhere else has man, through changing machines and ideas, effected such a variety of stages in landscape development—some totally new, others recurring as higher levels of previously known stages. Thus, in Maritime Europe, soils have been chemically altered through intense application of fertilizers; forests have been restored over vast areas once stripped of their tree cover; streams have been canalized and flows regulated; mountain valleys have been inundated and embayments drained; coastlines have been reshaped. Some minerals have been exhausted (the iron ore of England's Cleveland hills) or have been considered too expensive to continue to be intensively mined (Sicily's sulphur). Others, however, have recently been discovered (the Netherlands' oil) or have been taken out of economic obscurity (Ireland's peat). Areas where settlements have been abandoned have been restored. New lines and systems of transportation have been formed, some on recent, others on ancient traces.

Age and diversity present certain obstacles to continued development of the landscape but at the same time afford dramatic opportunities. One obstacle to development is that technically advanced industries have large-scale commitments in capital investment (machinery and men), and that it may not be feasible to shift to an even more advanced stage because of the attendant economic and social disruption. Another obstacle lies in the sharp differences in rates of development that exist both within and between countries. While in theory, the surplus from more advanced areas could be used to build up the more backward ones, in practice, this surplus frequently is invested to accelerate the progress of the more advanced area.

Countering these general obstacles to continued economic development are two important forces: 1) the destruction of plants and machinery during World War Two and the disruptive effects of the postwar division of the continent, which forced a good deal of Maritime Europe to renovate its manufacturing plant, and 2) the opportunities for progress that are presented by an advanced, highly diversified landscape through area specialization and area interchange. Intimate inter-area associations stimulate less developed sections to intensify their rate of progress, because of their desires to emulate the advances that are being made by neighbors. In Europe, economic decentralization does not carry with it the risks of political separatism, as in larger, more dispersed regions. On the contrary, the economic buildup of southern France or southern Italy enhances the strength of the central government. In modern European experience, therefore, economic decentralization and political centralization fortify one another.

The diversity that characterizes Maritime Europe is to a great extent the result of the responses of different peoples to different physical environments. But some of this diversity has been politically inspired or intensified. It is with politically inspired differences, if they do not serve valid economic and social uses of the landscape, that today's proponents of European integration have their strongest quarrels.

We might divide the entire European geopolitical scene into two periods: 1) Pre-World War Two separatism and 2) Post-World War Two integration. In the first period, starting with the emergence of Europe from feudalism and culminating in the modern national state, differences within the physical environment served to set European peoples apart from one another. The divides between river valleys, in particular, served as barriers. Within river valleys, concentrations of population and economic activities constituted core areas for the emergence of national states. Some were along middle and upper river valley crossings, such as Augsburg (Lech-Danube), Vienna (Danube-Morava), Belgrade (Danube-Sava-Morava), and Paris (Seine-Marne). Others were at the lower courses of rivers or at the key coastal plains, such as London (Thames), The Hague (Rhine), Bucharest (Danube), Copenhagen, and Stockholm. Although the contemporary map of Europe indicates that inland seas and gulfs serve to separate states, these have not been historic barriers like the land divides. Indeed, the North, Baltic, and Mediterranean seas, and their various arms, have had a longer history as connectors than as separators. These seas began to be used as political boundaries in the seventeenth century, but only in the nineteenth and twentieth centuries did they take on their significant present forms.

The political-barrier qualities of land divides in Europe are perhaps best underscored by the fact that the boundaries that follow them have tended to remain fixed over longer periods of time than those that cut across broad plains areas. In this context, compare the greater permanence of boundaries that have followed the Swiss High Alps, the Pyrenees, the Carpathians, and the Transylvanian Alps with those that have cut across the North European or Danubian plains.[6]

It is not simply the negative qualities of nature as a barrier to movement that has helped to frame the European national state. In Maritime Europe, access to the open sea from a state's core area enabled small territories to compensate for limited hinterlands by acquiring extensive colonial forelands across the waters. Indeed, a small land area could sometimes be turned to advantage in that short land frontiers required limited armies, while fleets, with minimal manpower requirements, could compete for world power.

We can therefore explain the map of national state Europe both in terms of the influence of the landmass and in terms of relationship to other parts of the world by sea. The deeply embayed submerged Atlantic coasts and the multiplicity of key river valley contacts with the sea contributed to the relatively large number of European states. Particular note can be taken of the role of glaciation in this context. Continental glaciation and its meltwaters provided the fjords and submerged the non-glaciated embayments which opened much of the landmass to the oceanic world. The young rugged ranges of the Alpine period and the mountain glaciation formed in these Pluvial times have formed convenient national boundaries. Even the land features associated with continental glaciation, such as the morainic ridges along the Baltic coast or poorly drained marshes have, by their barrier nature, served as boundaries. The hills and swamps of the southern Baltic coast, not the sea, barred Sweden from Poland and Germany. Also, as land communications improved, a power invading from the sea, like Sweden, lost much of its former mobility advantage, because opposing land forces could now concentrate with greater speed to oppose the sea invasion.

[6] For an appreciation of this, cf. figures 15 and 16 in S. Whittemore Boggs, *International Boundaries* (New York: Columbia University Press, 1940), pp. 114 and 116-117.

Differences in the physical environment, then, served to set Europeans apart from one another during medieval and early modern times. These differences formed frameworks for emergent national states. These states have since taken on political, economic, military, and psychological features, which have fortified the differences stemming from the physical environment. What intensified this process was the carving out of colonial empires, which compensated for domestic resource limitations and dispensed with the need for European states to act in consonance with their neighbors.

Jean Gottmann has suggested that *iconography*—the ideas that men hold about political units, especially the national state—constitutes one of the two principal forces that operate in the political partitioning of the earth. The second and contrary force is the *movement* of men, goods, and ideas across state lines.[7] Iconography seeks to maintain the *status quo;* movement reflects the dynamics of man's use of the land. It challenges the *status quo* because it puts pressure on the barrier features of existing political units.

In pre-World War Two Europe, when the age of political separatism prevailed, the national state was used as an instrument to interrupt movement from one part of Europe to another. Iconography was oriented to the national state, and stood in contrast to movement forces. Since the Second World War a regional iconography has appeared. *Integration* has become the motivating economic and political spirit within Maritime Europe (and also Eastern Europe). Broad patterns of unity within the landscape, such as the running together of national ecumenes and the building of efficient avenues of transportation and communication, are now held up as rationales for the framework of integration. Movement and iconography are now no longer contrary forces.

Specific factors promoting Maritime Europe's integration are:

1) Common economic recovery problems;

2) Common fear of military and political pressure from the Soviet Union, directly or through local Communist parties;

3) Loss of many dependent areas and consequent reduction of over-all commitments;

[7] J. Gottmann, "Geography and International Relations," *World Politics,* III, No. 2 (January, 1951), pp. 153-73.

4) American support of European integration concepts and programs;

5) Economic specialization;

6) Counter-moves to East European integration programs;

7) An inward, or more European, orientation by European statesmen and peoples. This is in part due to the factors listed above. In great measure, however, it is due to changes in world power status. The two greatest powers in the world that emerged in the wake of World War Two are non-European. For Europe to gain a similar position, individual national state activities are inadequate, and some form of integrated action has been proposed as a substitute.

The integration of Maritime Europe is, in one sense, a vague concept because it means different things to different persons. To some Europeans it means political integration; to others, economic integration; to the U.S.S.R. it means the crystallizing of an anti-Soviet bloc as a satellite of the United States, in more or less the same relationship that the U.S.S.R. has with its Eastern European satellites. To many Americans the integration of Europe conjures up the picture of a United States of Europe. An integrated Europe could, as we have pointed out, evolve into a superstate, but it would have to have new forms and geopolitical goals.

The Physical Framework

Proponents of European integration point out that Europe has a unity that stems from the interaction of its physical and cultural diversities. These diversities are not hard and fast barriers, because they blend into the greater whole that is Maritime Europe.

Among the physical elements that favor unity is size. Maritime Europe is quite compact, with a land area of approximately 1,220,000 square miles. Its national ecumenes merge, and it is possible to travel through many countries and cultural areas in a very short time. To many Europeans, certainly, the provincialism of peoples in other parts of the world is unknown. Maximum distances in Western Europe, as from London to Munich or from Paris to Rome, are under 700 miles. One of the longest conceivable intra-European journeys, from Madrid to Hamburg, is only 1,200 miles.

Another unifying element is shape. Most of the land is never far removed from the ocean or the interior seas. Irregular coastlines have stimulated settlements, shipping, and fishing. Moreover, the long northeasterly trend of the coast from Portugal to Norway increases the extent of the area served by the warming and moistening westerly winds and currents. Even that small part of Maritime Europe that lies north of 60 degrees north latitude is warmed by the Atlantic, so that, unlike other parts of the earth in similar latitudes, it is habitable.

Although climatic differences are to be found in Europe, they are not sharp, but grade into one another, acting as complementary units. In this sense, climate can be considered a unifying element. Western Europe's west coast marine climate (mild winters, cool summers, and well-distributed rainfall) grades into that of Central Europe (where cyclonic winds are weaker, rainfall maximum is in the summer, and the winter frost period is longer). The Mediterranean climate is distinct from these other two climatic regions, but there are transitional zones that interconnect Europe's south and north. These are the climates of the Po Basin, the southern edge of the Massif Central, and northern Portugal. They are characterized by summers that are cooler than those in the Mediterranean and by slight cyclonic activity that brings late spring and early fall rain. Thus, in those countries where the Mediterranean climate and agricultural patterns prevail, especially in France and Italy, there are transitional physical and human-use areas, like the central Rhone and the Po, that serve to link their countries to the Europe north of the Alps.

Although physiographic regions are diverse, there is nevertheless a pattern to these distinct regions that makes interconnection easy. The outstanding physical feature is the North European Plain, with its associated lowland basins in France and England. This plain is surrounded by highlands. These include the north Scottish and the Fenno-Scandinavian Massifs to the north and the various Alpine ranges to the south. Associated with these Alpine ranges are enclosed or outlying plateaus, like the Spanish Meseta, the Massif Central, and the Bohemian Massif. Also enclosed within these ranges are such basins as the Po and the Upper and Middle Danube. The Alpine ranges, from whose crests streams flow either north and westward to the Atlantic, North, and Baltic seas, or south to the Mediterranean, serve as the main water divide for Europe. East-west travel has always been easy, in conformity with the North European and Danubian Plains. North-south or northwest-southeast movement has to be channeled through key pass routes in the Alps or along such river valleys as the Rhine-Moselle-Rhone, Rhine-Doubs-Saone-Rhone, and the Rhine-Main-Danube. Railways, roads, and navigable waterways occupy most of these passageways and many European cities have grown up at shipping points along the transcontinental routes. Thus, mountain barriers, while sufficient to discourage political intercourse, have never discouraged economic and cultural ties. This can be seen by examining the extent of the European ecumene, which stretches from the Scottish Lowland to the Rhine, the Pyrenees, and northern Italy—with gaps only in the Alps and central France.

Movement and Integration

Maritime Europe's inland transportation system is undergoing radical changes. The system is being modernized, rationalized, and unified, furthering the general cause of economic and political integration. Movement, as we have noted, succinctly expresses the dynamics of man's changing use of the landscape. Prior to World War Two, railroads accounted for most of the goods shipped within Maritime Europe. Today, rail accounts for only half of the ton-mileage, road for 35 per cent, and water for 15 per cent. This trend is continuing. The fuels, ores, and building materials traditionally handled by the European railways often can be moved more cheaply by water. Moreover, roads are capable of competing with rails for food, agricultural products, manufactured goods, and in some cases building materials, partly because of the short hauls for which railroads are used. For example, in the United Kingdom, West Germany, and Italy, highway hauls average up to 150 miles—or more than the average for railway trips. Railroads are being improved by integrating various national systems in rate-fixing and in handling, and by changing coal-burning locomotives to diesels and electrics. However, the railroad has had its period of dominance. A by-product of reduced railroad trackage should be the conversion of this valuable space for new highways, as in urbanized portions of the United States.

The entrance of Maritime Europe into the automotive age has come with breathtaking rapidity. Motor vehicles carry two-thirds of all passenger movement. Annual automobile production of over four and a half million is already three-fourths that of United States production, and truck production is even higher—90 per cent of ours. The increase in production and use of motor vehicles has created considerably greater intra-European movement and must be reckoned as an important integrating factor. Maritime Europe now has approximately 30 million registered passenger vehicles (as compared to 15 million in 1954), or one car for every ten persons. In the United States the ratio is one car for every three persons.

Production of automobiles on a per capita basis in such countries as France, West Germany, and the United Kingdom, is fast approaching that of the United States, and the ratio of automobiles to persons is rapidly rising. This ratio probably will never match that of our country; because of excellent public transportation systems and less sprawling cities, fewer families in Europe need two cars than in the United States.

If such indices as automobile accident deaths and chronic traffic jams can be used, then Maritime Europe is already in the automotive age with a vengeance. With half as many automobiles, its traffic death toll exceeds that of the United States. Poorer roads and denser populations make driving relatively hazardous in Europe, and the building of modern highways in large, urbanized areas like London, Paris, and Rome is extremely expensive. The net result of the desire of Europeans to have automobiles may be to force them to suburbanize at a rapid rate—more rapid than some planning authorities may wish to see. Also, because it is financially and socially easier to build modern highways in less populous areas; the frontiers between different European countries are likely to receive new highway construction more rapidly than some of the older big cities. The attendant problems notwithstanding, Maritime Europe will benefit increasingly from the automotive age. Not the least of these benefits will be derived from the role of the automobile as a social and economic force for European unity.

The map of European movement is undergoing change in intensity, quality, and directional flow of passengers and goods. (See Map 15.) Several projects which show the scope of this change are under way or in their final planning stages. These include: 1) *The English Channel Electric Grid Link.* This will enable hydroelectricity that is surplus in France during the rainy winter to be sold to the United Kingdom. During the summer, surplus English coal-generated electricity will be sold to water-short France. 2) *The Mont Blanc Auto Tunnel.* This will be the first automobile tunnel through the Alps. It will connect France to Italy by funneling traffic under the northern flank of the highest mountain in the Alps and through the Val d'Aosta. The Mont Blanc tunnel is expected to handle hundreds of thousands of vehicles annually, connecting Turin with both Geneva and Chamonix-Paris. It should be an important stimulus to tourism and business, cutting time distance from Paris to Rome by about one-fifth. This tunnel seven miles long is being built at a cost per mile that is in actuality less than the cost of highway construction in built-up areas like Greater London. *The Great St. Bernard Auto Tunnel* is also under way and will act as a further spur to German-Swiss-Italian traffic. 3) *The Moselle Canal.* Canalization of the Moselle River, from Thionville to Trier along the Rhine has finally been agreed upon by France, Luxembourg, and Germany. Use of the canal will enable Ruhr coal to be shipped to Lorraine at about half its present cost. Its use will effect similar savings in the shipment of France's iron ore to the Ruhr and will enable French steel to be exported via the Rhine. 4) *Transcontinental Pipelines.* The appearance of transcontinental pipelines is part of a revolutionary shift in the location of petroleum refineries toward the center of the European markets, not along Europe's coasts or at the sources of supply. Lines from Lavéra, west of Marseilles, to Strasbourg and Karlsruhe, and from Wilhelmshaven to Cologne, are designed to pipe petroleum to inland Rhine refineries. Other pipelines are aimed at moving petroleum from Genoa northward to Switzerland and northeast-

MAP 15. Maritime Europe's Movement Links

ward to southern Germany. Lines from Italy to Austria are also under consideration.

Other movement links are indefinite but nonetheless worthy of mention. These include: 1) *the English Channel Auto-Rail link,* which is proposed as either a tunnel or a bridge; 2) *the Rhone-Saone-Rhine Canal* (from Marseilles to Mulhouse), which may have to await greater political stability in the Mediterranean; 3) *the Rhine-Main-Danube Canal,* whose building would only be warranted by large-scale East-West trade; 4) *the Lake Maggiore-Adriatic Sea Canal,* which would utilize the Ticino-Po riverways; and 5) *a Trans-Pyrenees Auto Tunnel* under the Pic de la Glère to link Luchon in France to Benasque in Spain. The Spanish are interested in such a mid-Pyrenees Tunnel to connect industrialized southwestern France with Madrid.

Internationalized waterways are also a Soviet-bloc concern (links between the Danube and the Oder and between the Oder and the Vistula have been proposed), as are east-west pipelines from Soviet petroleum sources to Central Europe and to the Baltic. The future for innovations in Europe's land and water traffic links appears bright. If Common Market Europe and Free Trade Europe succeed in bridging their differences, some of the projects that have been mentioned may materialize more quickly than expected.

Ideological and political interaction is also an aspect of movement. In this respect, the inter-European ties of various National Catholic and Socialist parties can be regarded as forces for European unity. So is the mobility of labor, which brings with it a need on the part of the host country to fulfill the cultural as well as the material wants of the immigrant worker. The settling of people of different national origins, not in frontier zones, but in the very center of European states, is still another trend to be noted. No longer must we look to Alsace, Savoy, and southwestern Sweden for the zones of cultural contact that have developed as the result of movement of people. Now, Paris, London, Liverpool, Liège, Düsseldorf, Frankfort, and Zurich all contain sizable nonindigenous populations. Since national boundary zones are no longer the only cultural frontiers, their barrier qualities tend to lessen. Considering the general examples set by Maritime Europe since the Second World War, the Austrian-Italian dispute over "Italianization" of the German-speaking Tyrol would appear to be an unpleasant throwback to the prewar Europe.

The Resource Base

Many of Maritime Europe's economic problems are related to the resource base. Two questions arise with respect to this resource base: 1) what are Europe's raw materials? and 2) if distributed rationally, would these resources be able to build up the present national economies in a substantial manner?

In answer to the first question, it can be said that Maritime Europe is moderately wealthy in domestic raw materials, not in comparison with Anglo-America or the U.S.S.R., but with a more varied base than that of any other similar portion of the earth. If we compare the raw material base of the ecumenes only, Europe is not far behind the two superpowers. Among the important raw materials that are available in ample quantity in Maritime Europe are the coal of Germany and the United Kingdom, the iron ores of France and Sweden, the potash of Germany and France, the mercury of Spain, the sulphur of Sicily, the magnesium of Austria, the timber of Scandinavia, the waterpower of the Alps and Scandinavia, and the specialized foodstuffs of the North European Plain and the Mediterranean (dairy and horticultural). The fact that the region has an increasing agricultural deficit must be noted. While rapid agricultural expansion is under way, especially in the Common Market-stimulated French sector, this is an expansion oriented to specialty crops. Consequently, relative self-sufficiency, even as practiced by the United States and the Soviet Union, is impossible. Only a revolutionary development of the Sahara as an agricultural storehouse for fruits, vegetables, and industrial crops could alter this picture. In the Sahara, however, surface, subsurface, and shallow waters are generally lacking and large-scale irrigated farming would have to depend upon desalted water from the sea or from deep subterranean sources that are claimed by some to exist.

Among the minor supplies of raw materials available to Maritime Europe are such minerals as: manganese (Sweden and Italy), chrome (Greece), molybdenum (Norway), vanadium

(Norway), copper (Norway, Sweden, Spain, Germany), lead (Germany), phosphates (France and Belgium), and petroleum (Austria, Netherlands, Germany, France, Italy). Again, limitations of petroleum frustrate possibilities of regional industrial self-sufficiency, unless Saharan oil is assured.

All of these raw materials provide a substantial base for industry and it is easy to see how greater exchanges of materials within an integrated Europe have facilitated rises in production. For example, coal from Germany has been used to boost nitrogen output for fertilizer industries in Belgium, France, Italy, and Switzerland. Ruhr coal has also helped Italy and France to increase caustic soda production. Small amounts of surplus hydroelectric power are being sold by Luxembourg to surrounding localities in France, Belgium, and West Germany. The Dutch steel industry has been expanded with the aid of Luxembourg iron ores. Norway, whose hydroelectric potential is estimated at five times present capacity, could sell its surplus to Denmark. French bauxite and Sicilian sulphur are other materials that could be more fruitfully exploited by other European countries under the new production and marketing conditions.

Obviously economic integration has affected some industry more than others. These include steel, petroleum, chemicals, and power. In such industries, greater exchange of raw and semifinished materials means higher production of finished products also. In the power industries, a wider European market will continue to stimulate hydroelectricity developments and is likely to hasten the exploitation of France's Saharan petroleum. Even atomic power, although initial opinions of its potential have been tempered by recent gluts in coal and oil, is likely to experience more rapid progress because economic integration will enable smaller countries to benefit from the know-how and facilities of their larger neighbors.

The free interchange of labor has been an important factor in the greater exploitation of Europe's domestic raw materials as well as in its ability to process foreign materials. Mining in France, Belgium, and Germany, agriculture in France, and forestry in Sweden have been expanded with the help of foreign labor. This manpower has also benefited the Belgian building industry, Germany's steel and chemical manufacturing, and Switzerland's tourism. The European exporters of manpower—Italy, Spain, Greece, The Netherlands, Denmark, and Finland—have in recent years contributed most of Germany's 600,000, France's 500,000, and Sweden's 100,000 foreign workers. Indeed, Italy is now so concerned with the outflow of its citizenry that its northern factories are trying to entice some *emigrés* to return. Spain, which has replaced Italy as the chief labor recruiting area for other European countries, is beginning to anticipate domestic labor shortage as a crucial block to its own industrialization. We may foresee the day when North African, West Indian, Hong Kong and South Asian areas will become the major sources of European labor recruitment, in the absence of a sufficiently broad regional labor pool.

Europe's experience with the labor market offers lessons to outsiders. Thus, the successful techniques employed by Europeans in stimulating people to move from depressed, overpopulated areas to labor-deficit areas, and the solutions of chronic depressed-area problems, are now being studied by American experts who are concerned with the depressed areas of the United States.

Greater population mobility cannot help but act as a unifying element within Maritime Europe. The present population is growing slowly as compared to population growth in other parts of the world. In 1940 the population was 257 million, while today it is 290 million. This represents an annual increase of about 0.5 per cent over the past two decades. However, since the end of the Second World War the rate of growth has tended to increase in key European countries at an annual rate of 0.7 per cent for France, 1.2 per cent for The Netherlands, and 2 per cent for Germany. This increase is important to the Western European countries, where production growth has tended to outstrip population growth. Moreover, the Mediterranean countries have been unable to absorb their increasing populations, despite the fact that the increase is under 1 per cent. Consequently, countries like Italy, Spain, and Greece, whose economic bases are narrow are still able to export labor in small but highly significant quantities.

Organizational Frameworks

Various organizations are working at different levels to integrate Maritime Europe. Some are functional; others are political. The functional organizations attempt to unify Maritime Europe for specific purposes, economic and military. Among them are: W.E.U. (Western European Union—the European component of NATO); O.E.E.C. (Organization for European Economic Co-operation); O.E.C.D. (Organization for Economic Co-operation and Development); E.C.S.C. (European Coal and Steel Community); E.E.C. (European Economic Community—the Common Market); Euratom; E.F.T.A. (European Free Trade Association); and C.E.R.N. (European Organization of Nuclear Research). Among the organizations devoted to the creation of a united Europe through political means are the Council of Europe and the European Movement.

Unlike most of the functional organizations, the Council of Europe is not an intergovernmental agency, because its Assembly of Members of Parliament from the represented countries speak only for themselves. When efforts to turn the Council of Europe into a Federal Union failed, its leadership began to spur the idea of supranational specialized authorities possessing treaty powers granted by the participating states. The Coal and Steel Community was the first such supranational body, since followed by the Common Market and Euratom.

The most important act that has occurred in the postwar European integration process has been the creation of the E.E.C. —the Common Market of the Six. The constituent countries—France, West Germany, Italy, and the Benelux states—are the core of Maritime Europe. The Common Market, when organized in 1957, had as its purpose the extension over the entire economic field of the type of co-operation that was already being realized within the Coal and Steel Community. In these few years, the pace of reduction of internal customs dues and quotas has been more rapid than projected, labor has achieved free mobility, and capital movement-restrictions have been mostly eliminated. The market free from national discrimination is emerging. On the other hand, tariffs towards third states can be increased, and this is a major fear of the United States as well as of the rest of Maritime Europe.

Certainly Common Market countries could impose tariffs against outside raw materials and foodstuffs. If the 180 million population of the European Six were, in itself, the only market with which E.E.C. industry had to be concerned, higher tariffs upon outside materials might not have far-reaching internal effects. But to continue to prosper, Common Market Europe will have to continue to export. Wherever higher-cost domestic raw materials are used behind a protective tariff screen, the advantages in foreign trade that have been gained with such remarkable success are likely to be thrown away. If, for example, low-cost American coal is excluded by tariffs from Belgium to protect the Belgian coal industry, will Belgian wire be able to maintain its current price advantage that has given it half of the total U.S. market?

In general, the advantages that the Common Market offers its members in supplying a big internal market and an unrestricted flow of domestic raw materials should be sufficient to afford the import of foreign materials and products without economic discrimination. But specific industries could suffer if they sought tariff advantages, either from driving up export prices or from provoking foreign tariff retaliation.

Perhaps more than any other industry, agriculture has been represented as seeking to protect itself by Common Market walls. Small-scale, relatively inefficient German farming is not likely to survive the onslaught of French agricultural competition within a Common Market, unified-farm-pricing structure. But France in turn has been accused by critics of hoping to isolate its relatively high-priced farm products from the competitive effects of external competition. While such an eventuality is by no means impossible, there is no reason to assume that France's Common Market partners will blithely accept higher food costs and consequently lower living standards. Nor need we assume that French agriculture cannot follow the path of French manufacturing and adjust itself to both the demands and the opportunities of the Common Market. Indeed, the modern agricultural revolution that has swept over the American farm since 1940 has every possibility of capturing France's peasant base. True, deeply ingrained local practices and customs have kept French agriculture in a self-satisfied, static state. But part of the reason for the failure of the French farmer to modernize has been lack of market incentives and absence of pressures from forms of urban competition, like job opportunities and city-life amenities. The Common Market can change the situation overnight. New incentives represented by a European market that is four times the French market can inspire a chemical and mechanical revolution in French agriculture. Fast trucks, modern food processing, supermarkets, and home refrigerators are bound to create new demands for the mass production and marketing of foodstuffs, which will provide tremendous opportunities for French agriculture. With its rich and varied soil and climatic base, this agriculture should prove no less capable to responding to the challenge than French manufacturing has proved. At the same time, new employment opportunities in manufacturing and improved housing conditions in urban areas are likely to lure increasing numbers away from the farms and to spur the social land-use revolution that is bound to accompany the chemical-mechanical farming age.

Does all this mean that outside farm products would lose ground in their fight for the European Six Market? Not necessarily. Europe can well become self-sufficient in food grains and dairy products if it so desires, but the fertile "limon" soils of the Beauce need not remain essentially in cereals and in sugar beets. Under more intensive farming conditions, they can, in part, be converted to horticulture (though probably at the expense of Belgian and German farm interests). Extensive grazing in the Massif Central may lose out to intensive cattle rearing and fattening along the Loire and the Garonne. Viticulture may disappear from parts of the humid east in response to the pressure of horticulture and dairying. Intensification and change in French agriculture could well affect the competitive position of outside dairy and meat-producing countries, but is less likely to affect outside cereal producers (who might partly shift their market emphasis from food to feed grains). And in the long run, the modernization of horticulture, not only in France, but in Mediterranean Europe, could shift the internal emphasis from livestock also, increasing the market potential for outside producers.

In response to the Common Market's emergence, the E.F.T.A. (Free Trade Europe of the Outer Seven) and the O.E.C.D. (the Organization for Economic Co-operation and Development) have been formed. The latter organization, including the United States and Canada as well as eighteen European countries, has been conceived by the United States as a replacement for the O.E.E.C. Its goal is greater North Atlantic economic co-operation and co-ordinated aid to underdeveloped countries. The E.F.T.A., initiated by Britain, was designed to secure greater economic co-operation among its participants, while maintaining existing external associations. For while tariffs among member countries are to be eliminated, separate tariffs can be leveled by individual states upon third parties.

The fear voiced by many that E.E.C. and E.F.T.A. would crystallize as separate and rival blocs in Maritime Europe seems to have been exaggerated. Certainly Britain's decision to seek entry into the Common Market reflects the preponderant strength of the forces that are driving towards economic integration.

We may well view the present trade conflicts and negotiations as an important stage in an evolutionary process. Integrated Maritime Europe needs a core and this can best be provided by the Europe of the Six. Integrated Europe also needs to maintain strong associations with the outside world. While the French Community is representative of such ties, Free Trade Europe, which has been formed around Britain and its Commonwealth, has even stronger extra-regional bonds.

If the core can be firmly consolidated without destroying outside associations, the results will be mutually beneficial to Maritime Europe and to those former colonial countries that maintain close economic and cultural ties with Europe. In the event that these ties cannot be maintained, the rupture will have grave political-ideological consequences. For the Commonwealth and the French Community represent the best chance that the Western world has for maintaining sound global contacts that cut across racial and religious lines. Without such ties, our divided world might well become an assortment of hopelessly isolated blocs.

A European Capital

"Wanted—a capital city: centrally located, good accessibility, cosmopolitan in flavor, spacious, moderate climate, economically and politically stable, and with a 'European' tradition." Europeans have been searching for such a city since 1950, but with no success to date.

As the number of organizations charged with integrating Europe proliferates, administration and personnel overlap. To help achieve co-ordination and rationalization of the integrating activities, their localization in one city seems highly desirable. Beyond the economic-social aspects of such localization, a central seat can fulfill broader political-psychological functions. If Maritime Europe is to be united it needs a capital to symbolize this unity, as well as to centralize it.

At present, the chief European organizations are located in four cities: Brussels, Luxembourg City, Paris, and Strasbourg. All told, eight different cities house seventeen major European organizations. Even the European Community—the "little Europe" of the Six—has not been able to fix upon one capital. The Coal and Steel Community is housed in Luxembourg City, while the Common Market and Euratom are in Brussels. O.E.C.D., the major economic organization, is centered in Paris, and the Council of Europe is in Strasbourg. (See Map 16.)

Table 8 is a selected list of major European organizations. Some, like E.C.E. and the European W.H.O., are United Nations-sponsored agencies; O.E.C.D. includes, as associated members, the United States and Canada. The European Organization for Space Research includes one non-European state—Australia. This addition makes available to Maritime Europe the Australian empty space. To European countries other than France, the use of the Sahara is politically complicated as long as France's relations with North Africa remain in their present uncertain state. On the other hand, the Australian range at Woomera affords its European users the room for launching satellites, without attendant political problems.

It is one matter to describe the qualities needed by a national

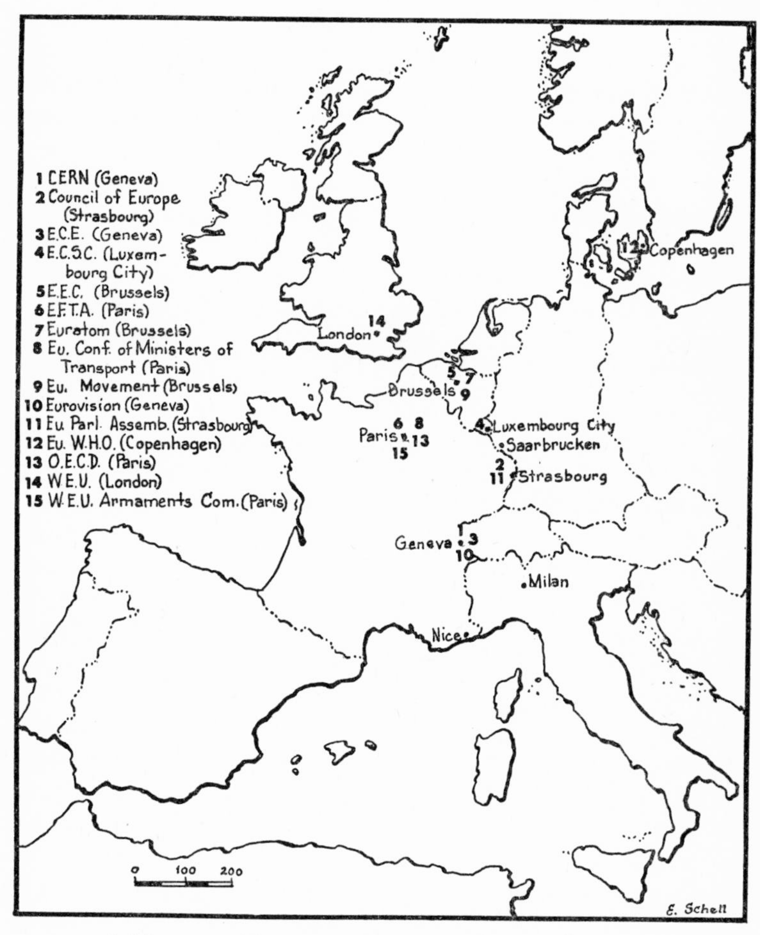

MAP 16. Maritime European Organization Headquarter Cities

TABLE 8

Maritime European Organization Headquarter Cities

Name	City	Number of Participating States
CERN (European Organization of Nuclear Research)	Meyrin (Geneva)	14
Council of Europe (and Consultative Assembly)	Strasbourg	15
E.C.E. (Economic Commission for Europe)	Geneva	29
E.C.S.C. (European Coal and Steel Community)	Luxembourg City	6
E.E.C. (European Economic Community)	Brussels	6
E.F.T.A. (European Free Trade Association)	Paris	7
Euratom (European Atomic Energy Community)	Brussels	6
European Conferences of Ministers of Transport	Paris	17
European Movement	Brussels	15
Eurovision	Geneva	15
European Parliamentary Assembly	Strasbourg	6
European World Health Organization	Copenhagen	30
Nordic Council	none	5
O.E.E.C. (Organization for European Economic Cooperation); (currently being supplanted by the Organization for Economic Cooperation and Development—O.E.C.D.)	Paris	20
Western European Union	London	7
Western European Union, Standing Armaments Committee	Paris	7

capital; it is quite a different matter to sketch out United Europe's requirements for a capital seat.

The chief function of a national capital is to unify the state. The capital city is the center from which radiate the various political and cultural influences that have "nationalizing" effects. Generally, capitals are found within the historic core of the state—that is, within the area of political and population concentration from which the state evolved. Paris is one such example; ancient Rome was another. Historic cores tend to be centrally located within their states. Where they have been eccentric, capitals have often shifted from them to a more central location, such as in the case of Madrid. Sometimes centrality of location corresponds with the compromise choice of a site against two or more competing cities. Warsaw is an example, chosen over two former capitals, Poznan and Cracow. All capitals, whether central or eccentric, seek easy accessibility to the entire state.

Defensive qualities have been important considerations for locating capitals, as far as both specific sites and general locations are concerned. Budapest is the defensive point where the Danube enters from its last gorge onto the central plain. Ankara was chosen by Ataturk because of its remoteness from the sea.

Border capitals have fulfilled both defensive and offensive functions. Vienna was essentially a frontier-defender from its foundation to the late seventeenth century. Then, with the decline of the Turkish threat, it began to take advantage of its situation's excellent accessibility to three natural passageways: the Austrian, Moravian, and Hungarian gates. Other frontier capitals have been assigned offensive-colonizing roles. These are the *Wachstumspitzen* or forward points, like fifteenth-century Berlin and modern Jerusalem. Rawalpindi (Islamabad), the new capital of Pakistan, is another example.

Once a city becomes a capital, it generally grows rapidly because of its political importance to the state. Rome's growth was supported by the tribute of an empire, Washington's by the taxes of an entire nation. As Whittlesey put it, "the capital city reflects the wealth, power and political organization of the state of which it is the administrative center . . . (capitals) incarnate the corelands that have evolved as nationalities." [8]

However, Europe is not looking for the capital of a nation—it is looking for the capital of a group of nations. Perhaps Europe's capital should possess the locational qualities that federal capitals possess. Federal capitals have been located so as to avoid ill-feeling and jealousies between constituent units and to be as neutral of regional politics as possible. Washington, Ottawa, and Canberra are such cities. Brasilia, chosen partly

[8] Whittlesey, *The Earth and the State,* pp. 159, 196.

for such a purpose, was also chosen as a frontier focal point which could unite Brazilians in a drive to conquer the interior.

When we consider Maritime Europe's needs, there is no interior frontier that requires the development-assistance of a capital. Nor is there much enthusiasm over the advantages of an extraterritorial middle-ground type of location, such as has been suggested for a 100-square-mile area along the German-Dutch-Belgian border, an area that has been in dispute since 1940. Many Europeans feel that it is more important to locate the capital in a country that is lukewarm about unity than to select a country or an area that is a small intermediary. This is not unlike the thinking that strongly favored locating the United Nations headquarters in the United States to keep the interest of the American public in the United Nations at a high pitch. Whether or not to seek a frontier capital along the Iron Curtain represents still another challenge to the location-seekers. The defensive liabilities of such a measure are obvious; on the other hand, it might be argued that the forward thrust of a European capital could have political-psychological advantages in maintaining close physical contact with Eastern Europe.

Among the cities that have been considered likely candidates for the capital seat are Brussels, Strasbourg, Milan, Nice, Luxembourg City, Paris, Geneva, and Saarbrucken. How closely they meet locational needs can only be judged by matching their qualifications with a list of "ideal" prerequisites. A European capital should, in our opinion, possess the following characteristics: 1) centrality within the European ecumene; 2) accessibility of air, rail, and highway routes; 3) size and economic diversity sufficient, not simply to "house" the capital, but to develop large and rich "European" cultural and economic institutions befitting a capital; 4) architectural blend of traditional Europe and the modern; 5) political and economic stability within the city so as to isolate the governing institutions from mob violence, terrorism, and more subtle forms of pressure; 6) high degree of multilinguism, a feature that is prevalent in many of Europe's cities.

Of the cities that have been considered, neither Saarbrucken nor Geneva has strong backing today. Had the Saar become an autonomous district within the Western European Union, the choice of Saarbrucken would have appealed to many. Rejection of a Europeanized Saar in the referendum of 1955 has left Saarbrucken with few of the necessary qualifications for the capital. Geneva's location, facilities, and traditions as an international center are well known, and the city is busy absorbing hundreds of United Nations and European civil servants. However, Switzerland has remained aloof from the Council of Europe, Western European Union, and E.E.C., in an attempt to maintain neutrality in political and military matters. Its strongest concession to joint European action, to date, has been membership in E.F.T.A.

The core of integrating Europe is the Europe of the Six. This is the Europe that has the greatest immediate need for one capital, and it is from within this Europe that such cities as Brussels, Strasbourg, Milan, Nice, Luxembourg, and Paris have been suggested as capital sites. Today's capital of Europe's Six is likely to be tomorrow's capital of Maritime Europe and eventually of Maritime Europe and the Maghreb. London, Copenhagen, and Vienna are too eccentric to fulfill the function of a capital, and the latter two are overly exposed frontier cities besides. The choice of a city should be made within the core and with an expanded, unified Europe in mind.

Cities like Nice, Luxembourg City, and Strasbourg lack some of the necessary qualifications. Nice appears to be too small, too eccentric, and too one-sided in its economy. Luxembourg City, while more central, is nonetheless not especially well served by road or airplane. Moreover, it is a very small city (only 75,000 population). Strasbourg reflects much of the north-south unity of Europe in its location and architecture, and is on good east-west rail and automobile lines. The Mont Blanc and Great St. Bernard Auto Tunnels will improve road accessibility from the Mediterranean. Strasbourg is also multilingual. It is, however, a small city (under 250,000 population), does not have a broad economic base, and is not quite as well served by air as are larger European cities.

Brussels and Milan, the cities with over a million in population among core cities thus far mentioned, have many desirable qualities as capitals. Milan, the trade crossroads of the past, is both an ancient and a modern city. It has a strong, vibrant, diversified economic base and many cultural attractions, and it is close to the Alps, which provide recreational amenities. With access to the entire Mediterranean, Milan would be able to symbolize the need for European-Maghreb unity. The city does, however, have some liabilities. It would be eccentric to Maritime Europe-Maghreb as a whole, and certainly eccentric to the broader North Atlantic region; it is not multilingual; and it is a city in which industrial tension and Communist party strength can pressure governing bodies.

Brussels is perhaps the most central of all large cities within the European ecumene; it is highly accessible to the United Kingdom, the North Atlantic, Northern Europe, and Europe north of the Alps; it possesses beauty, culture, and economic strength; its industries are light and spread throughout the suburbs; and it has not been especially subject to industrial strife. While the Flemish-Walloon tensions that have plagued parts of Belgium are present in Brussels, such tensions are sporadic and not serious enough to jeopardize the normal workings of government. If the recent violence should persist or intensify, this would diminish the desirability of Brussels as a capital site. While it is a North European city by virtue of its location in Flemish Belgium, Brussels is French in character and multilingual in speech. Flemish, akin to Dutch, is a Germanic tongue spoken by many. The majority of the city, however, speaks French and is attractive culturally to all of the Mediterranean region. Finally, Brussels is representative of a zone that has been Western Europe's neutral zone in the past.

No European city has to grapple with the problems of racial discrimination that beset cities like Washington and New York, hindering their functions as national and international capitals. On the other hand, cities that can be subjected to violence and terrorism, like Paris, owing to the 200,000 North African Muslims in its midst, are probably not the most feasible candidates for the seat. If peace in North Africa should be fully realized, then this negative quality would turn into an important asset. This, added to the many obvious advantages that Paris possesses, could fortify its claim to the capital seat of the Maritime Europe-Maghreb region.

Relations with the Maghreb

The relationship of Maritime Europe to North Africa can, in part, be explained by the form and vicinal location of the Mediterranean Sea. The Mediterranean is an interior arm of the Atlantic. Structurally, the basin consists of four distinct units, exclusive of the Black Sea. In form, however, geographers have considered the sea as having three basins: the Western, the Eastern, and the Black—or two: the Western (to be precise, the Northwestern) and the Eastern (Southeastern). The latter division omits the Black Sea. Whichever the case, the Mediterranean is not a unit, structurally or morphologically. Moreover, the character of its littoral is quite varied. Newbigin has said, "The Mediterranean Basin is not a unit; its shores belong here to the desert area, and there to Central Europe; only at intervals are they truly Mediterranean." [9] The coastlands are diverse, and the relationship of their parts to adjoining power cores adds to this diversity.

When we consider the above factors, it is little wonder that political separatism, not unity, has characterized the Mediterranean basin. Only Rome succeeded in unifying the sea completely. The Phoenicians, Greeks, Carthaginians, Moors, Turks, and West Europeans failed to do so, although the Greeks and Turks did unify the Eastern basin geopolitically. France, now that it acts in harmony with its European Mediterranean neighbors, can be said to have unified the bulk of the Western basin strategically, for the time being.

For most of its history, the Eastern Mediterranean has been under Middle Eastern-Asian influences. Unlike its western counterpart, this basin possesses several major passages into the interior lands. The Black Sea provides the opening into the Ukrainian steppes and the Lower Danube; Asia Minor's coastal streams into the Anatolian Plateau; the Syrian Saddle and Syrian Gate into Mesopotamia; the Isthmus of Suez and Red Sea to Arabia; the Nile Delta into the Valley proper; the Vardar-Morava

[9] Marion Newbigin, *The Mediterranean Lands* (New York: Knopf, 1924), p. 211.

Rivers into the Middle Danube; and the Gulf of Trieste-Klagenfurt and Ljubljana passes into the Upper Danube Valley.

Because it is accessible to these populous and well-endowed interior reaches, the fate of the Eastern Mediterranean has been tied to the rise and fall of its hinterland powers. Unity has been imposed from all sides of the basin—from Egypt, the Levant, and the North, as the core of power has shifted along the littoral. Balanced strength among these bordering nations has meant political separateness within the basin.

The Western Mediterranean basin has experienced a different history of political development. With the line from Sicily to Cape Bon as its boundary, the Western Mediterranean's narrow coast is, for the most part, encircled by young, fold mountains. There are few breaks across these mountains and no significant ones through the desert, such as the Nile. In addition, the Western Mediterranean contains a number of islands that are accessible to both northern and southern coasts (the Balearics, Corsica, Sardinia, and Sicily). Long ago settled by Europeans, these islands are outposts for European states in their strategic relationships with the southern shores.

The absence of effective breaks across the surrounding mountains has, until modern times, made the issue of control an internal or "family" matter within the Western basin. Thus, Carthage, Rome, North Africa, Spain, France, and Italy vied for control of the basin, with little outside interference. Because of the weaker North African support base, the Moors (as well as the Carthaginians before them) did not penetrate effectively beyond Spain, Sardinia, and parts of Sicily. During the Middle Ages, Spanish-French-Austrian rivalry over Italy diverted the attention of the European powers from the North African coast. With modern times came two changes: 1) improvements in land communications across Western Europe to the Mediterranean, and 2) the Anglo-French alliance, which controlled both the western entrance to the Mediterranean and the trans-Mediterranean sea lanes. As a result, France was enabled to attain strategic control over most of the Maghreb, entering Algeria in 1830, Morocco in 1875, and Tunisia six years later. However, Spanish and Italian counterinterests, as well as recurrent strife with Germany, prevented France from gaining unchallenged mastery of Western North Africa. Moreover, the geopolitical patterns of colonial association that France forged with this part of the Muslim world proved incompatible with Muslim demands for equality and political self-determination.

France's greatest omission, from the standpoint of its need to forge enduring geopolitical ties with North Africa, was that it did not populate the region adequately with Frenchmen or other Europeans.

During the European conquest of Africa, many Europeans saw in the southern continent an outlet for mass settlement, as well as a source of raw materials and potential markets. The fact is, however, that not even a favorable settlement locale like Mediterranean North Africa, let alone the unfavorable tropical reaches of most of the continent, succeeded in attracting mass European migration. North Africa measured its annual immigration in the thousands, not the tens or the hundreds of thousands. After the first fifty years of French colonization in Algeria, the European population numbered only about 400,000. A half-century later, this figure had increased to 800,000, with natural increase accounting for the major share of the growth. In 1961 the figure was about 1,000,000. France did not populate Algeria on a larger scale for two reasons: 1) France lacked surplus population at home, and 2) France was not suffering from the hopelessness of economic plight that had driven most of its neighbors to become large-scale immigrant exporters. French farmers and workers were reluctant to move to Algeria as colonists, where they had to face the competition of cheap Muslim labor.

It is always tantalizing to speculate how different the geopolitical map would took today had European co-operation been as advanced a century ago as it is today. Had there been joint action on colonization even between France and Italy during the great period of emigration, North Africa today would be part of Europe. This presupposes that the increased immigration would have been more adequately supported by manufacturing than it has been in the actual course of North African economic development. A broader resource than is available within most of the European Mediterranean, a European laboring class, and greater pressures on France to support North

African industrialization, would have favored such a process.

Leon Gambetta, France's Prime Minister during the occupation of Tunisia, is quoted as having said in 1880 that the configuration of the French coasts and the establishment of French rule in Algeria had made the Mediterranean, and especially the Western Mediterranean, France's "scene of action."[10] History has borne him out, but not in the geopolitical form that he had envisaged. For after 125 years of colonization and acculturation activities, France's political influence in the Maghreb is still tenuous. From recent events it has become apparent that France alone cannot maintain the necessary European association with North Africa. A united Maritime Europe, however, could assert its strategic dominance over the Maghreb if driven to take such a step—a situation that is quite similar to Soviet-Eastern European and United States-Caribbean geopolitical relations. It would utilize its control over Atlantic and trans-Mediterranean sea lanes and the Mediterranean islands to do so. Then applying its economic strength and cultural attraction, it could organize the geopolitical framework within which to unify the Western Mediterranean.

The participants in such a geopolitical program would be Maritime Europe and the Maghreb—not outside forces. For outside intervention could be attempted from distant bases only. The nearest are militarily weak and economically underdeveloped states in West Africa and the Middle East. These states lie across broad desert barriers. This is not to say that such states *must* play a negligible role in the Western Mediterranean. For in the past few years, Egypt has been a prominent sponsor of the Algerian revolution, and Black African support of the F.L.N. has been a significant factor in the halls of the United Nations. But these outside areas can only influence the situation when the leaders of the Muslim Maghreb wish to invite such influence. In comparison with either West Africa or the Arab Middle East, the Maghreb can more than stand on its own feet in leadership cadre, cultural levels, military forces, and stage of economic development. Ultimately, this should prove the decisive element in fashioning an accommodation within the Western Mediterranean.

[10] Quoted in Norman Harris, *Intervention and Colonization in Africa* (Boston: Houghton, Mifflin, 1914), p. 238.

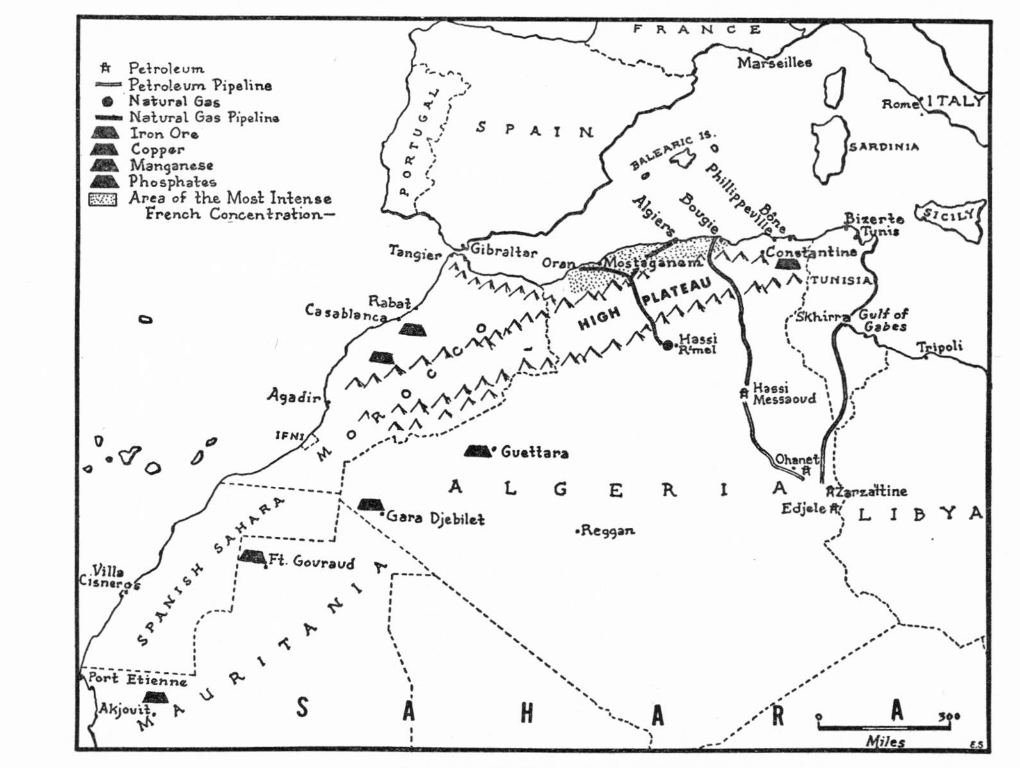

MAP 17. The Maghreb's Mineral Resources

The initiative for such geopolitical accommodation must come from the European side and, under the leadership of Charles de Gaulle, such initiative has finally been exercised. A unified Maritime Europe would possess the capacity to formulate a political and economic agreement that could satisfy the pressing interests of the Muslim Maghreb, without sacrificing European strategic requirements.

Can Europe and the entire Free World afford anything short of such accommodation? Were the Maghreb to turn away from the West and become a Soviet base, the wartime defense of Western Europe would be nearly impossible. Attack upon Europe from the East by conventional land and air assault would be difficult enough for NATO to repel. Were it to come from the Mediterranean as well, the attack could hardly be stemmed. Foreseeing such an eventuality, the alternative left to Europeans would be either nuclear holocaust or surrender. Even without war, an encircled Maritime Europe would be subject to currents that would expose southern Europe to extreme pressures of subversion, as well as isolate most of the African continent from Europe. Spain, Portugal, France, and Italy would become targets of individual and group activities that could operate with relative impunity from North Africa, unless Europe should draw a new Iron Curtain across the Mediterranean.

Another aspect of strategic location, empty space, has already been mentioned. To France today, as well as to United Europe tomorrow, the availability of vacant reaches for nuclear bomb testing and for missile shoots is strategically important. Reggan, in the central Algerian Sahara, has been the site of French nuclear bomb testings. Even if atmospheric testing of such devices should be banned, the need for use of such a vacant area for other military and civilian space-age projects would be no less. (See Map 17.)

To distinguish economic from locational strategic necessity is not easy. For what makes an area important is not simply where it is, but what it contains. To imperial Rome, North African wheat became a strategic necessity because of the remoteness of the Egyptian supply and the exhaustion of Sicily's grain lands. Centuries later, France returned to North Africa, where she developed its wheat, vine, and citrus products. Considering the wealth of the Metropolitan French agriculture, these commodities can scarcely be described as strategically vital. Indeed, until 1959, arguments as to the strategic economic importance of North Africa to France were spurious. North Africa's role as a breadbasket, a supplier of iron ore and phosphates, and a source of manpower for the French armed forces was more than counterbalanced by the French expenditures in social services and in policing the area. As a protected market, North Africa and other parts of the French Empire acted as "opiates" to French factories, which did not feel bound to modernize and to innovate as rapidly as many of their European neighbors. Only after Tunisia and Morocco had gained their independence and Algeria had been torn apart by revolt was the strategic-economic element injected into the conflict—the discovery of petroleum, which began to flow in significant commercial quantities from the Hassi Messaoud fields in 1959.

Petroleum is France's most important raw material strategically. Its cost of import represents an annual drain of half a billion dollars, and 15 per cent of all imports. Far more important than foreign exchange expenditures, however, is the strategic dependence that France has had upon the Middle East for its supply of oil. During the Sinai-Suez campaign of 1956, this supply was cut at both the Suez Canal and the Syrian overland pipeline routes. With ample Algerian oil, France will never again be vulnerable to Middle Eastern economic or military pressures. To a lesser extent this can also hold true for a unified Maritime Europe.

The flow of Algerian petroleum to France has exceeded expectations. The three major fields at Hassi Messaoud, Edjele, and Zarzaitine have been connected to the coast by 24-inch pipe lines (at Bougie, Algeria and Skhirra, Tunisia) and interconnected by a 30-inch pipe line from Ohanet to Hassi Messaoud. The 1962 goal of 20 million tons is being met with high quality crude oil. Moreover, 1965 production goals of 50 million tons seem quite within reach, considering the fact that Algerian oil reserves are now estimated at three-quarters of a billion tons. Since France consumes 35 million tons of petroleum annually, Algerian oil is likely to become available to other Western European countries in quantity. In addition, very rich natural gas deposits in the Central Sahara at Hasi R'Mel have been connected to Oran and Algiers by pipeline. Plans are to export much of this gas in liquid form, via tanker or underwater pipeline.

Less significant strategically, but of great economic potential value, is the iron ore of the Sahara. Fort Gouraud in Mauretania has hemitate reserves of 200 million tons, but Gara Djebilet, in Western Algeria, has reserves that are estimated at three billion tons. This is a surface deposit that is considered to be larger than any other single deposit in the world. Smaller desert deposits of manganese at Guettara and copper at Akjouit (in Mauretania) add to the favorable picture of mineralization. Finally, the Saharan environment could become the world's major base for solar energy production.

Although France temporarily detached the Saharan departments, administratively, from Algeria, the political future of this area will be tied to Algeria if Algeria remains associated with France. Morocco claims much of the Western Sahara, including Mauretania's portions, and has already encroached upon Algerian territory. Tunisia has sought a frontier change along the Algerian border, the gain of which might touch off further claims upon oil-bearing territories farther south at Edjele. To compound the complications, France and Spain have failed to agree upon accessways for transporting the mineral wealth of the Western Sahara. Fort Gouraud's iron ore needs an outlet to the Atlantic. The French-proposed rail line to Port Etienne would have to pass through southeastern Spanish Sahara. The Spanish counter-proposal is to build a railroad half as long as that suggested by France to the Spanish Sahara's port of Villa Cisneros. If the vast iron deposits of the Saoura Department are to be exploited, then the logical outlet for them might be via rail to Agadir in Morocco, or through Moroccan territory to the Spanish enclave of Ifni, which is also claimed by Morocco.

It is clear that the Saharan departments cannot exist in political isolation. Charles de Gaulle put it thus:[11] "Our line of conduct is that which safeguards our interests and which takes reality into account. . . . The realities, they are that there is not one Algerian . . . who does not believe that the Sahara should be part of

[11] Fifth Press Conference, Paris, September 5, 1961, Charles de Gaulle.

Algeria, and that there would not be one single Algerian Government, whatever may be its orientation with regard to France, who would not ceaselessly proclaim Algerian sovereignty over the Sahara." On the other hand, it is equally clear that French interests in the Sahara concerning oil exploitation and transit rights are also realities—strategic realities. With Saharan oil France will not only be free from Middle Eastern pressures; it will also be able to play a more dominant role within the Common Market. In recognition of the need to safeguard these French interests, de Gaulle has said, "If neither this safeguard (of French interests) nor association are possible on the Algerian side, we must create, out of all that stone and all that sand, something special as long as and insofar as, for us, the disadvantage be no greater than the advantage."[12] The solution in the Sahara will await the final solution in Algeria. To assume that the Sahara can be separated from North Africa and be geopolitically attached to Black Africa would flaunt geographical and military realities.

Without the Saharan lands, Algeria takes on most of Mediterranean California's physical characteristics. Containing two-thirds the population and land area of California, Algeria has a threefold climatic and landform division: 1) A semihumid zone: the densely settled coastal plain, rolling hills, and Tell Atlas Mountains. The climate is Mediterranean, with from 30 to 60 inches of winter rainfall; (2) a semiarid zone: the high intermontane plateau, with 12 inches of rainfall, or less; and 3) the Saharan Atlas Mountains, with 20 inches of rainfall on the northern-facing slopes and desert on the southern side.

Productive land in Algeria covers 17,000 square miles, or about four-fifths of California's crop land. Sizable deposits of iron ore, phosphates, and manganese, when added to the oil, natural gas, iron, and copper of the Sahara, provide Algeria with as favorable a mineral base as California's.

However, the two regions differ fundamentally in several respects, mostly related to human use. Among the major differences are these: 1) cultural and technological level of the bulk of the inhabitants in agriculture as well as manufacturing;

[12] *Ibid.*

2) high degree of urbanization and industrialization in California, compared to the fact that 70 per cent of Algeria is rural; 3) availability to California of water resources from the humid portions of northern California and the Rockies-fed Colorado River system; 4) difference in political status of the two units.

Algeria requires both farm reform and a broad manufacturing base to lift its nine million Muslims out of their present poverty. Algeria also needs increased possibilities for large-scale emigration to help relieve its population pressures. Not only France, but all of Maritime Europe can provide such an outlet. Agriculture, especially, has been molded to the desires of Europeans, not to the needs of native farmers. Over 500,000 acres, for example, are in vineyards. From these are produced 500 million gallons of wine annually that are mostly sent to France as cheap table wines. These are among the best lands and ought to be in food crops. The French do not need additional wine and the Muslims do not want it. Grains are grown on nearly 80 per cent of all farm land, mainly under primitive, dry farming conditions. While cereals are badly needed locally, an increase in their production can undoubtedly be accomplished through intensification and modernization, while at the same time some of the acreage currently in grains can be turned over to vegetables, citrus, and livestock. Land reform (one-third of all land under cultivation is owned by Europeans), education, irrigation, and rural electricity can change the agricultural face of Algeria. In recognition of this, the Constantine Plan of 1958 put forth agrarian reform as one of its major goals, fostering land distribution, cooperatives, modern farm techniques, and crop change-over. Without peace, however, agricultural and all other fields of economic reform have remained will-o'-the-wisps.

The Algerian referendum of July, 1962, confirmed the Evian agreements between France and the Algerian nationalists on Algerian self-determination. While the basis for agreement is cooperation and economic association between Algeria and France, the schism within Algerian nationalist ranks over this issue is deep. If the Algerian nationalists choose association with France, the future can be bright economically. Such a choice, however, will mean clear-cut political-military identity with Maritime Europe and with the latter's global views and commitments.

The driving forces behind association are diverse. They include the strategic, political, economic, and cultural-psychological elements that have been noted. Petroleum and natural gas, especially, can serve as unifiers between France and Algeria, provided that the Algerian economic stake is not relegated to the production and transportation of these minerals. If Algerian industrial and consumer wants should become highly dependent upon an uninterrupted flow of these fuels, then the Algerian need to maintain a common front with France will become a matter of practical politics. Syria had little to lose (save a small transportation royalty) when as a reaction to the Anglo-French intervention in the Sinai campaign, it cut the petroleum pipeline from Iraq to the Mediterranean. Its economy was not directly related to the "black gold" that flowed across its territory. An Algerian economy that used Saharan fuels to the point where it could not survive without them, would be a strong element for political, as well as economic, association with France.

The second outstanding force for association is emigration. Industrialization cannot solve the Algerian overpopulation problem in this generation. Indeed, the very wealth of Algeria's minerals and the availability of large amounts of French investment capital could stimulate the development of a high value, modern, manufacturing economy in Algeria that would not be able to absorb large numbers of workers. Oil refineries, chemical plants, steel mills, construction materials factories—the reflections of Algeria's specialized mineral base—are likely to be built in modern, automated forms, especially if Algeria seeks to keep pace with Common Market Europe. If manufacturing should be based upon a small, skilled, well-paid group, in contrast to the broad, rural population base, with its limited income, then financial and social frictions would become sharp. It appears probable that the Algerian manufacturing base will not be able to absorb hundreds of thousands of workers in the next few years. Emigration to Maritime Europe will be necessary to absorb this surplus population and to contribute financial support to the Mother Country. Without association with France, and through France with the rest of Maritime Europe, such an outlet will not be available.

Perhaps the leadership of the New Algeria will reject the road of association because of the Cold War involvements which it must bring. In our opinion, Algerian plans for neutralism are likely to prove illusory. For there is no possibility that an Algerian neutralism that might open the gates to hostile forces from the East could be left unchallenged by Europe. If association between France and Algeria should be rejected, what then? Partition is no longer a possibility because of the flight of Europeans from Algeria that was touched off by the O.A.S. War of Terror during the spring of 1962. When de Gaulle first returned to power, partition could well have been imposed by the concerted action of the French Government, the French Army, and the European settlers. With Oran (60 per cent European) and Algiers (55 per cent European) as cornerstones, a French Algerian department could have been extended eastward from Oran to Bougie and southward to the Tell Atlas crests. French minorities in Philippeville, Bône, and Constantine, along with Muslims who desired to reside in the French area, might have been relocated. It was possible to have conceived of a partitioned Algeria, 400 miles in east-west extent and 50 to 70 miles in north-south depth. A population with the 1,000,000 Europeans in the majority would have had at its disposal an area larger than that of Switzerland, Israel, or Puerto Rico, with the Mediterranean as the economic and military link to the Mainland France support-base. Such a partitioned area would have been reminiscent of the first partition of Algeria, when France received at the Treaty of Tafna (1837) the Oran area (from Oran to Mostaganem) and Algiers and its hinterland (the Mitijda Plain).

Because partition is no longer a realistic alternative, France and the West have no recourse but to make sure that the Evian agreements are upheld. Our reaction to a temporary turn to neutralism by Algerian nationalism should not be passive acceptance or "hands-off" disillusionment. Instead, such a term should be accepted as a challenge to the determination and ingenuity of France and its allies to create the geopolitical unity of Maritime Europe and the Maghreb that is so vital to the well-being of both parties and to the Maritime World as a whole. The presence of the French Army in Algeria and the question of control over Saharan petroleum remain trump cards for the West in the months of critical negotiation that lie ahead.

If the efforts to integrate Maritime Europe and the Maghreb

were to have as their goal the creation of a superstate that would duplicate and compete with the other two superstates, the goal would prove illusory. Because of its limited size, its lack of effective national territory, its agricultural deficiencies, and its intermediate location between the ecumenes of the United States and the U.S.S.R., the European superstate cannot be an imitation of the others.

Moreover, Maritime Europe has to be unique because it is a world trader, not a continental or a pan-regional one. Half of all international trade is carried on by Maritime Europe, and over half of this region's trade is conducted with non-European areas. Even within the Common Market, where trade among the six members has increased by 50 per cent in the past three years, three-fourths of the international trade is carried on outside the Common Market framework. Finally, historical-cultural bonds within the southern hemisphere and strategic involvements in Anglo-America and Africa south of the Sahara make any form of "superstate self-containment" unthinkable.

If Free Europe has a new destiny to fulfill, it will fulfill it through internal consolidation together with reinforced external associations. For European unity cannot be achieved behind economic and military frontiers. It can only be achieved along a new pathway, which will combine historic benefits of regional specialization stemming from global associations and the modern advantages of regional consolidation emerging from the breakdown of national differences.

·6·

THE SOVIET UNION

Frontiers and Their Geopolitical Dynamics

Two basic locational conditions characterize the geopolitical positions of the U.S.S.R. and the United States. First, these two superpowers have grown up in physical isolation from one another. They are still physically remote, save in a time-distance, air-age sense. Second, the Soviet Union lives in direct land or narrow seas contact with a large number of sovereign states; Americans have few neighbors.

The first condition may help to explain why the Cold War has not erupted into a shooting war. The second condition underscores the fact that the U.S.S.R. places a very high priority on its military relations with its neighbors, while the United States cannot find security through military hegemony over its neighbors alone.

The Arctic is the major barrier between the two superpowers. It is, in a sense, the political "refrigerant" of today's divided world, helping to keep the Cold War "cold." Because of polar seas and peripheral frozen land masses, the United States and the U.S.S.R. have no common area, either land or narrow seas, sufficiently endowed with people and raw materials to serve as a major arena of Cold War conflict. True, Soviet and American territories are separated by only 26 miles of water in the Bering Straits, and the polar air and waters are arenas of friction and sources of potential conflict for air and submarine forces. But the mutual strategic threat posed by the Arctic is as the arena of Hot War, not Cold War.

The major sphere of Cold War clash today is the Old World Rimland, where the land and sea boundaries of the U.S.S.R. meet those of fifteen diverse national states—allied, opposing, and neutral. To the U.S.S.R., regional security with respect to bordering states could in effect mean global security, because of the size and diversity of its economic base. If such security were to be obtained on Soviet terms, however, it would mean United States global insecurity. In contrast, United States boundaries, which meet only three different national states outside of the Arctic, present relatively minor security problems. Regional security for the United States, even when fully attained, cannot possibly mean global security. The wheel therefore has turned. American regional security, the prized goal of our Founding Fathers, to be obtained through enforced isolation from Europe, has lost its meaning. We continue to guard our frontiers, and this can be easily accomplished, for such security can be attained without infringing on other powerful national states. But this security, in isolation from what occurs in other parts of the world, has little significance.

Thus, while many geopolitical similarities may be noted between the U.S.S.R. and the United States, particularly those stemming from land-resource use and development, a fundamental difference remains—the comparative outlooks on regional and global security. We shall deal in this chapter with the changing geopolitical map of the U.S.S.R. as related to this security outlook.

The Soviet Union is in the process of altering its landscape, both by making new uses of it and through territorial additions. This process affects both the internal and the external scenes. No longer does such a geographical quality as continentality alone serve to shape the U.S.S.R.'s geopolitical character; nor do the traditional ideas about Russia's drive to the seas fully explain her needs and aims.

Continental expansion of the Soviet Union has led to borders that are either wastelands or heavily populated marginal seas. Continental expansion of the United States has led to well-endowed coastlands and oceanic contacts with distant lands. To the United States, then, oceanic borders have been suitable, both for drawing up defensive national boundaries and for launching expansionist international contacts. To the Soviet Union, land and marginal sea frontiers have not been able to serve this dual purpose. Where, as in Central Asia, the frontiers have been the basis for defensive boundary lines, they have not been useful international contact zones. Where, as along the marginal seas, the frontiers have provided good international contact zones, they have not been adequate defensive boundaries.

The Changing Political Environment

The U.S.S.R., like all states, is the expression of the interaction of its people and the landscape which they occupy. The political marking off of this landscape produces a national landscape—the arena of the people's activity; changes in this area cause or reflect changes in national characteristics and objectives. A national landscape becomes altered in two ways: vertically, or through new internal uses, and horizontally, or through the addition of external areas. Vertical changes cut across the existing grain of the national landscape. They occur as new sets of physical, environmental conditions emerge (as through climatic desiccation, soil erosion, rising water tables, and forest removal), or as new uses of the physical environment are conceived (as through mining, new crops, or urban sprawl). The Netherlands, Japan, Sweden, Israel, Malaya, and Jamaica furnish examples of both changes. Through specialized concentrations of national energies, increasing populations can be supported.

Horizontal change does not affect the existing grain of the national landscape; rather, it produces a new national landscape by annexation, loss, or substitutions of national territory. East Germany, without the former agricultural areas east of the Oder, has become more manufacturing-oriented within its reduced field of activity. Jordan, through its annexation of Eastern Palestine, has diversified its national agricultural base without any fundamental changes in the separate parts of the landscape. However, annexation has upset the political stability of the former desert kingdom by adding an ambitious, sophisticated, Palestinian leadership elite and a dissatisfied refugee element.

Historically, national states have matured, first through enlarging their territorial bases—that is, through horizontal change; and then through intensifying the use of this base—that is, through vertical change. Today, because of the pressure of population and because of the ease of transmitting technological experience, the two processes tend to occur simultaneously. As a state alters its character through boundary changes, it also alters its character through new uses of the landscape.

It is to this dualism in geographical change that we can look for a greater understanding of Soviet national interests. The following three topics have been selected as the basis for an analysis of the implications of geographical change within the U.S.S.R.:

1) The expansion of the national territory.
2) The response to the challenges of frontier areas.
3) The development of the national territory, not solely through progressive advance from the primary core of the state, but also from secondary core areas along the borders.

TERRITORIAL EXPANSION

The territorial expansion of the Russian Empire and its twentieth-century heir is a centuries-old process that may well not have run its course. Certainly memories of Soviet annexations effected during and in the wake of the Second World War are fresh enough to cause us to speculate about future expansion. While one might suggest that the projection of ideological power through international Communism minimizes the importance of national boundaries in many ways, there is, nevertheless, a profound distinction between an area that has been internally absorbed within the boundaries of a state, and a satellite state. In the case of the Soviet Union, the annexation of specific areas within its territorial framework has converted these areas into internal components whose political relationship to the remainder of the state is quite stable. Such stability stands in contrast to the volatile nature of ties between the U.S.S.R. and its satellites.

The boundary of any national state marks the limit of its internal political authority. Such a line is more than a mark of sovereignty. It becomes a symbol, orienting the landscape towards the national core, and is thus a powerful centralizing element. Because it functions as a separator of one state from another, the boundary has strong defensive qualities.

A boundary line also cuts through frontier zones. Political frontiers tend to be intermediate, or transitional, human-use areas between adjoining political units. Usually, the very process of moving a boundary within a frontier zone affects the character of the zone as a whole. For what happens to the portion of the zone that becomes included within the new boundary cannot help but alter the political value of the remainder of the frontier. This, in turn, becomes more strongly attracted to, or repelled by, the power that has changed the boundary, depending upon the counterforce that can be exerted by the neighboring state.

As the Soviet Union has annexed territory, it has made every effort to convert these newly acquired areas into inwardly oriented, integral parts of the state. By the same token, however, these borderlands cannot be rigidly separated from contiguous non-Soviet territory, because of the goal of regional integration that the U.S.S.R. seeks with its satellites, especially those to the west. The result is, therefore, that the annexed lands serve both defensive and offensive functions. As they have been absorbed within the Soviet state, and tied to Soviet core areas, some of their former transitional human-use characteristics have been eliminated. Such integration is not part of a simple, monolithic state-building process, for many of the annexed areas have been added to non-Russian Union republics rather than to the Russian Soviet Federated Socialist Republic. The net effect of this annexation is to strengthen the country's defensive posture. These new lands are also being used as political and military spearheads for the external application of Soviet power towards the satellite states—and this is essentially an offensive posture.

As many states have expanded territorially, they have rationalized this expansion in terms of their need for "natural" boundaries. The term "natural" boundaries usually means physical features that can serve as the framework for political boundaries. The concept of "natural" boundaries as an historic necessity has frequently been repudiated by geographers and historians.[1] While nature provides us with features that can effectively serve as political boundaries, these features are our servants, not our masters. They become political boundaries only when we choose to make them serve this function. Herbert Luethy, in his lucid study *France Against Herself*, has this to say on the subject:

> . . . the natural frontiers of France are nothing but a figment of the jurists—entirely devoid of reality. Centuries of mole-like advance were required of the French monarchy before it could think of, let alone come anywhere within sight of, the Pyrenees, the Mediterranean, the Alps, the Jura, and the Rhine. Until the end of the Middle Ages, it was concerned exclusively with its own vassals, and those frontiers never provided it with security. They represented a claim, not a line of defence.[2]

The problem of "natural" boundaries is not, however, to be resolved simply by dismissing it as a pseudoscientific concept. If a people believes in "natural" boundaries, and ascribes to certain features of the physical environment a mystical, irrational function, then this belief becomes an unshakable basis for national action. At various periods in the development of the United States, such physical features as the Mississippi-Missouri watershed, the Sabine River, the Rio Grande, the Continental Divide of the Rockies, the Pacific shoreline, and the islands of adjoining oceans were designated as "natural" boundaries. These boundaries were attained through settlement, negotiation, or war. They were accepted by the public as providing the prerequisite territorial framework for geographical unity and military security. These features became part of the expansionist myth. For six million people living along the eastern seaboard in 1800 to begin a process of expansion that would lead to an ocean-to-ocean setting may not have been reasonable or necessary. But some men believe that states, like nature, abhor

[1] Jan Broek, "The Problem of 'Natural' Frontiers," *Frontiers of the Future*, University of California, 1940, pp., 3-20.

[2] Herbert Luethy, *France Against Herself* (New York: Praeger, 1955), pp. 10-11.

vacuums. As the myth of continental expansion became a national ideal, it acquired real substance. In these terms, the illogic of the following quotation from A. E. Parkins is the logic of United States history:

> Disgraceful as the Mexican War seems to us, three-quarters of a century removed from the spirit of those times when territorial aggrandizement was the factor that dominated our national policy, we must confess that American expansion to the Rio Grande and the Pacific was in full accordance with the laws of geographic adjustment that a virile nation makes when its potential economic energy is devoted solely to land-using occupations . . . Coastlines that give ready access to the world ocean, mountain ranges, and desert tracts are the logical geographic locations for national boundaries.[3]

German geopoliticians were not unaware of the theoretical deficiencies of "natural" boundary concepts.[4] On the other hand, they were quick to point out the inconsistencies and unacceptability of many "artificial" (political) boundaries. The solution of the geopoliticians was to introduce a vague term—the "organic" boundary. This was described as a political boundary set up in accordance with the geopolitical character of the state and shifting as the needs of the state dictates. Such boundaries were expected to function within their broader zones as either offensive or defensive tools, depending upon the state's needs. The German geopoliticians made a unique contribution to the discussion of boundaries by emphasizing certain anthropogeographic elements—especially race, language, and culture—as being the most important element of the "organic" frontier.

Does Soviet geopolitical theory or practice seem to have derived any inspiration from such myths as "natural" or "organic" boundaries? Soviet geography rejects environmental determinism, as is illustrated by the following: "Economic geography of the U.S.S.R. is an active geography; it narrates about conscious and planned transformation of nature carried out by socialist society on the basis of advanced science under the leadership of

[3] Almon E. Parkins, *The South* (New York: Wiley, 1938), pp. 114-15.

[4] Andrew Gyorgy, *Geopolitics* (Berkeley: University of California Press, 1944), p. 228.

the Communist Party of the Soviet Union."[5] Certainly such a philosophy is not likely to conjure up "natural" or "organic" boundaries as Soviet foreign policy objectives. Indeed, the violence of Marxist-Leninist attacks by Soviet geographers upon "environmentalism" in European and American geography seems to dispose of this as even a remote possibility. Moreover, the thesis that the "urge to warm waters" has been a persistent geopolitical aim in Russian history has been effectively discounted by students of the topic.[6] It is true that the acquisition of certain corridors to the sea was a persistent aim of some of the Czars who were in search of trade outlets and other forms of contact with Europe. But the approach has been pragmatic and opportunistic, concerned, above all, with lands athwart Russia's interior and marginal seas. It has not been based upon appeals to geopolitical deterministic slogans.

St. Petersburg, founded by Peter the Great in 1703; Odessa, first taken by Catherine II in 1774; and Vladivostok, founded in 1860 after annexation of the Amur provinces from China, spearheaded Russia's marches to the Baltic, Black, and Pacific waters. Significant earlier footholds on the sea had been Archangel in 1584 and Okhotsk, the first Russian settlement on the Pacific, in 1649. None of these coastal footholds, however, were to lead, ultimately, to broad openings on the world oceans, partly because of Russian defeats in the Crimean and Russo-Japanese wars, and partly because of the distance and physical barriers that separated the Russian ecumene from such waters.

Since 1939 the U.S.S.R. has acquired new lands on the Baltic, Black, Okhotsk, and Barents seas. These acquisitions have, also, been on interior and marginal seas, and consequently have defensive rather than offensive significance. New footholds on open seas have been developed through the medium of political satellites—an important strategic gain for the U.S.S.R., to be sure, but not indicative of the launching of a full-scale "warm waters offensive." (See Map 18.)

Soviet territorial expansion has three objectives as its basis:

[5] N. Baransky, *Economic Geography of the U.S.S.R.*, translated by S. Belsky (Moscow: Foreign Language Publishing House, 1956), Preface.

[6] John Morrison, "Russia and the Warm Waters," *U.S. Naval Institute Proceedings*, 1952, pp. 1169-79.

strategic, economic, and nationalistic. Historic claims seem to be important only as they relate to the above factors and play an unimportant role within the Soviet propaganda mechanism. The strategic objective is defensively motivated in seeking to assure command of interior and marginal seas and land gateways. It also serves an offensive function in increasing the vulnerability of neighboring states to Soviet pressures. Economic objectives play a major role in providing the Russian ecumene with improved port facilities in the Baltic for foreign trade. They play a minor role with respect to the needs of specific localities. Thus Leningrad uses the hydroelectric stations of territory annexed from Finland, and Kiev takes natural gas and petroleum from Western Ukrainian lands formerly belonging to Poland. Nationality objectives relate not only to Pan-Slavic ambitions but also to the unity of minority peoples that operate within the Soviet nationality-administrative framework. Not only were Russian-inhabited parts of Latvia annexed to the R.S.F.S.R., and Ruthenian portions of Poland to the Ukraine, but much of the Karelian-inhabited portion of east central Finland was added to Soviet Karelia.

To weigh the relative importance of these objectives in assessing the motives behind Soviet territorial annexations is difficult, and it is complicated by the fact that two or three of these objectives can be simultaneously served. If, however, we were to single out two overriding elements, one would be the strategic needs of some of the most important cities of the U.S.S.R. for defensive depth, and the second would be fear of invasion from Germany.

Consider the fact that the principal international ports of the U.S.S.R., in 1939, were Odessa, Leningrad, Murmansk, Archangel, and Vladivostok. Of these ports, all save Archangel were frontier cities. Odessa was twenty miles from the Romanian border, Leningrad twelve miles and Murmansk fifty miles from Finnish territory, and Vladivostok thirty-five miles from Japanese Manchuria. Soviet Harbor, developed during the Second World War on the Gulf of Tartary as a deep-water naval base and commercial port for the Amur Valley, was only seventy miles from Japanese-held southern Sakhalin. With the territorial changes that have since occurred, Odessa is now fifty, Leningrad ninety, and

Murmansk eighty miles from the borders of the Soviet Union, and Vladivostok is shielded by both southern Sakhalin and the North Korean satellite.

That this security problem is completely resolved from a Soviet point of view is questionable. Batum, the Black Sea port terminal and refining center for much of Baku's petroleum, is only seven miles from the Turkish border. Baku itself is about fifty miles from Iran. Until the emergence of the U.S.S.R. as one of the two great world powers with nuclear bomb capabilities, Soviet fears as to the exposure of her ports were realistic and well founded. Today, what security fears may motivate her to seek defensive depth for Caucasus oil ports or others would seem to be highly irrational. Indeed, had the U.S.S.R. held her present position of power eminence two decades ago, it is unlikely that she would have had to seize the territories that she did, at least from the standpoint of security motivation.

The second major element in Soviet territorial annexations was fear of invasion from Germany. Hitler's first plans for "Operation Barbarossa," for example, were to strike the Soviet Union simultaneously through several corridors: 1) Northern Finland against Murmansk and Archangel; 2) the Baltic, via southern Finland and the Baltic states towards Leningrad; 3) White Russia, from along the Warsaw-Bialystok-Minsk land corridor north of the Pripet Marshes and thence northward to Leningrad; 4) Southern Poland and the Western Ukraine south of the Pripet Marshes to Kiev and the Donbas; 5) Romania to Odessa and the Black Sea.

Table 9 and Map 18 show how most of these approaches to the U.S.S.R. have been annexed as Soviet territory since 1939.

These land acquisitions represent an area of 265,000 square miles. They have increased the size of the Soviet Union to 8,606,300 square miles, which is 50,000 square miles more than the territories held by the Czarist Empire at its 1904 zenith. But far more than additional land, they represent significant strategic, economic, and nationality acquisitions.

Annexation of the Pechenga district in northern Finland, including the western Rybachiy peninsula, provides greater security to the ice-free port of Murmansk and nearby Kola Peninsula apatite resources. The latter mineral has freed the U.S.S.R. from its dependence upon imported phosphates. South of Pechenga

TABLE 9

Survey of Soviet Land Annexations Since 1939

Area	*Former Owner*	*Present Soviet Status*
Pechenga District	Finland	Murmansk Oblast (R.S.F.S.R.)
Karelia (Salla)	Finland	Karelian A.S.S.R. (R.S.F.S.R.)
Vyborg District	Finland	Leningrad Oblast
Northern East Prussia and Memelland	Germany	Kaliningrad Oblast (R.S.F.S.R.) and Klaipeda Oblast (Lithuanian S.S.R.)
Estonia	Independent	Union Republic
Latvia	Independent	Union Republic
Lithuania	Independent	Union Republic
Eastern Estonia and Latvia	Estonia and Latvia	Pskov Oblast (R.S.F.S.R.)
Eastern Poland (Western Belorussia)	Poland	4 oblasts in Belorussian S.S.R. and Vilna Oblast (Lithuanian S.S.R.)
Transcarpathia (Ruthenia)	Czechoslovakia	Transcarpathian Oblast (Ukrainian S.S.R.)
Western Ukraine	Poland	6 oblasts in Ukrainian S.S.R.
Northern Bukovina	Romania	Chernovtsky Oblast (Ukrainian S.S.R.)
Central Bessarabia	Romania	Moldavian S.S.R.
Southern Bessarabia	Romania	Izmail Oblast (Ukrainian S.S.R.)
Tannu Tuva	Independent	Tuva A.S.S.R. (R.S.F.S.R.)
Southern Sakhalin	Japan	Sakhalin Oblast (R.S.F.S.R.)
Kurile Islands	Japan	Sakhalin Oblast (R.S.F.S.R.)

lies Russian Pasvik, which was annexed by Finland in 1920 to provide access to Pechenga. This corridor and its nickel resources are now in Soviet hands; as a consequence, Norway possesses a common border with the U.S.S.R. Its taconite ore mining town of Kirkenes lies exposed, and the population of northern Norway as a whole is subject to strong Communist propaganda pressures.

MAP 18. Soviet Boundary Changes in Europe Since 1939

Despite all these changes in the north, the entrances to the Barents Sea are still not in Soviet hands. The Svalbard island group is owned by Norway, which has rejected Soviet claims to this coal-mining Arctic archipelago. Soviet denunciations of NATO exercises off North Cape suggest that the possibility of efforts to seek further territorial accessions from both Norway and Finland should not be dismissed. In addition to Svalbard, we should recall that Finland's Inari district, once common to Sweden, Russia, and Norway, became Russian in 1809 and was joined to Finland, then under Russian control, in 1833. Were the U.S.S.R. to find a means to absorb Inari, Norway's Finmark County, including the coastal reaches of Hammerfest and North Cape, would become exposed to increased Soviet pressures.

The most important boundary change that occurred was the annexation of the Baltic republics. A Soviet geographer sums it up aptly: "Owing to its geographical position, the Soviet Baltic region is of prime importance for the external connections of the U.S.S.R. . . . [it is] a natural harbor which serves the Central U.S.S.R."[7] Although not entirely ice-free, Riga, the largest city and a major rail terminus, presents the Soviet Union with its best Baltic port. Klaipeda (Memel), and Ventspils (Windau) have newly developed oil ports, and Tallin has become a natural gas terminus. Kaliningrad (Königsberg) is an important ice-free addition to the eastern Baltic ports. Slight internal territorial changes have strengthened the Russian position in the Baltic, vis-à-vis both satellite states and non-Russian Soviet republics. Most important, the Kaliningrad Oblast, cleared of Germans and populated by Russians, is part of the R.S.F.S.R., and provides direct access to the Polish and East German satellites' ports of Gdnask, Szczecin, and Rostock. A portion of Estonia lying along the right bank of the River Narva has been detached to be added directly to the Leningrad Oblast. Finally, Russian-inhabited rural districts of Estonia (Petseri) and Latvia (Abrene and Kačanava)—east of the Gulf of Riga—were detached, and added to what is now the Pskov Oblast within the R.S.F.S.R. Pskov, at the southern end of Lakes Peipus and Pskov, is a key to Leningrad. Also following the principle of nationality boundaries, a Lithuanian-inhabited

[7] Baransky, *op. cit.*, p. 384.

strip of Belorussia was added to the Lithuanian S.S.R., which had reincorporated Vilna from Poland. With Vilna and Pskov now both Soviet territory, the "Vilna Corridor" that follows the high Baltic end-moraine northeastward to Leningrad, is more secure. Soviet actions in the Baltic, in a broad sense, can be described as defensively oriented, owing to the exposure of the Russian core to the European lands to the west.

The westward shift of the boundary in Belorussia has brought the Pripet Marshes completely within the Soviet fold. This boundary follows the "Curzon Line" of 1919, east of which Poland pushed after its 1920 war with Russia. Return to the Curzon Line has completed Russian control over the Vilna Gap, as well as occupying the high ground from Brest to Minsk that skirts the Pripet Marshes' northern edge. Moreover, Western Belorussia was claimed on nationality basis, White Russians being in the majority over Poles.

The Western Ukraine lands that have been taken from Poland include Lvov and Drogobych. The former is a rail hub on the upper Bug River whose industries serve the agricultural areas to the east. The latter is a district on the northern slopes of the Carpathians that used to be Poland's major petroleum-producing region. Its denial to Poland as well as its availability to Kiev has strategic economic implications. In the case of the Western Ukraine, unity of the Ukrainian people was an important basis for the claim, although the fact that the Soviet border is now but 130 miles from Krakow and just another 50 miles from industrialized Upper Silesia would seem to be another basis for Soviet interest.

With the absorption of Transcarpathia, the Russians accomplished much more than the union of Ruthenians with their kindred Ukrainians. This land annexation has given to the Soviet Union complete control of the Eastern Carpathian Mountains and a base on its southern slopes from which to overlook the Tisa River and all of the Hungarian Plain. Czechoslovakia and Hungary have common borders with the U.S.S.R., and Budapest lies exposed to a Soviet border that is only 150 miles away. And Belgrade and Vienna are not unaffected by this new Danubian position of the U.S.S.R.

The border changes in Northern Bucovina and Bessarabia also

were justified in terms of absorbing predominantly Ukrainian peoples, but, again, they serve broader Soviet interests. For now the lands between the Dneister and the Prut are Soviet, as is the northernmost mouth of the Danube. The Ploesti oil fields and Bucharest are about 125 miles from the Soviet border—still another example of the vulnerability into which a satellite state has been pushed.

Recent boundary changes in Siberia have been far less important than those in Europe. Sakhalin and the Kuriles point a double dagger towards northern Japan, and enclose the Sea of Okhotsk. However, these annexations have not affected Russia's Sea of Japan coast and Vladivostok. In the case of the latter regions, the Sovietization of North Korea is likely to be regarded as a security goal for Vladivostok, irrespective of Soviet-Chinese relation in Manchuria.

Annexation of nominally independent Tannu Tuva in 1944 may well have been desired as a precedent for eventual Soviet annexation of the Mongolian People's Republic. A lightly populated and underdeveloped land, the Tuva A.S.S.R. is at the headwaters of the Yenisei and overlooks Irkutsk and the Trans-Siberian Railway from the eastern end of the Western Sayan Mountains.

It would be unwise to assume that territorial annexations along the periphery of the U.S.S.R. have run their course. The Soviet Union has shown itself quite capable of reviving territorial claims previously renounced. In the past, Russia's borders have included the upper Aras, upper Kura, and middle Çoruhk river basins. These are now in Turkey and claims to their major towns, Kars, Ardahan, and Artvin, as belonging to Soviet Armenia and to Georgia, were revived in 1945, at the time of Soviet demands for control of the Straits. Indeed, claims of Soviet Georgian professors for all of northeastern Turkey up to Samsun, on the grounds of its once having been Georgian, were given wide publicity at that time.[8]

Iran, too, is not free of Soviet land annexation pressures. For a brief period (1723-32), all of the southern shore of the Caspian Sea was held by Russia. Soviet interests have been somewhat

[8] *The Middle East—A Political and Economic Survey* (London: Royal Institute of International Affairs, 1950), p. 46.

more restricted, to date, encouraging separatist movements in Persian Azerbaijan and in Kurdish Iranian areas south and west of Lake Urmia. From such positions, Turkey would be hemmed in on two sides, and northern Iraq would be directly exposed to the Soviet Union. In Chinese Central Asia, the Dzungarian Gate —the grassy plain headwaters region of the River Ili that connects Chinese Turkestan and Russian Central Asia—was once briefly occupied by Russia (1871-81). While present circumstances hardly suggest the raising of a claim to this region, it might be reactivated in the event of Sino-Soviet friction or simply as part of a strategic-area "swapping" process.

Whatever the future territorial claims of the Soviet Union may be, their formal basis is likely to continue to be on nationality lines. Natural features and historic claims become objectives as they coincide with nationality frontiers. Demands based upon nationality can be a very effective weapon for territorial expansion, for within the border reaches of the U.S.S.R. are many minorities with ethnic ties to peoples in neighboring states.

These include Armenians (with kinsmen in Turkey); Kurds (with fellow-Kurds in Turkey, Iraq, and Iran); Azerbaijanis (with counterparts in Iran); and Tadzhiks (with related tribesmen in Afghanistan). Soviet minorities also have kindred groups in Outer Mongolia (the Mongols) and in Chinese Turkestan (the Turko-Tatars). Sustaining exiled groups who have kinsmen within U.S.S.R. border areas is an advantage that the Soviet Union has never been loath to exploit, and the demographic pattern that finds minority groups overlapping borderlands fits in well with programs of internal subversion within neighboring states. Only along the Manchurian border are significant border-overlapping minorities absent.

To secure one of her most vulnerable areas, the Far Eastern provinces, Czarist Russia for decades sought a position of influence in Manchuria. Whether ideological bonds with China will alone be sufficient to secure this area today is debatable. But certainly, the dependence of the Manchurian and North Chinese economy upon Soviet machinery, transportation equipment, and markets for raw materials helps to weld Sino-Soviet ties and thus to enhance the security of the lands of the Amur Valley. So does Soviet control of North Korea.

Growing Soviet influence in Afghanistan appears to offer little serious threat to South Asia in and of itself. For Afghanistan is a dead end in terms of economics and transportation. We disagree with those like Toynbee who, harking back to that period in history when a disorganized Northern India fell prey to Afghan chiefs, consider Afghanistan to be one of the key powers in the East-West power struggle. This would be so only if Afghanistan, as a Soviet satellite, were able to further the cause of Pashtunistan inciting the Pathans to open revolt against Pakistan. But an open Soviet-Afghan alliance with strenuous efforts to dismember Pakistan probably would produce the contrary effect of bringing Pakistan and India closer together to face the common threat.

The region that is likely to remain the most persistent focus of Russian pressure is the Middle East. In addition to the specific land claims on Turkey and Iran already discussed, the broader problem of the Straits remains a major concern to the Soviet Union. Soviet support of renewed Bulgarian demands for Greek Thrace territory could be conceived of as one way to outflank the approaches to the Dardanelles. With the elimination of the Suez Canal as a Western base, and with various Soviet port activities along the Mediterranean (Latakia and Alexandria) and the Red Sea (Hodeida), Russian interests in the waterways to the Far East have taken on new vigor. Past emphasis upon the Black Sea and the straits was essentially defensive, for Soviet fear of attack through the water routes was well founded. Today's emphasis, however, is far more offensive, in the total political-economic-military sense. Never before has Russia had so large a potential stake in the Suez Canal-Indian Ocean-Far East sea route. If commercial and military traffic to China, Egypt, Iraq, India, and Indonesia continues to increase, the U.S.S.R. may exert unprecedented pressures and take considerable risks to gain the virtual control of the Straits and Persian Gulf that have heretofore been considered desirable, but not strategically essential. Thus, we can describe the Black Sea-Mediterranean as the Soviet "Offensive zone," in contrast to its Baltic "Defensive zone."

Vladivostok and the Manchurian ports of Port Arthur and Dairen could become less important to the Soviets than the rail routes that run directly to north and central China and the sea route around South Asia. Many have heretofore considered the

Soviet northern sea route as the "Mediterranean" or Panama Canal of the U.S.S.R. Its limitations, however, are perfectly well known. In the long run, a combination of the European Mediterranean and Indian Ocean sea route, and the overland rail routes to China, will probably be the key to the U.S.S.R.'s contacts with the Far East. As we have said, this will increase the Soviet Union's appetite to secure control of strategic approaches, like Suez, the Persian Gulf, and the Straits of Malacca. But there is another lesson to be learned from this. As long as the Free world retains control of the key points along peripheral Eurasian sea lanes, ever increasing Soviet trade dependence upon these routes will make her more aware than ever of her strategic vulnerability to Free World counterpressures. If we are to counter the Soviet threat to our Suez lifeline, we can do this most effectively by strengthening our control of the Black Sea approaches and Indian Ocean and Far Eastern lanes.

CHALLENGE OF THE FRONTIER REGIONS

The challenge of the frontier is far older in the Russian experience than in the American. By 1533, the northern Urals had been crossed, as Ivan IV broke the Tatar power that had confined his predecessor to Muscovy and Novgorod. Soon after, the fall of Kazan on the Volga opened the gate through and around the southern Urals. Finally, in 1581, Sibir, capital of the Siberian Khanate, was taken and sixty-eight years later a Russian settlement was planted on the Sea of Okhotsk. Thus a people of less than ten million had spanned the 4,000-mile gap to the Pacific. By the end of the seventeenth century, colonizing families extended from above the mouth of the Amur to the northern edge of the Bering Sea.

This early start in Russian colonization was accomplished with the help of Cossack tribesmen and in the face of the limited opposition offered by the few, weak, indigenous people of Northern Siberia. But Northern Siberia was a land valuable for its fur, lumber, and minerals. It could not attract large farm and commercial centers. Siberia's promising pioneering regions were at the southern edge of Northern Siberia, in the Caucasus in Central Asia, and in the Far Eastern provinces. The military fate of these more populous native areas, bordered by such powers as Turkey,

Persia, and China, was not resolved until 1860-65. Without a Russian military victory, not only would there have been little Russian settlement in Central Asia and along the Amur, but the Tomsk-Lake Baikal-Chita strip at the southern edge of Siberia could not have been fully developed.

But more than weapons were needed to colonize Soviet Asia. A national pioneering effort was required. Czarist Russia never wholeheartedly favored and supported pioneering in Siberia, save during the period 1891-1911. Even when government policy favored colonization by farmers, fishermen, and lumbermen, the Czars opposed industrialization outside of the European Russian and Ukrainian cores. Immigration came, not in waves, but as a "groping forward";[9] it occurred in the form of seasonal labor as well as permanent settlement. Increasing population pressure in rural Russia finally combined with political considerations to convince the last of the Czars that settlement in Asia should be encouraged. Heavy colonization then took place in the Western Caucasus, northern Central Asia, and—above all—in Siberia. Following the revolution, this process became more thoroughly planned and directed, for industrial as well as agricultural purposes. Moreover, while Czarist settlement in Asia was primarily for the purpose of exploiting the resource base so that its materials could be processed in Russia, today's settlement is directed towards partly self-contained, agricultural-industrial, regional complexes within a broader framework of national interdependence.

Much has recently been said by Soviet leaders about colonialism. That the word is frequently misused is clear. Strictly speaking, a colony is a territory of which the soil is principally owned by settlers from the mother country. Colonialism, as a process, involves settlement from a mother country, generally into empty lands and bringing to these lands the previous culture and organization of the parent society. Imperialism, as distinct from colonialism, refers to rule over indigenous people, transforming their ideas, institutions, and goods.

Where colonialism occurred in relatively empty lands, it has been described as "secondary colonization." Where it occurred

[9] Georges Jorré, *The Soviet Union,* translated and revised by E. D. Laborde (London: Longmans, 1960), p. 162.

in settled areas, being superimposed on indigenous societies, it has been called "primary colonization." [10] Primary colonization means, in effect, colonialism-imperialism, because it involves both settlement from the outside and the transformation of the native society as a result of the pressures of the colonists.

Most of the United States frontier was settled by a colonial process, because the American Indian population was so limited in number and because most of the land lay in a virgin state. Only in Texas and California was colonialism-imperialism operative, when English-speaking minorities settled and imposed their rule upon Indian-Spanish majorities. But the numbers involved were, again, quite small. Texas had 90,000 Indians and Spanish and 30,000 Americans in 1840, and California had a total of 92,000 people, mostly Indians, when it joined the Union in 1850.

As practiced by the Czars and their Communist successors, however, colonialism-imperialism has been imposed upon millions of people. Certainly, this is a distinction in frontier development that is as important as any historic parallels that we may care to draw between the American and the Russian experiences.

No other people have colonized so extensively, in so heavily and indigenously populated an area, as have the Russians throughout their empire. From 1859 to 1897, six million Russians migrated, to increase the total of Russians east of the Don to 16 million. At this same time, there were approximately 25 million indigenous inhabitants in the area. Today, east of the Don, there are 45 million non-Slavs. They are not only clasped to the Soviet Union in an iron grip; they are often locally outnumbered by the 30 million Slavs who live in their historic homelands. On a regional basis, Russians are the majority in the Trans-Volga steppes, the western Caucasus, and Siberia. Natives predominate in the rest of the Caucasus and in Central Asia.

In addition to such factors as national policy and the opposition of native groups and nearby foreign powers, physical environment has influenced the character of frontier development in Czarist Russia and the U.S.S.R. It is estimated that about seven and a half million square miles (87 per cent of the total land area) present serious limitations to settlement, particularly

[10] S. Herbert Frankel, *The Concept of Colonization* (Oxford: Clarendon Press, 1949).

farming. As a result, these lands of deficiency either have been bypassed, or have inspired revolutionary changes so as to become opened up to farming, manufacturing, mining, and transportation.

In his essay *Orographie de la Sibérie* Prince Kropotkin noted the similarities in landforms of the Russian Empire and Canada.[11] He compared the traverse from the Baltic across Central Russia, the Urals, the Middle Siberian plains, and, finally, the mountains and plateaus of Transbaikal, with a trans-Canadian traverse. Canada's maritime coast was likened to Russia's Baltic; her eastern forests to Central Russia's forests; her Great Lakes to the Caspian Sea; her Laurentian uplands bordering Lake Superior to the Urals; her prairie provinces to the Siberian steppes; her barrens to the Siberian tundra; her Rockies and Pacific ranges to East Siberia's mountains. Kropotkin observed that there was one fundamental distinction between the two: beyond North America's Pacific coast mountains there was no broad coastal plain, while beyond the Transbaikal Mountains lay the broad plains of the Amur, Manchuria, and North China.

The geopolitical consequences of this distinction are important to our understanding of Russian frontier psychology. Because of the existence of heavily populated, foreign-controlled areas along the Pacific, the "sea-to-sea" goal could not have the same meaning to Russians as it had to Americans. More significant a goal has been the settling of the Continental Interior, as a means unto itself, not as a steppingstone to the Pacific. And the waterways that have the most geopolitical meaning to the U.S.S.R. continue to be the Baltic and Black seas—not the open ocean. If we characterized the United States as a Maritime-Continental nation, then we must characterize the Soviet Union as a Continental nation with the beginnings of a Maritime personality that is not likely to compete with the state's continental outlook for many years to come.

Canada does not, by itself, provide an adequate analogy to the Soviet Union. We would have to add to this picture the Great Lakes-Middle West industrial-farm belt of the United States,

[11] Pierre Kropotkin, *Orographie de la Sibérie*, Institut Géographique de Bruxelles, Publication 9, 1904, pp. 40-42 (translated from the Russian, originally published in 1876).

which can be likened to the Ukraine; the Western Desert and Mountain province, which can be likened to Central Asia; and the Californian Mediterranean, which has similarities with Transcaucasia. Such a composite view provides the American reader with a clearer idea of the immensity and diversity of the Soviet landscape.

NATURE'S LIMITATIONS

Because of latitude, remoteness from open seas, the barrier effects of mountains, and continentality, the U.S.S.R.'s climate leaves much of its territory too cold or too dry for large-scale permanent settlement. Permafrost, alone, covers three and a half million of the eight and a half million square miles. Not only is the subsurface frozen solid in the winter; in the summer the thaws tear up roads, railway beds, and building foundations. Most crops cannot grow in the permafrost area because of the cool, short summer, which also lacks adequate moisture. Farther south, in the brown soils and the chernozems of the wooded steppes, when the growing season does permit agriculture, the 10 to 15 inches of annual precipitation are highly effective because of low evaporation.

The second area of climatic deficiency embraces two million square miles of desert and semidesert lands in Central Asia. With 8 to 12 inches of rainfall annually, mostly in the spring and summer, intense evaporation reduces effective moisture to a minimum. These lands differ from the cold areas in that they can be made highly productive under specialized conditions of irrigation farming. An important feature of Soviet agriculture has been the large-scale development of industrial crops, vegetables, and fruits in the oases of Central Asia.

In addition to climatically deficient areas, there are two million square miles of rocky, mountain forest soils, immature hill soils, and peat bogs that are unsuited to cultivation. Although drainage is being expanded, less than 5 per cent of all Soviet crop land has installed drainage.

Within this framework, 10 per cent of the U.S.S.R. (900,000 square miles) is devoted to crops, and 16 per cent to permanent meadow and pasture. Of the crop lands, the most important area is the wedgelike triangle from Leningrad to the Black Sea to

Krasnoyarsk along the Yenisei River at the edge of the Central Siberian Plateau. This triangle contains mixed forest podsolic, deep chernozem, and brown soils. East of the Urals, the triangle becomes quite narrow, and rainfall is marginal. But along this belt lie the manufacturing cities and farmlands of Siberia—a belt which, along with the Amur Valley, Central Asia, and, to a lesser extent, the Caucasus, represents the Soviet Frontier Region. (See Map 19.)

SOME INTERNAL CHANGES

We turn to some examples of internal change, not because these are sharply differentiated from the external affairs of the U.S.S.R., but precisely because they affect them so profoundly. First, with respect to agriculture, we are aware of the priority that is being given to increased agricultural production in the U.S.S.R. today. This cannot be otherwise in a country whose rural populace is 52 per cent of the total, and whose agricultural workers are 42 per cent of all workers. The primary aim is to improve the lot of a rapidly urbanizing Soviet society. If the result also achieves an agricultural surplus, the U.S.S.R. will have added an important Cold War weapon. To date, large-scale export of farm commodities has been carried on by the Free World, and particularly by the United States. In the long run, Soviet exports like cereals and industrial crops could become as significant a weapon in the race for the support of the uncommitted world as machinery and manufacturing know-how. For the moment, however, Soviet leadership is grappling with farm problems that partly stem from the development lag between modern industry and modern agriculture.

We have mentioned the agricultural triangle that extends from the Baltic and Black seas to Krasnoyarsk. In this area, 600,000 square miles are under crop cultivation. Here two revolutionary land-size changes have been made in the past several years: 1) the pushing of grains to the north and the southeast, and 2) the relocation of certain crops and the planting of new ones.

It has been quite some time since the Ukraine—the historic center of the agriculture of the Russian Empire—has led Soviet republics in the production of any commodity save sugar beets. After the First World War, agricultural expansion occurred in the

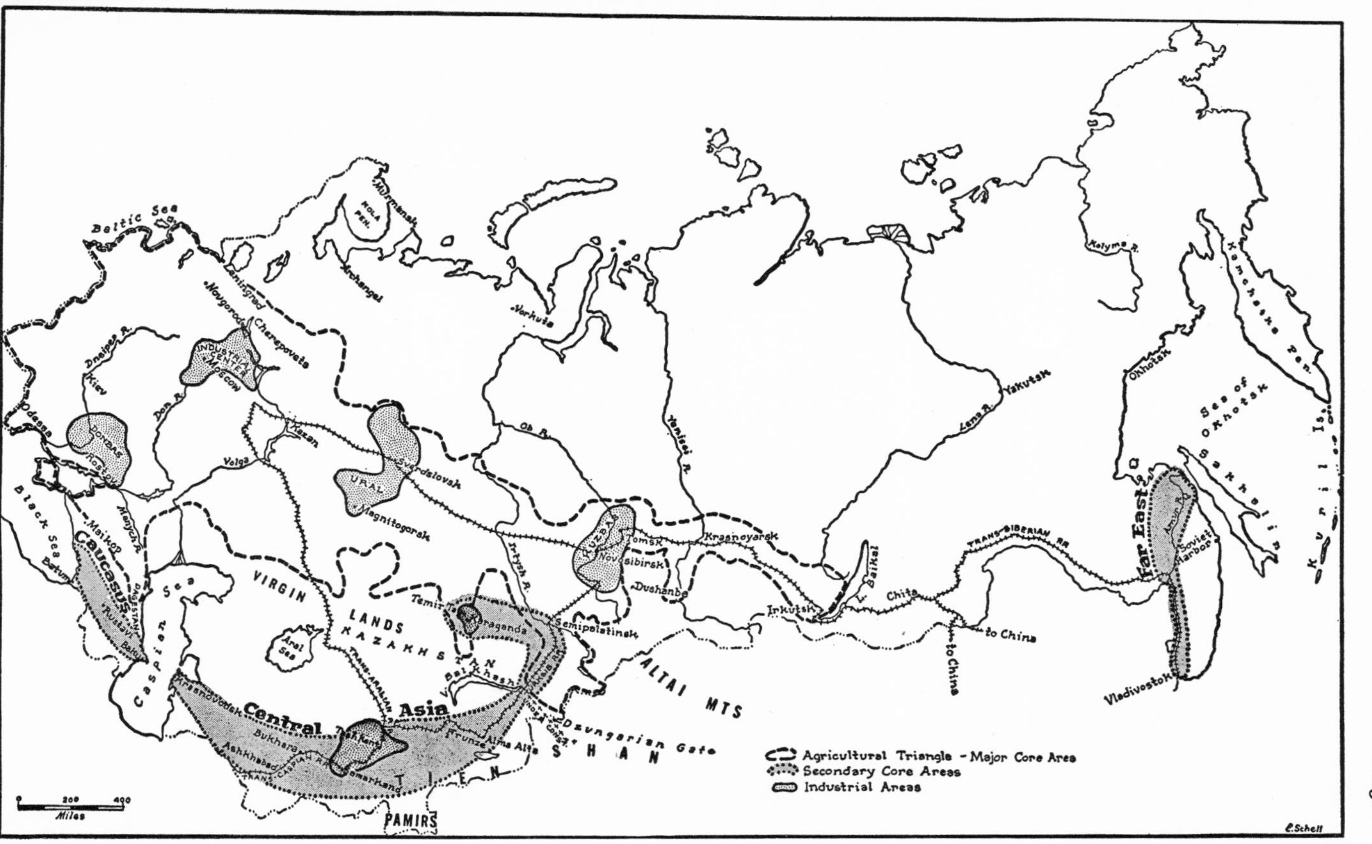

MAP 19. Soviet Development Cores

coarse grain and dairy lands of White Russia, and in the grain and root crop districts of Moscow. Then came the extension of cereal farming to eastern European Russia, especially the Volga lands, and finally into Siberia. There, spring wheat has been cultivated in the Yakutsk area, various cereals in Kazakhstan, and fruits and industrial crops in Transcaucasia and in Turkestan.

With agricultural expansion has come diversification. Grain production today accounts for 60 per cent of the total crop area, while in 1914 it covered 90 per cent. While significant increases in yields and acreage have been made along many lines, relatively little headway has been made in dairy and meat production. This has occasioned the launching of a grandiose plan for new farm expansion and crop diversification. The first phase of this plan deals with growing wheat in the subhumid and semiarid "virgin lands" in the east, from the Volga to Karaganda to Tomsk. The other phase consists of converting coarse grain lands west of the Urals to corn and hogs. One hundred and fifty million acres are involved. Despite climatic liabilities, poor drainage, the need for summer fallow acreage, inadequacies of transportation, and labor shortages, considerable progress was made in the first stages of the plan.

The U.S.S.R. is gambling with this radical shake-up in its agricultural plant. The gamble is particularly great, considering that it is based mainly on dry farming—not irrigation, and the 1962 revelations of Soviet farming inadequacies reflect, in great measure, this risk. For if dry farming is emphasized, much land must either lie fallow or have considerably more chemical fertilizers added so as to avoid soil exhaustion. The meeting of production targets in meats, dairy, and vegetables will, of course, affect domestic events. Success in grains and industrial crops will also have bearing upon foreign affairs. The 1965 grain target is 180 million tons. Wheat is by far the leading grain—nearly half of the total now grown. Rye, oats, barley, millet, and corn complete the picture, save for modest production of rice. In recent years, grain production has varied between 100 and 140 million tons. The real question is not whether the goal can be reached but whether it will have to be reached at the expense of energies that could be devoted to livestock or vegetables. At stake are both consumer needs and the grain export market to Eastern Europe. Perhaps, eventually, grain exports will become important factors in the pattern of Soviet trade with underdeveloped countries.

Irrigated land is only 5 per cent of total plowland and since 1957 costly irrigation projects have been reduced. Only cotton and sugar beets are being emphasized in new irrigation programs. Even here, in a water-conservation effort, some cotton is being grown without irrigation in a belt extending from the Eastern Ukraine to the Caspian Sea. Soviet cotton is now about one-quarter of the world production, and more and more of it is of the long-stapled Egyptian variety. It is small wonder, then, that cotton imports from Egypt are being resold to Maritime Europe at less than the purchase price. We can assume that the Russians will dump cotton if they deem it economically necessary or politically desirable to do so. With over 40 million tons of sugar beets, there is an ample supply of sugar and its by-product, and sugar dumping can also be anticipated as a result of Soviet-Cuban trade. As crucial as the agricultural goals are, it is even more important that they be met while the agricultural labor force is simultaneously decreased. As has frequently been noted, the U.S.S.R. may experience serious manufacturing labor shortages unless her agricultural work force is reduced. Current demands in the U.S.S.R. for increased tractor production reflect this pressure on labor. In sum, irrigation facilities, fertilizers, and machines will all be required in greater quantities than they have been heretofore, if the U.S.S.R. is to remove the gamble from its efforts to solve its farm problems. Unless more of the national capital now being devoted to heavy industry is shifted to agriculture, spectacular advances are likely to remain limited to a few farm sectors.

Industrialization

The abundance and variety of mineral and forest resources, stemming from the size and diversified geologic structure of the U.S.S.R., gives to its industry a most significant advantage. No other political area is, potentially, so self-sufficient. The shortages that may exist in tin, cobalt, molybdenum, and tungsten are supplemented by the resources of satellites. The Soviet Union is better provided with mineral resources than any other single country, and new reserves are constantly being uncovered. Also, together with Eastern Europe's forests, the forests of the Soviet realm form more than one-third of the world's total forest areas, and timber is important as an exportable commodity.

But if space provides an advantage in the variety of resources that it has to offer, certain disadvantages stem from the distances between raw materials and markets. Manufacturing in the U.S.S.R., even more than agriculture, has to contend with transportation costs and problems that few other parts of the world must face. The mineral resources of the U.S.S.R. are spread much farther than are its people. Where one resource and a market may coincide, the other resources vital to the manufacturing process may be hundreds of miles distant. A classic example is the Urals-Kuzbas Combinat, wherein coal and iron ore are exchanged over a 1,200-mile distance.

A more recent example of the magnitude of the transportation problem can be seen in the building of a huge, integrated steel plant at Cherepovets. This plant, with an annual output of five million tons of steel, furnishes Leningrad's machinery manufacturing plants with their major source of steel. The steelworks have been located 300 miles east of Leningrad in a position intermediate to raw materials and market (from here Moscow, too, can be supplied, if necessary). The coal comes by rail from the rich, new Pechora-Vorkuta fields at the northern end of the Urals—a distance of 1,200 miles. Iron ore is shipped by sea from the Yena mines in the Kola Peninsula to Archangel, and then by rail for 500 miles to the steel plant. New plants like those at Cherepovets, Temir Tau (Kazakhstan), Magnitogorsk, and Rustavi (Georgia) have raised Soviet steel production to 70 million tons. But the cost of producing steel under such conditions is high, and the drain on transportation is considerable. Certainly, the export of steel under completely competitive circumstances, cannot meet the export prices of steel made in equally modern Western European or American plants.

The basic solution to the problem of distance is not only to move factories to the resources, but also to create markets nearby. The process of successful industrial decentralization is tied to that of population decentralization, and the Soviet government is making energetic strides in this direction. One of the consequences of such a process is the trend to decentralize economic planning and bureaucratic controls. Stalin decentralized plants and markets, but kept a highly centralized control of the various regions in Moscow. Khrushchev has recognized the strangling effects of centralization and has turned over planning as well as production to the regional centers.

THE ADVANCE OF THE RUSSIANS

Plans that are concerned with developing mineral resources, decentralizing industry, or opening up new lands to agriculture have political as well as economic significance. Because this diversification is being spearheaded by Great Russians, a profound change in the population distribution map is taking place. Great Russians, who are 60 per cent of the country's total population, occupy key urban and mining areas in Kamchatka, Northern Siberia, the Amur Valley, the Kolyma Basin, the Siberian Wedge, the Ob and Yenisei valleys, Turkestan, the Western Caucasus, Karelia, and Kaliningrad. This population is in a position to submerge many small nationality groups, especially of the Turkic and Mongol stocks. Some idea of the trend can be seen in the fact that from 1955 to 1958 about two million young people, mainly Russians, migrated to the "virgin land" areas of Northern Kazakhstan.

The major Russian colonizing thrust was, and still is, an eastward one into Siberia. Settlement efforts by Russians in Central Asia and the Caucasus have had to contend with both existing native populations and less favorable physical environments. Nonetheless, over the broad sweep of time the process of Russian dispersion throughout the land seems inevitable. The Middle Volga, once Asiatic, is now two-thirds Russian. The Lower Volga and Ural River valleys, still largely Asiatic, contain growing Russian industrial centers. North Kazakhstan, the contact zone between Siberia and Central Asia, is now mainly Russian, as are areas in eastern Central Asia, like Semipalatinsk and Alma Ata, which have recently been opened to development by the building of the Turksib Railway. Farther north, the mining areas of the Western Altai Mountains are mainly Russian. The Trans-

Caspian railway, which traverses southern Central Asia, has touched off Russian settlement along the eastern Caspian Sea, at Ashkabad and at Samarkand.

While Western Ciscaucasia (the Kuban) has long been Russian and is part of the R.S.F.S.R., the Caucasus as a whole remains essentially native. There are, however, Russian enclaves in Dagestan and Baku. Along the country's western frontiers, there have been significant population changes in Karelia and Kaliningrad (formerly northern East Prussia), which now have Russian majorities, and in Western Belorussia, where, in the wake of the emigration of Poles and the extermination of Jews, White Russians now predominate. Even where Russians are not in the majority, the introduction of Russian settlers into selected localities where industry, mining, or farming is being developed injects a Russian influence that cannot be measured in mere numbers. Urbanization means Russian settlement throughout the Soviet Union—a phenomenon that Harris first observed from his studies of Soviet census data over two decades ago.[12] For example, recent Soviet policy has been to set industry in the countryside, away from the major manufacturing centers. In many instances, these new centers have replaced older market towns, whose function has long since disappeared as a result of the collectivized agricultural framework. These new industrialized cores are Russian enclaves within the rural native habitat, setting the pace for the modernization that affects farming as well as the city.

It is true that political and cultural recognition of the 169 nationalities was a farsighted response by Soviet leadership to the problems created by the cultural diversity of Czarist Russia. The political-administrative framework that has evolved is based essentially upon this heterogeneity of nationality. But both strategic and economic needs motivate the Russians and their allied Slavic groups to continue to spread throughout the land. The very fact that the technical and administrative know-how needed to exploit the raw materials of the Soviet Union's frontier lands resides essentially in Russian minds and hands, makes immigration necessary and endangers the cultural position of

[12] Chauncy Harris, "Ethnic Groups in the Soviet Union," *The Geographical Review*, July 1945, pp. 466-73.

national minorities. The construction worker, the foreman, the plant engineer, and the administrator are all needed to develop backward rural areas, and most of these are drawn from the older, industrial centers. The success of this exploitation of resources, in turn, makes the European Russian corelands increasingly dependent, economically, upon the frontier reaches. This is because regional interdependence, rather than regional self-sufficiency, is the basic goal of Soviet planning.

> The Industrial Centre represents, as it were, the main knot which ties up the principal threads of the country's inter-regional connections . . . As a result of this construction (in industry, agriculture and transportation), the U.S.S.R. could develop its productive forces to such an extent that it is now no longer dependent on foreign countries both for industrial equipment and raw materials . . . The rapid development of industry in the regions of the Volga, the Urals, Western Siberia, Kazakhstan and Central Asia . . . has greatly strengthened the ties of these regions between themselves and with the Industrial Centre.[13]

Interdependence is something more than dependence, to be sure. Nonetheless, each day brings with it greater Russian need for raw materials and products of national minority lands. As a consequence, nationality distinctions and freedoms are likely to yield increasingly to the centralizing forces and pressures of the Russian majority. What long-term meaning, then, slogans of political autonomy and economic self-sufficiency can have to the nationalities of this federal state, in the face of centralized Russian controls and Russian population dispersal, is highly questionable.

SECONDARY CORE AREAS

The lands of the Czars were harsh, somber, and untamed. So is much of the present Soviet landscape. When we think of the conquest of the frontier, we should not think of this advance into the wilderness as a slow, evenly paced advance from the primary core. Frontier settlement consists rather of a multitude of developments of various sizes and types. It consists of dots on the land-

[13] Baransky, *op. cit.*, pp. 406-11.

scape, like mining towns; of ribbonlike stretches of farms and cities along railroads and rivers; of clusters of urbanized, industrial complexes; of broad sheets of plowland. The high proportion of territory that is in Arctic tundra, northern coniferous forest, mountains or deserts, has only superficial value to our assessment of Soviet national power. What is important is the specialized economic qualities of these distinct landscapes, and the manner in which they are being exploited. This can be measured by the numbers and sizes of the various points or locales of exploitation, and by the type and quality of lines of transportation.

In the development of Anglo-America, settlement did not occur through a uniform westward progression. Footholds were established along the mouth of the Mississippi (New Orleans), the southwest Pacific coast (San Francisco, Los Angeles), and the Columbia River basin, to support settlement back into the interior. These footholds were in areas sufficiently well endowed by nature to become rapidly self-supporting. As we contemplate the American scene, we see that the process of filling in the United States from these secondary core areas has been intensified in the past two decades.

In the same manner, the Far Eastern, Caucasus, and Central Asian regions of the Soviet Union serve as secondary core areas to supplement the extension of the frontier from the main European core. The progressive movement of Russians from the Don to the Kuzbas is therefore the major, but not the only, direction of frontier development. For the specialized resources of the Amur Valley and the Pacific coast, and of the mountains and adjoining plains of southern Central Asia and the Caucasus, have provided a basis for agricultural and industrial activities that can also help push back the frontier.

The Far East, historically, has been the strategic Russian key to the Transbaikal region. When it could not deny its enemies the use of Vladivostok as an ocean-supported base, the Soviet government of 1918 was helpless to take counteraction against the Czech-Japanese forces in Eastern Siberia, nor could it influence events in northern Manchuria. On the contrary, the four-year stay of the Japanese in Vladivostok was the key to Japan's control of the Chinese Eastern Railway and North Manchuria.

Although lightly populated today (under five million), the highly urbanized Soviet Far East has a manufacturing and mineralized economy, with petroleum, machine tools, transport equipment, building materials, and fish as items that can support developments in the Transbaikal sector of Eastern Siberia. Moreover, grains and livestock are shipped to all of Eastern Siberia from North China via Vladivostok.

Another secondary-support core region is the Caucasus. For the most part, the Caucasus has remained quite distinct from the rest of the U.S.S.R. in a physical and cultural sense. However, Western Caspian and Maikop petroleum has been an important factor in the industrialization of the lower Don (Rostov and Kamensk) and the lower Volga. Also, Caucasus timber and farm production have played an important role in the emergence of Rostov as a great, national farm machinery producing center.

Underway in the North Caucasus is a large river canal project, designed to connect the Manych River, which flows into the Don at the Sea of Azov, with the Caspian Sea (following the remnant of an old watercourse). The riverway will be used for irrigation, as well as navigation. The Manych was traditionally regarded by Russian geographers as the boundary between Russia and Asia. With the completion of the project, the poorly developed "White Steppes" that border the northern Caspian Sea will gain support for irrigated agricultural development from the Caucasus base.

By far the most important of the secondary core regions is Central Asia. It is no accident that powerful, Central Asian, Turkic Khanates were able to resist the Czars until less than a century ago. For these Muslim empires lay at the mountain foot of Central Asia. Waters from the Pamirs, Alai, and Tien Shan supported large oasis civilizations in Bukhara, Samarkand, and Tashkent. Besides, the Aralo-Caspian desert served to bar the way from the north. But today these southern oases and many newly founded towns have become important Soviet agricultural and industrial centers. River waters have been stored and canalized to become the basis for the country's cotton-growing industry. Fruits and vegetables, sugar beets, rice, and tobacco are also important. Industry has kept pace with the modernization of agriculture. From Krasnovodsk (oil terminus and chemicals), to Ashkabad (textiles, glass, food), to Dushanbe (textiles, tannery, food), to Alma Ata (chemicals, food, publishing), to Frunze (textiles, cannery, food), vital industrial activities have been developed. Tashkent, the railway junction of the Turksib, Trans-Caspian, and Trans-Aralian lines, is the leading center, with large textile, machinery-making, and food-processing plants. Its satellite towns have developed hydroelectric power and copper refineries.

From these industrialized oases flow materials and market potential that aid significantly in the development of Northern and Central Kazakhstan, and of Western Siberia. Railways that converge on these southern cities (like the Turksib along the east, the Trans-Caspian along the southwest, the Karaganda-Balkash cutting north-south through the heart of Kazakhstan) have attracted settlers and furthered industrial developments. At the same time, the railroads have made it possible for these southern oases to help support the development of the desert and steppe portions of Central Asia.

The East European Satellites

Europe outside of Russia is divided into two parts: West and East. Central Europe is no more. It is a mere geographical expression that lacks geopolitical substance. The disappearance of Central Europe was foreshadowed by the dismemberment of Austria-Hungary in 1918, when the dual Empire, with fifty-one million people and 141,600 square miles, fell apart, its lands being allocated to seven different states. The conquest of Austria and Czechoslovakia by Germany in 1938 and the Nazi-Soviet Nonaggression Pact of the following year led to the division of Central Europe between German and Russian power. The war, and Germany's defeat, brought on the sweeping changes in the ethnic and national boundary maps of Europe that have culminated in today's crushing reality—Central Europe is gone. Its eastern two-thirds belong to Continental Europe; its western one-third belongs to Maritime Europe.

Central Europe generally was taken by geographers to refer to that part of Europe lying between the Rhine on the west and Russia and the Balkans on the south and east. Eastern

Europe meant, essentially, European Russia. It is instructive to recall that, while most geographical works following the First World War continued to speak of, and to regionalize in terms of, a Central Europe, Halford Mackinder, in 1919, spoke of the real Europe as being divided between East and West Europe.[14] To Mackinder's incisive mind, East Europe included the area from the Elbe to the Urals. Its Tidal Lands, or Middle Tier of states that lay between Germany and Russia, were, in his eyes, the key to control of all of Eastern Europe.

What Mackinder assumed was that Europe between the Rhine and the Volga must not be permitted to unite, and that it could be prevented from uniting by the creation of a tier of independent states from Finland to the Black Sea. Mackinder wrote: "You must have a balance as between German and Slav, and true independence of each . . . The condition of stability in the territorial rearrangement of East Europe is that the divisions should be into three and not into two state-systems. It is a vital necessity that there should be a tier of independent states between Germany and Russia." [15] Mackinder pleaded for what he called an "adequate" subdivision of East Europe with a Middle Tier of "really independent" states. He called for seven states based upon the seven different Middle Tier peoples (Poles, Bohemians, Hungarians, Romanians, Serbs, Bulgarians, and Greeks), totalling more than sixty million in population, interconnected by railways, and having access to the Adriatic, Black, and Baltic Seas.[16]

Hindsight tells us that the *cordon sanitaire* failed for two major reasons: the hopeless divisions among these Middle Tier states, and the need of these countries for co-operation with and support from the Soviet Union. Without this support they were helpless against German economic and military pressure. Conversely, without German support they were helpless against Soviet pressures. Even a united Middle Tier could not have resisted simultaneous pressure from both powers. Yet no less a geopolitical observer than Isaiah Bowman was moved to state that extension of Poland through Galicia, and of Romania through Bucovina, linked these countries as a continuous belt from the Black to the

[14] Mackinder, *Democratic Ideals and Reality,* map on p. 21.
[15] Mackinder, *Ibid.,* pp. 157, 158.
[16] Mackinder, *Ibid.,* p. 171.

Baltic Seas, enhancing their ability to stand together as a bulwark against Bolshevism.[17]

Opposition to Germany and the Soviet Union was not an adequate basis for the emergence of the Middle Tier as a third and balancing force in Eastern Europe. The antagonisms within and among the states concerned were too great to be surmounted by common fears of outside pressure. On the contrary, the various small states concerned sought support from either Russia or Germany in their schemes against their neighbors. Thus it was that these tidal lands of the German, Slav, Magyar, Romanian, and Jew—from the Oder to the Dneiper—sought to devour one another when Nazi Germany broke the *status quo* in the east. Capitalizing on the Munich Pact, Poland seized the Teschen area and Hungary absorbed the Magyarized southern border of Slovakia's Hungarian Plains, from Ruthenia almost to Bratislava. Later Ruthenia was turned over to Hungary by Hitler. In 1940 Hungary was further rewarded by its Nazi ally with Northern Transylvania. At this same time Bulgaria seized southern Dobruja from Romania. After the German invasion of Yugoslavia, both Hungary and Bulgaria were awarded spoils. Hungary took two portions of the southern Danube Plain, the Baranja (along the Middle Drava) and the Bachka (the Danube-Tisa "Mesopotamia"). Bulgaria seized Macedonia. It also occupied sections of Greek Thrace, from the Struma River to Alexandroupolis, in pursuit of a long-desired outlet to the Aegean Sea via the Maritsa River.

The ideal of national self-determination that was sponsored by the victorious allies after the First World War meant self-determination for some, but not for others. In every newly created state the national majority had to contend with large minorities that were frequently in the majority in specific cities or portions of the country. The Czechs and Slovaks were only two-thirds of their country's population, the Serbs half of theirs, the Romanians three-quarters of theirs, and the Poles two-thirds of theirs. The extermination and deportation of millions during the Second World War, and the population transfers that followed, have made Poland Polish, East Germany German, Czecho-

[17] Bowman, *The New World* (Yonkers N.Y.: World Book, 1922), p. 294.

slovakia Czechoslovak, Romania Romanian, and Bulgaria Bulgarian. Germans, White Russians, Ukranians, and Jews are to a great extent gone from Poland; Poles from Germany; Germans, Ruthenians, and Jews from Czechoslovakia; Germans, Slovaks, South Slavs, and Jews from Hungary; Germans and Italians, from Yugoslavia; South Slavs, Jews, and Bulgars from Romania; and Turks from Bulgaria. Many Magyars were expelled from Slovakia and from the Voivodina, especially the Yugoslav portion of that region. A new type of political boundary has been created—*a culture-molding boundary*—by which the demographic characteristics are reshaped to conform with the political boundary. We could, modifying Hartshorne's suggested terminology,[18] call this a "superimposed-subsequent" boundary. The boundary is marked off without regard to the original cultural landscape, and is therefore "superimposed." Then the cultural landscape is completely altered by population movement, and new cultural features emerge with which the boundary now conforms. What Europe has "perfected" on a mass scale was preceded in Turkey, and has since been followed in India-Pakistan, Israel, Korea, Vietnam, and Dominican border areas, among other places.

This coincidence of nationality and national boundary is one condition of East European geopolitical life. A second is the far-reaching effects of regional economic integration that has been brought about both by Communist co-operation and by external pressure from the U.S.S.R. Economic life in the Soviet satellites has been transformed, particularly through heavy industrialization. Intra-regional trade is quite heavy, though still less than the trade of individual countries with the Soviet Union.

The rapidity of the drive to industrialize Eastern Europe follows Soviet patterns quite closely. However, it must be pointed out that industrial strength is uneven. East Germany and Czechoslovakia are industrial countries, Hungary and Poland are partly so, and Romania and Bulgaria are still agricultural. The problems of industrialization are therefore not uniform throughout Eastern Europe.

Steel production has been made the measure and guidepost

[18] Richard Hartshorne: *Suggestions on the Terminology of Political Boundaries*, Leipzig, 1936.

of Eastern European industrial development, as it has been in the U.S.S.R. Today's steel production for Eastern Europe is over twenty million tons, or three times the 1938 output. The heart of Eastern European steel production lies in one great complex, the Silesian-Moravian coal, iron ore, and zinc region. Here two-thirds of all of Eastern Europe's steel is made. The Polish and Czech industrial areas have been connected by railways and canals, and iron ore from Krivoy Rog in the Eastern Ukraine has largely replaced the supplementary iron ore that was formerly imported from Sweden. Countries like Hungary and East Germany must rely upon imported raw materials for their steel. Heavy industry's expansion in Eastern Europe rests, therefore, upon two pillars: greater intra-regional trade, and greater dependence upon the Soviet Union.

A reflection of the industrial dependence on the U.S.S.R. is the development of an extensive pipeline system from Soviet territory, bringing petroleum and natural gas to Czechoslovakia, Hungary, East Germany, and Poland. Warsaw and Krakow have for some time received natural gas from the Western Ukraine, and now petroleum is being pumped from the Caspian and Black Sea areas to East Germany and to the Danube Valley.

Nonferrous metals, coal, pig iron, industrial raw materials for light industry, and timber are other imports from the Soviet Union. Only in chemical fertilizers, soda, and sulphuric acid, does the U.S.S.R. lag in supplying its satellites with raw materials for heavy industry. The net result is that from 60 per cent to over 90 per cent of the foreign trade of individual Eastern European countries is with satellite neighbors and the U.S.S.R., and there is little to suggest that this trend will be altered.

While growth characterizes heavy industry, light industry has made relatively little headway save in already advanced countries like Czechoslovakia and East Germany. Trade patterns with the U.S.S.R. are in complementary industrial raw materials and heavy industrial products, not in consumer goods. Because of this, the bulk of whatever products Eastern Europe does import from the West are engineering supplies, chemicals, drugs, consumer goods, and foodstuffs.

Eastern Europe has lost its traditional role of food exporter. Czechoslovakia and East Germany are major food importers today, and even Poland must import some grain. The stagnation of agriculture in Eastern Europe has left townspeople in a worsening situation of less available stocks at higher prices. Failures of the region's agriculture can be partly attributed to peasant resistance to collectivization, and partly to unbalanced emphasis on investment in manufacturing and transportation at the expense of agriculture. Essentially, however, it is the inevitable consequence of the change-over from a subsistence, national, agricultural economy to an industrial-commercial, agricultural economy, based upon regional specialization. If the U.S.S.R. can succeed in building up exports of grain and industrial crops (the latter, directly or through barter with third parties), then Eastern Europe's dependence upon Moscow will be further heightened.

The final condition of Eastern European geopolitical life is its strategic dependence upon the U.S.S.R. Between the Black and the Baltic seas, the Soviet Union has common borders with Poland, Czechoslovakia, Hungary, and Romania. As we have already noted, all of these countries are subject to pressures and the threat of instantaneous reprisals from Soviet soil. In addition, because of post-World War Two boundary changes and population expulsions, Poland and Czechoslovakia seek security from future German demands; Bulgaria from Romanian counterclaims in Dobruja; Czechoslovakia from Hungarian counterclaims in Slovakia; Yugoslavia from Hungarian counterclaims in Voivodina; and Romania from Hungarian ambitions in Northern Transylvania. Even if local Communist parties did not require Soviet assistance to maintain their control over the satellite countries, or if such parties become or are replaced by nationally oriented parties, the strategic dominance currently exercised by the Soviet Union makes independence of action in the face of Soviet opposition highly unlikely.

Trade as an Economic Weapon

Much of the struggle between the Free World and the Communist bloc manifests itself in economic clash. The Soviet bloc has already enjoyed considerable success in capturing overnight much of the foreign trade of a few neutral, and even Western, nations. Egypt, Cuba, and Guinea are prime examples, but Afghanistan, Iceland, and Turkey are cases where a substantial share of the business has turned to the Soviet Union and its satellites. Through extending credits, grants-in-aid, and barter, and through buying up large quantities of raw materials like cotton, coffee, sugar, wool, and fish, a major power can redirect the foreign trade of subsistence or single-commodity countries.

On the other hand, states that suddenly shift to the Soviet market have reason to be cautious. Unless the U.S.S.R. has a long-term need for the commodities it decides to import, it may suddenly reverse its decision to make such purchases, leaving the supplier without alternative markets. Moreover, Soviet purchases of commodities that are already produced in quantity in the U.S.S.R. is apt to lead to "dumping." Cotton from Egypt has already been dumped on the European market. In the future, machine tools, paper and pulp, and petroleum could be dumped.

With respect to petroleum, it should be noted that from the tanker ports on the Baltic, Caucasus, and Emba, crude and refined products can be shipped to northern and western Europe. Also, from Danube Valley pipelines there can be connections to Italy to bring petroleum to the Mediterranean. Russian petroleum dumping could become a fantastic nightmare if the U.S.S.R. should gain control of some Middle Eastern sources. Even without Middle Eastern oil, there is enough surplus petroleum in the Soviet Union to warrant large-scale exports to a few selected countries at very low prices. Vast North African, Venezuelan, and Canadian resources could be an adequate counter to the capture of Middle Eastern oil by the U.S.S.R. Moreover, Common Market-type agreements in Europe and the Western Hemisphere could close the Maritime World to Soviet dumping attempts, and conceivably leave the U.S.S.R. with quite a petroleum surplus if it should try to step up internal production or use Middle Eastern resources for trade purposes. Anti-dumping measures will probably not succeed, however, unless Western oil companies can be induced to set lower, more realistic pricing policies than the present United States Gulf Coast-dictated levels.

The U.S.S.R. can be expected to apply its economic advantage with considerable vigor so long as it uses foreign trade selectively as a weapon. The Maritime World cannot duplicate this procedure because it is committed to spreading assistance throughout most of the world, out of economic, strategic, and humanitarian considerations.

We need not assume that, in the long run, the economic path of the U.S.S.R. will be smooth. The Maritime World's advantage in terms of capital accumulations, know-how, and present near-monopoly on international trade will be enhanced by certain permanent Soviet international trade liabilities:

(1) The development of Soviet resources is moving manufacturing farther and farther into the interior of the country. The more successful the development of the Siberian and Central Asian frontier, the greater the distance from the export market. This means increased transportation costs and a permanent disadvantage vis-à-vis ocean-located states.

(2) The diversity of the raw material base of the U.S.S.R. means that, in the long run, large-scale purchases of minerals and industrial crops from underdeveloped countries will only duplicate Soviet resources. In the absence of major Soviet consumer goods imports, these are the only types of imports that can be brought in. Soviet self-sufficiency, in other words, is a long-term hindrance to international trade.

A shorter-term liability to trade stems from the lower living standards in the U.S.S.R. This makes it unlikely that large-scale capital surplus will be exported on a sustained basis during this period of Soviet development.

In our appraisal of the changing Soviet geographical scene we have touched upon several points. Outward expansion of the Soviet state to present borders poses serious threats to neighboring states. In the process of Czarist and Soviet territorial expansion, large non-Russian minorities were absorbed. To resolve the problems of colonialism-imperialism that attended this expansion, Marxist-Leninist theory created a federated state format that offered theoretical equality to all nationality groups. To insure control of the national territory in a practical sense, however, Communist leaders are carrying out large-scale Russification programs within these peripheral areas.

In the Soviet Union, agriculture, mining, and manufacturing are moving eastward—away from major sea lanes and optimum transport conditions for international trade. Emphasis in agriculture continues to be on dry farming under hazardous climatic conditions, rather than on more stable but far more expensive irrigation facilities. The result is that greater investment capital is available for manufacturing—an economic strategy that can prove sound only if the agricultural gamble succeeds.

Within the Soviet state, a degree of self-sufficiency is being achieved that is unique among today's modern states. This self-sufficiency is likely to be a major stumbling block to Soviet trade relations with other parts of the world—particularly those areas that are throwing off European imperial and colonial rule, which continue to depend heavily upon the export of raw materials in their foreign commerce.

In Eastern Europe, despite efforts of nationalist Communism to take up more independent economic and ideological positions, the strategic vulnerability of the region to Soviet pressures appears to preclude any possibility of its breaking away to become part of some genuinely neutral Central European buffer zone. The Soviet Empire has, with the exception of Yugoslavia, Austria, and Finland, expanded to its full continental European limits. Elsewhere in World Island, the contest for the Shatterbelts intensifies. Beyond these regions of direct strategic concern lies the zone of global conflict, wherein military and economic goals are secondary to ideological ones.

We must recognize that Soviet international policy goals differ from place to place because of the differences in their geopolitical values. Economic unrest, radicalism, and vestiges of Western imperialism are exploited by the Soviet Union wherever they occur, as a means of expanding Soviet influence. But over and above this, specific locales have uniquely important qualities from a Soviet standpoint. Achieving defensive depth for border ports, securing land gateways into the U.S.S.R., unifying minority nationalities, using global sea lanes for international trade—these are among the more important territorial considerations that have motivated recent Soviet foreign policy. Proper assessment of these values in each instance will better prepare us to cope with Soviet global designs.

Part Three

SPHERES OF CONTACT AND INFLUENCE

·7·

THE MIDDLE EAST AND SOUTHEAST ASIA

Today's Shatterbelts

We have discussed the characteristics and functions of Shatterbelts in Chapter III. The Shatterbelt is defined as a "large, strategically located region that is occupied by a number of conflicting states and is caught between the conflicting interests of the Great Powers." At present we recognize two such regions —the Middle East and Southeast Asia. Each is a zone of contact between the Continental Eurasian Realm and the Trade-Dependent Maritime World, easily reached from them, and commanding transit lanes and significant mineral wealth. Both regions, recently emerged from colonialism, have been unable to attain the economic and political unity to which many of their leaders aspire. Instead, internal divisions have become accentuated by the East-West struggle, and the Shatterbelts have become areas of contention rather than neutral buffers.

This chapter presents brief surveys of the two regions. The primary purpose is to explain their geopolitical functions more fully. However, a study of these Shatterbelts can shed light upon the conditions under which new Shatterbelt regions might emerge. For as the Central European Shatterbelt has disappeared from the map, so might the two present ones disappear, to be replaced by other regions caught up between new constellations of opposing Great Powers.

The Middle East

Consideration of the Middle East as a distinct geographical region is a point of view that meets with general acceptance. Names[1] applied to this area may vary and boundaries[2] may change, but the concept of a Middle Eastern region is implicit in international affairs, and especially in political and military strategy.

In discussing a part of the world like the Middle East, it is easy to become involved in an analysis of some very specific and exciting item of crisis. Such an approach is tempting, but the path is strewn with pitfalls. First, it is likely to become hopelessly out of date. Second, each event can acquire full meaning only when it is related to the broad pattern of events that occur within and around the Middle East.

The most dramatic change that has taken place within the Middle East in its modern history has been its sudden conversion to the status of a Shatterbelt. British-French control of the region has been replaced by a variety of conflicting internal and

[1] The terms *Near East, Nearer East, Levant, Hither East, Classical Deserts, Arab World, Cradleland of Civilization, Southwest Asia,* and *Most Ancient East* are among those which have been applied to parts or all of this region.

[2] a. The Middle East Supply Centre established by the British government in 1941 included the area from Tripolitania eastward through Iran and southward through the Sudan, Ethiopia, and the Somalilands. Cyprus and Malta were also within the Centre's framework, while Turkey, because of its neutral position, was omitted.

b. The United Nations Commission to Foster Economic Development in the Middle East includes the countries from Greece through Pakistan and south through Ethiopia.

c. The British geographer, W. B. Fisher, in his definitive study *The Middle East* (London: Methuen & Co., Ltd., 1950), includes the area that extends from Western Cyrenaica and Egypt through Turkey and through Iran.

d. The U.S. Department of State's Office of Near Eastern Affairs covers Egypt, the Sudan, the Arabian Peninsula, the Levant, and Iraq. In addition, there is an Office of Greek, Turkish, and Iranian Affairs. Both offices are included within the Bureau of Near Eastern Affairs.

external forces that threaten to divest it of whatever qualities of regional unity it might have possessed formerly.

If we were to measure the density of national tensions and stresses in terms of unit areas, the Middle East would lead all other regions. There is not a single Middle Eastern state that lives at complete ease with its neighbors, and almost every Middle Eastern state struggles with internal tensions that are the product of deep-rooted cultural clashes and geopolitical immaturity. Truly, the Middle Eastern geopolitical environment is a jungle. Territorial disputes rage, or are liable to flare up, between Turkey and Syria, Egypt and the Sudan, Israel and her neighbors, Saudi Arabia and Jordan, Saudi Arabia and Trucial Oman, Saudi Arabia and Yemen, Iraq and Kuwait, Iraq and Iran, Iran and the United Kingdom (over Bahrein), Afghanistan and Pakistan, and Yemen and Aden. Over-all political tension exists between Egypt and Iraq, Iraq and Iran, Turkey and Syria, Lebanon and Syria, and Israel and the Arab states, to name just a few. Military dictatorships rise and fall with rapidity, and iron-fisted monarchs cling to tenuous thrones. Everywhere the struggle is to consolidate states in the face of internal divisions and external pressures.

Overshadowing the entire region looms the pressure of the Soviet Union. The U.S.S.R. has unresolved claims against Turkish and Iranian border provinces. It is increasing its influence upon Iraq, through both Iraqi Arab Communists and Kurdish Nationalist elements. It is making strong inroads in Egypt and Yemen through general trade and specific naval base activities. Above all, it has evinced its ability to forestall counteractions to the spread of Nasserism or other anti-Western movements. This ability was demonstrated in events that started with the Suez crisis. It prevented any Western countermeasures to the revolution in Iraq. It influences Israel's relations with its neighbors. It may affect Western ability to act against future coups in Iran.

Shatterbelts evolve from both internal fragmentation and external pressures. While the U.S.S.R. fashions one ring of pressure around the Middle East, the Maritime World, from the Mediterranean and from Africa south of the Sahara, forms a counter-ring of pressure. And the Indian subcontinent is not without some influence in the region. These pressures are cultural and economic, as well as political and strategic. Middle Eastern cultures, economies, and even races reflect the outside world. Western customs, dress, and speech, Western economic patterns, and Western-sustained Christianity and Judaism are present along with Indo-Iranian and African influences to help shape the Middle East. We can view Pan-Arab aspirations of modern Arab nationalism as being in basic revolt against the forces that have conspired to make the Middle East a Shatterbelt. But such a revolt can by no means hope to sweep the entire region by its own efforts, for it runs headlong into forces of internal fragmentation, as well as outside opposition.

In Chapter 3, the geographical region has been defined as a "community of physical, biotic, and societal features that depict, or are functionally associated with, man's occupance of an area." While the Middle East meets the standards of this definition, its regionality is not easy to perceive because of two factors: the strength of its geographical components or sub-regions, and the political divisions that have tended to fragmentize the entire cultural landscape.

The Middle East lacks a single core and therefore it cannot be described as a nodal region. Rather, it is a uniform region wherein uniformity is most clearly expressed on a sub-regional basis. These sub-regions are organized through features that are functionally associated in groupings of different sizes or ranks. Attention must therefore be directed to diverse components, such as physiography, climate, agriculture, industry, religion, and strategic space, and to the area patterns these features form within the Middle East. When superimposed upon one another, such patterns constitute new sub-regions that are often more significant than the over-all region. If there is a broader uniformity to the region, it expresses itself most clearly in over-all location terms as a crossroads for the three continents, in its movement patterns, and in its environmental and cultural distinctiveness from neighboring regions.

The political consequences of the existence of geographical sub-regions within the Middle East qualify the significance of some of the regional generalizations that are so often bandied about—namely, that the region is the crossroads of the earth's greatest landmass; that land, sea, and air points of transition make the Middle East of importance to the West, the U.S.S.R., and the African-Asian world; that within the region is the single greatest storehouse of petroleum; and that the Middle East is the focal point for Islam and a potential bridge between the Muslims of Asia and Africa.

If we recognize the difficulties of trying to treat the Middle East as a monolithic region, our political approach finds firmer footing. We know that its various parts are experiencing differing rates of development, and these differences are rooted in the environment and in the people. This is a region of rainy mountains and lowland deserts, of dry interior plateaus and wet coastal fringes, of broad river valleys and isolated oases, of bare rock, sands, and gravels, and of alluvials. This is a region of nomadism and sedentary agriculture, of landlocked peoples and seafarers, of westernized contact zones and eastern cultures, of foreign trade and economic isolation. Whereas internal diversities such as these have not prevented other regions from unifying politically, Middle Eastern diversities are heightened by the fiercely competitive drives of modern nationalism and by the centrifugal pressures that outside interests bring to bear upon the region.

It is because internal differences are so marked, and because they are found in a region that is crushed between outside interests, that we have defined the Middle East as a Shatterbelt. The maps on the following pages are presented to illustrate some of the internal diversities.

The map showing the Middle East's structural units relates directly to mineral resources. (See Map 20.) In the Northern Zone we find a great variety of metallic minerals, iron, coal, and petroleum. In the Median Zone we find the sandstones that have trapped oil in their slight foldings to create the storage places for the world's richest petroleum reserves. Potash, phosphates, and limestone are also widespread there. The Southern Zone's crystalline rock platform is mineral-poor, save where overlaid by sedimentary deposits, as along the Isthmus of Suez, or where broken up by highlands, as in the case of the iron ore-bearing East Egyptian highlands near Aswan. The significance of these structural zones is that they relate to the ability of the various countries to obtain foreign exchange and to broaden the base of local industry.

Differences of climate are of overwhelming importance because the Middle East is so dependent upon agriculture and grazing. Rainfall variations form striking patterns. (See Map 21.) In essence, these rainfall patterns and their attendant soils and vegetation influence the formation of three Middle Eastern agricultural zones: 1) winter and summer farming, 2) irrigation farming, and 3) grazing. The critical rainfall line is the 16-inch isohyet. Those areas with 16 inches or more rainfall annually can engage in year-round farming operations, with either dry cereal farming and tree or vine crops in summer, and grains, fruits, and vegetables in winter. Unless they practice irrigation, those areas with less than 16 inches of rainfall can carry on only winter crop cultivation, and summer grazing and olive culture. Below 8 inches, only grazing is possible, although the 4-inch isohyet is sometimes accepted as the absolute minimum for grass.

The 16-inch isohyet has political, as well as economic and social significance, for it is a potential key to stability and strength within Middle Eastern agrarian societies. This is the line that divides normal, year-round farming operations from part-time agriculture, grazing, or irrigation farming. In the majority of cases, these latter three types of activities, suffering from inadequacies of water or soil resources, are carried on within a framework of overcrowding, unrest, poverty, and tenancy. Fertile riverine soils and water for irrigation—the very attractions of the great oases—are, in a social sense, their greatest weakness. This is because oases are not easily enlarged. The major exception to this within the Middle East today is the Tigris-Euphrates Valley, which appears capable of absorbing considerably more people.

The accommodation of rural populace to its land and water resources is a valuable guide to economic and social structures in the Middle East. Those countries, the majority of whose farmers live in areas with over 16 inches of rainfall or in the Tigris-Euphrates Valley, do not suffer from agricultural overcrowding. This is in marked contrast to the countries of the southern Middle East and the Levant, east of the Jordan Rift Valley. It should be noted that climate is not the only cause of

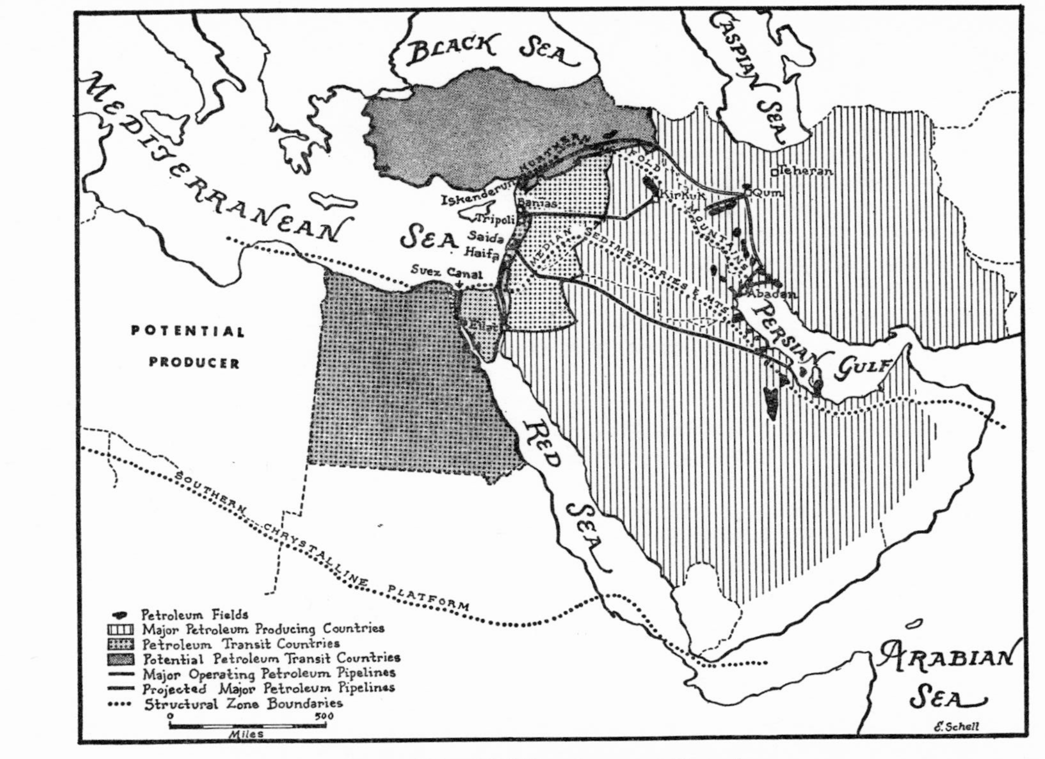

MAP 20. The Middle East and Petroleum

overcrowding. Lebanon and Yemen are also agriculturally over-populated, not because of lack of rainfall, but because of lack of level land.

Middle Eastern industry reflects the region's mineral distribution, its agricultural and water base, and its capacity to import raw materials. Turkey, Egypt, and Israel are the major producing countries of the region. Turkey leads in total output of industrial electricity, steel, and woolens; Egypt leads in general electricity output, cement, fertilizers, and cotton textiles. Israel, the most industrialized and urbanized of all, in a relative sense, has a highly varied output that ranges from food processing and textiles to industrial diamonds, tires, automobiles, fertilizers, and a steel mill. The three countries lead in rate of manufacturing growth, manufacturing employment, mechanization of agriculture, and caloric intake.

Turkey has the broadest industrial base within the region, with its minerals, foodstuffs, and employable labor force. Israel, with its skilled labor force, outside capital, chemicals, and locational advantages, should continue to forge ahead. Egypt's industrial future is more dependent upon its agricultural base than is that of Turkey or Israel, although, as in the case of the new steel mill at Helwan, industry is charting a pioneer course.

Today's Middle Eastern industry is concentrated along the Mediterranean coast, emphasizing the significance of imported raw materials. Elsewhere, the only industry of note is Persian Gulf petroleum refining. While this pattern shows a division along east-west lines, there is reason to believe that the progress of interior Turkey and southern Israel, and developments in Iraq and possibly Syria, may some day extend industrialization to the north, and to the drier sections of the Levant-Persian Gulf. It is interesting to note how little relationship there is between the map of Middle Eastern petroleum and industrial activity. While petroleum production is about one-fifth of the world's total, refining amounts to only 6 per cent, and domestic consumption to only 1.5 per cent. This points out the almost purely extractive nature of the Middle Eastern petroleum industry and its extra-regional service function.

A final illustration of the diversity of the Middle East is its religions and peoples. (See Map 22.) It would be fallacious to

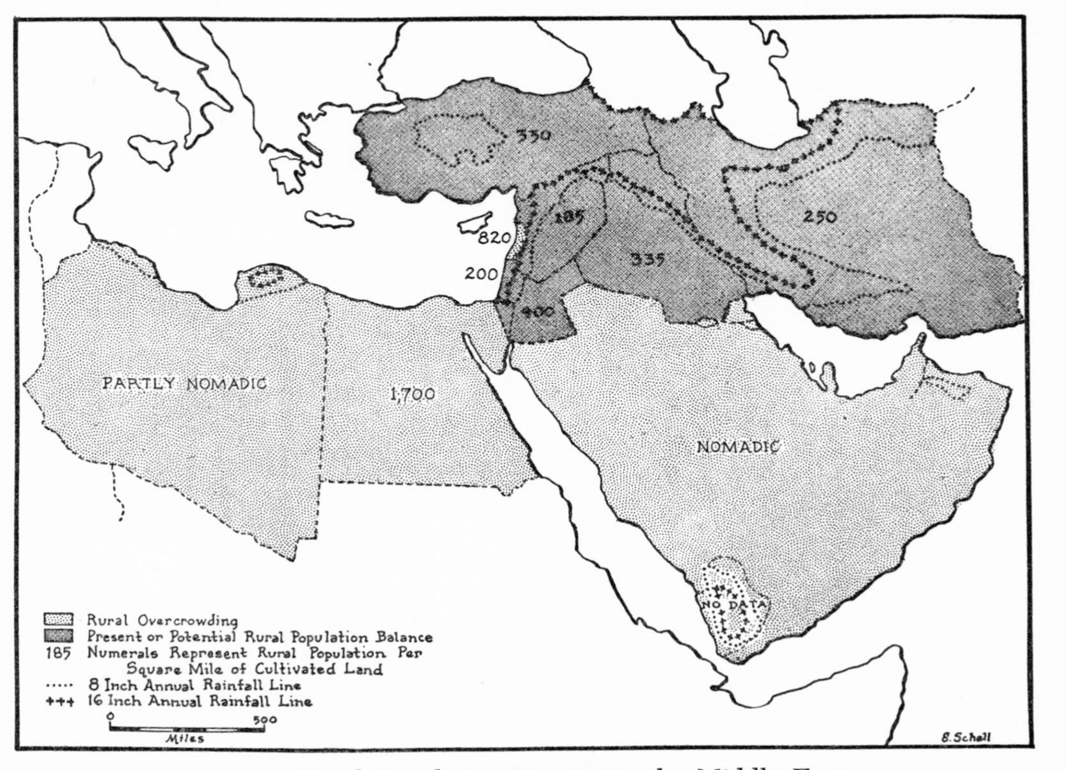

MAP 21. Rural Population Density in the Middle East

equate the Middle East with the Arabic Islamic World, and to ignore sectarian differences within Islam, or the differing political roles that Islam plays within various states, would also be a mistake. Thus, Shiite Iran has little in common with Sunnitic Egypt, and Muslim Turkey is a secular state, while the influence of Islam is strong in the political affairs of Saudi Arabia.

All of these diversities help to explain why there is little likelihood that one power center within the Middle Eastern Shatterbelt will be able to unify and dominate the entire region. Iran, Turkey, and Israel together have as large a population as the entire Arab world combined. Historically, the Turkish and Iranian plateaus have housed power centers independent of the Arab world. Today, with Ankara and Teheran emerging as associated seats of power, there is practically no possibility that they will be merged with an Arab coalition dominated by Cairo or by Baghdad.

What stands as the crucial problem today is whether the Middle Eastern Shatterbelt will remain as it is; whether it will become divided into two hostile blocs, Arab and non-Arab, one or both supported by an outside Great Power; or whether three blocs can emerge. The latter might be most desirable, because an intermediate group of states could act as a buffer, in terms of both internal regional politics and Great Power rivalry. Moreover, a three-bloc Middle East would be in closer conformity with sub-regional geographical patterns. Before Egypt took over the mantle of Pan-Arab leadership, such a three-fold division might have evolved, if the British-backed Greater Syria scheme had been successful.

If the Middle East should become a two-bloc region, it would do so through Arab unity, which would stand distinct from, and in opposition to, the non-Arab parts of the region. In the event that Arab unity should emerge under the leadership of Cairo, then, under the most favorable circumstances, the neutrality of the Arab bloc would be colored by a violent anti-Western bias that might be partly balanced by an anti-Soviet point of view. If Arab unity should emerge through a Communist take-over in Baghdad or Damascus, then a new Iron Curtain would be drawn between the Western-oriented and Communist worlds in the Middle East. A Communistic take-over of the Arab world through

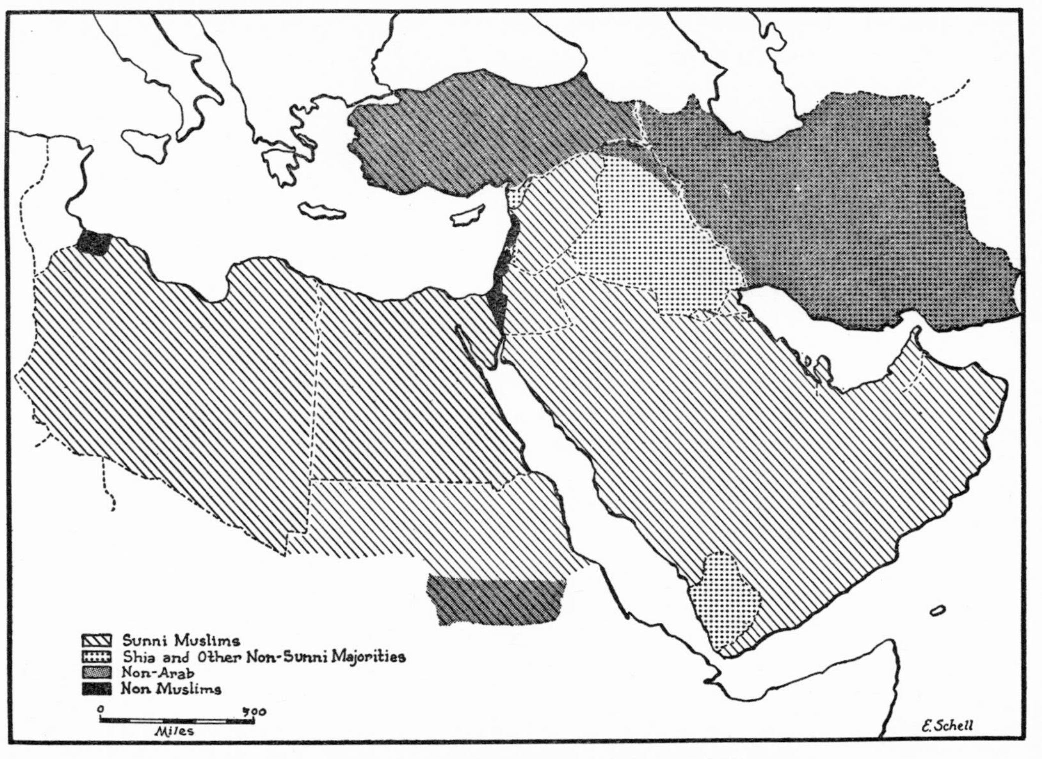

MAP 22. Religions and Peoples of the Middle East

a process of internal subversion and infiltration has been prevented to date only by the efforts of Arab military leadership. Whether this military leadership, if backed to the wall, could invoke Western intervention against Communist pressures is doubtful. For the unremitting anti-imperialist sloganeering of Arab leadership during the past few years would make it most difficult to maintain the support of the masses under such turnabout circumstances.

Because of the manner in which Egypt sought to absorb Syria, and the failure of this project in Arab unity, it is not likely that a federated, let alone a centralized, Arab state will be realized for a long time to come. The split within the Arab world will probably polarize even more strongly around Cairo and Baghdad. In this process, the Levantine and Persian Gulf Arab states will remain the key pawns in the power struggle. Their ability to retain a neutral footing within this field of internal Arab struggle is already being sorely tried, and there is likely to be little stability within the Arab world until the fate of these intervening countries is resolved.

The divisions within the Arab world are reflected in various issues. To Nasser, Arab nationalism has meant Arab internationalism—that is, political unification of the entire Arab world under a centralized government. To Kassem, Arab nationalism has been viewed through the traditional nation-state framework, and some form of Pan-Arab Federalism. To both, Arab nationalism means vaguely defined social reforms. To Iraqi and Syrian Communists, social reform means thorough nationalization and socialization under a Communistic framework. To the Saudi rulers, social reform is hardly a tenet of Arab nationalism. To petroleum "have-nots" of the Arab world, Arab nationalism means a sharing of regional wealth. To the petroleum-rich states, such ideas of sharing the wealth are anathema.

POLITICAL ALIGNMENTS

To relate rigidly political alignments in the Middle East to the various physical and human activity groupings already cited, is not possible, if only because the boundaries of those various sets of zones are not coextensive. Nevertheless, the construction of two broad political zones with flexible frontiers, and a third and intermediate one, has geopolitical validity and strategic tenability because these zones reflect three geographical sub-regions.

The Middle East has rarely been united. Instead, several fixed loci of power have been the bases of regional rivalries.[3] The contests between Babylonia and Assyria; Babylonia and Egypt; the Graeco-Romans and the Parthian-Sassanians; the desert empires of Petra, Palmyra, Nabataea and their neighbors; the Ummayads and the Abassids; the Crusaders and the Saracens; the Mongols and the Mamelukes; the French and the British—all had their roots in opposing power centers. The periods of political fragmentation represented by these various conflicts were far longer than those of unified regional control (as achieved by Babylonia, Alexander the Great, and Rome). Even during the Arab and Turkish eras (each of which lasted for four centuries), strong central government held only brief sway.

Time and technology have changed the significance of some of these loci of power. The desert way stations, for example, lack the land and manpower base necessary to regain for them their past imperial glories. Underpopulated Mesopotamia, open to invasion from the north, cannot, by itself, stand fast. Turkey and Persia were rival seats of empire during the sixteenth and seventeenth centuries because of their size and isolation. Today they are emerging as an allied power center, because of a common fear of Soviet aggression and with the help of improved transportation and communication. Certainly, if they should try to stand in isolation they would be more vulnerable to political and military infiltration.

The airplane, train, automobile, and ship have consolidated and regrouped the Middle East's loci of power within its geographic sub-regions. Today three significant zones stand out: 1) the Northern Plateaus, 2) the Nile and the Red Sea, and 3) the intervening "Intermediate Maritime Zone." The latter, though

[3] These areas are:

a. The Nile River Valley, one of the two most extensive areas of irrigated land in the Middle East.

b. Mesopotamia, the region's other great river valley.

c. The "Fertile Crescent" land area, which connects the Nile and Mesopotamia. Within the "Fertile Crescent" are the Levantine ports, the interior access ways, the Assyrian Piedmont, and the Syrian desert oases.

d. The Anatolean Plateau and rimming southern and eastern mountains.

e. The Iranian Plateau and rimming western mountains.

smaller and less populous than the other two, has coastal ports, interior accessways, and petroleum, as strategic sources of strength. (See Map 23.)

The Northern Highland Zone

The non-Arab northern highland countries of Turkey and Iran contain the single largest population grouping in the region (50 million persons); they have the broadest land bases, potentially the most stable agricultural economies, and the possibilities for wider industrialization thanks to fuel, mineral, and capital resources. Kurds and Azerbaijani are separatist elements within their countries. Their very existence, however, forces their governments to greater centralization efforts, such as the expansion of internal communications. Finally, Sunnitic Mohammedanism is weakest in this zone, and Orthodox Islam can, therefore, not be cited as a reason for political ties to the rest of the Middle East.

In general, the northern political zone corresponds with the northern structural and climatic zone. The one area of overlap is Khuzistan in southwestern Iran—west of the Central Zagros, which lies within the median structural and southern climatic zones. As a source of petroleum and a foothold overlooking Mesopotamia, southwestern Iran gives added strength to the northern political grouping.

The Southern Desert Zone: The Red Sea Bloc

The lands of the southern deserts and irrigated oases, extending from Libya through Arabia, are coming under the increasing threat of domination of Cairo. Nearly two-thirds of the zone's entire population of 45 million lives along the Nile Valley, and the Suez Canal is the most significant geopolitical asset of this part of the Middle East.

Until now, Egypt's attentions have been focused northward, toward the Levant and the rest of the Arab world. But Egypt and some of its neighbors are only peripheral to the Middle East. Their concern with areas and events taking place to their south and west may one day be as great as the concern that the northern states now have with the U.S.S.R. Egypt, especially, may have to involve itself more deeply in African affairs, and look

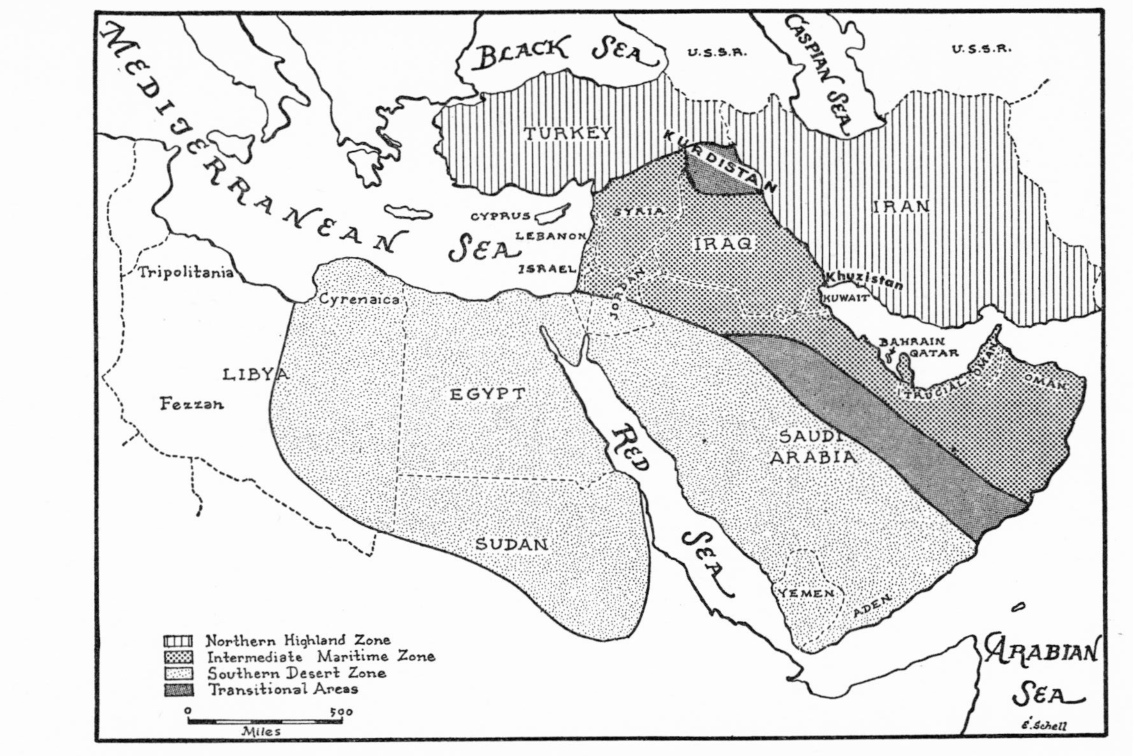

MAP 23. The Middle East in Three Geopolitical Zones

southward to the sources of the Nile. In this respect, ambitious Egyptian rulers regard the Sudan as only the first and the immediate objective of the extension of Egypt's sphere of influence into Africa. In the future, the Central and East African Nile headwater areas may become the focus for Cairo's geopolitical ambitions. In the very long run, these may extend to the Muslim world of North and Black Africa, and to the entire continent.[4]

Libya is transitional, for its westernmost sections are culturally and agriculturally parts of the Maghreb. This recently created state is finding difficulty in retaining its unity, since it is composed of two different culture worlds—the nomadism of Cyrenaica and the North African coastal farming of Tripolitania. As a measure of containing Egyptian influence, it is in the interests of the Western world to encourage the strengthening of ties between Libya and the Maghreb.

Saudi Arabia, too, has dual characteristics. The bulk of its population lives along the moister Red Sea coast—or northern interior desert—part of the southern structural unit. Petroleum, however, the basis for the country's wealth, lies along the Persian Gulf coast of the median structural zone. This separation of population concentration from the major mineral resources may some day lead to greater political divisiveness in the Arabian Peninsula, although, conversely, the petroleum could conceivably buy for the Saudi Arabian government the political and military power to strengthen its kingdom's unity, and to maintain a Persian Gulf orientation, free of Egyptian dominance. Whether this petroleum can one day stimulate the growth of a large industrial population along the Gulf is doubtful in view of the cultural pull of Mecca-Jidda and the feudal nature of the state. Indeed, the very element that might strengthen Saudi Arabia's orientation to the Persian Gulf—industrialization—contains within it the seeds of revolutionary nationalism and the pull to the Egyptian-controlled southern zone.

A critical issue is the rivalry between Saudi Arabia and Britain, which once helped to turn Saudi Arabia politically toward Egypt. Britain's influence in Kuwait, Bahrein, and Oman has aroused Saudi opposition to "British imperialism." At the same time, Iraq

[4] For an insight into this problem, see Gamel Abdel Nasser, *Egypt's Liberation* (Washington, D.C.: Public Affairs Press, 1955).

claims Kuwait and Iran claims Bahrein. Perhaps, eventually, this issue of Arab-Persians versus the West can be removed by allowing Iraq and Iran to establish direct political footholds in those principalities to which they have historic claims. This need not be accomplished by annexation but rather by some loose federal arrangement. Under such circumstances, rivalries within the Persian Gulf area would become internal, with Britain and the United States acting as interested, but not directly involved, parties to conflicting Saudi and Iraqi-Iranian pressures. The timing for such a move would be related to the speed with which Saharan oil can be exploited as a supplement, and, if need be, a substitute for some of the Middle Eastern production.

The Intermediate Maritime Zone

With both the northern and southern blocs exercising pressures against the intermediate areas, we must now ask ourselves whether an intermediate zone, oriented toward both the Eastern Mediterranean and the Persian Gulf, is politically viable. Political instability has characterized this area in the past, for it has the characteristics of an internal Shatterbelt.

But this intermediate zone does stand apart from its neighbors. It has a large measure of unity that stems from common and interdependent human and physical resources. We find forces for unity in the ports of the Eastern Mediterranean and their accessways (like the Tripoli-Homs Gap, the Col du Beidar, and the Valley of Jezreel) to the deserts that lead eastward; and in the petroleum of the Persian Gulf fields and their land bridges to the Mediterranean (the 1040-mile TAP-line to Saida, the 530-mile IPC pipeline to Tripoli, and the 556-mile IPC pipeline to Banias). These pipelines carry about 40 million tons (almost all crude), or about 40 per cent of all of the Middle East's petroleum that is exported to Europe, North and West Africa, and North America. We find potential unity in the dependence of landlocked Jordan and interior Syria upon the ports of other Levantine states for effective outlets to the sea. We find a force for unity in the intra-regional trade of the Levantine states that is higher than that of the Middle East as a whole. We find such a force in the fact that countries like Lebanon and Kuwait are too small to solve their economic problems in isolation. Lebanon needs the markets of neighboring states to modernize its agriculture, replacing grain with fruits and vegetables. Kuwait needs the markets of its neighbors to enable it to invest some of its surplus capital in modern factories that could give to the Kuwaiti populace a productive and purposeful economic role. We even find unity in the religious and ethnic diversities within this zone—for these diversities set apart the zone from the non-Arab Islamic North and the Arabic Islamic South. They make of it a cultural, ethnic, and religious mélange which may one day recognize that its survival rests upon some form of political unity.

Thus, while location has made the intermediate zone vulnerable to pressures from both sides, and while a bipolarized Middle East is neither inconceivable nor lacking in historic precedent, this unique area has within it a basis for political distinctiveness. A coalition of Levantine-Persian Gulf states, standing as a neutral between the northern and southern zones, could give greater stability to the region as a whole, and might serve to isolate petroleum as an issue in East-West politics. However, the emergence of such an intermediate zone requires, first, the creation of an Iraqi, Syrian, and Jordanian Federation, and second, peace between Israel and her neighbors. Neither eventuality is likely to occur within the next few years, and the intermediate zone should be considered as a long-range hope, not a short-range target.

To sum up, treatment of the Middle East as a threefold political-economic region, rather than as a unitary one, finds support within its geographic framework. The distinguishing elements within the northern political zone are: 1) proximity to the U.S.S.R., 2) mountainous terrain and minerals including petroleum, 3) non-Arabic peoples, 4) a stable agricultural base. Those which distinguish the southern political zone are: 1) The Suez Canal, 2) deserts, 3) Egypt's Nile as a center of population and local power, 4) a subsistence agricultural base. To distinguish the intermediate political zone there are: 1) Levantine ports and accessways, 2) petroleum, 3) smaller but heterogeneous population, 4) historic and cultural associations with the Western world. This is not to suggest that a rigid ternary approach be adopted for the Middle East. This would be unrealistic owing to the overlapping zonal characteristics of some of the countries concerned. The threefold political approach, based as it is upon physical and human-use tiers, should therefore be accepted as a broad, flexible framework, constantly open to reevaluation. It should serve as a guide, not a dogma, to understanding the Middle East.

FREE WORLD FOOTHOLDS

The Shatterbelt status of the Middle East can be more easily maintained if some degree of internal stability is realized, as against the current patterns of sudden political squalls and upheavals. The West has tried to buy friendship within the intermediate zone through past alliances with Iraq, Saudi Arabia, and Lebanon. We failed. Now we seek to encourage neutrality in some of these countries and in Syria. Perhaps a lesson from the past suggests that Jordan be encouraged to take a similarly neutral position, rather than to try to maintain its shaky stance as a Western ally.

Obviously there is no guarantee that avowedly neutral nations will not become neutral in favor of the Soviet Union. This is a chance that we take when we offer to extend economic aid, and even to sell arms to countries that announce their neutrality and indicate, by deeds, a willingness to accept accommodation and arbitration in international economic disputes. But the chance is worth taking, so long as we do not neglect our most pressing task—the safeguarding of allies who want and deserve our support.

Many reasons can be cited for not recommending Arab states as footholds for the Free World. The most telling one is that Arab nationalism is, on many issues, bound to be anti-Western. The legacy of European imperialism; the issues of Israel and Algeria; the Suez Campaign; the rivalry for Africa south of the Sahara; the existence of military bases in Libya and Aden; the control of Nile headwaters by European-influenced political areas; the distribution of petroleum profits—these are all part and parcel of Arab nationalism. We must recognize that accommodation on some of these issues will not be possible for many years to come.

It has become obvious that the West's most advantageous associations rest, not with the Arab world, but with Turkey,

Iran, and Israel. Turkey furnishes a Black Sea base for overseeing the Ukraine and the Caucasus. The Turkish Straits can be used to cut off Soviet shipping as a counter to any Soviet-backed move by Egypt to close the Suez Canal to the West. Most important, the people of Turkey are ideologically oriented to the West—to them, westernization is a thoroughly acceptable ideal.

Iran overlooks the Caspian and the Muslim-inhabited portions of the U.S.S.R. If necessary, its petroleum can fill half of all Maritime Europe's Middle Eastern oil needs. Strategically, Iran dominates the Persian Gulf oil principalities and Iraq's Mesopotamian Valley.

Israel has the most skilled manpower pool in the Middle East and is a genuine democracy. Its location separates Egypt from the rest of the Arab world, and provides a land route that is an alternative to the Suez Canal. It has the only Middle Eastern army capable of foiling Arab advances without necessarily precipitating a Great Power conflict over the region. In this context, lack of formal military alliances between Israel and the Western world may have some advantages, provided that all of the tangible elements of an alliance are enjoyed. Above all, these three countries know and fear the consequences of Soviet intervention in their affairs—something that, for the most part, Arab states have taken as a lesser evil than Western intervention.

Military and economic assistance alone is not enough. These countries need help and encouragement in the realm of social and political advancement. Turkey needs judicious counsel with respect to the restoration of political freedoms. It also should be included in as many Maritime European organizational activities as possible to strengthen its ties with the West. The Shah of Iran needs our continued encouragement in carrying through his land-reform program and deserves preferential oil-policy treatment. Israel needs assistance in its drive to westernize Jewish refugees from Arab lands, and to solve its Arab minority problems. No "crash" economic assistance program to these countries will be meaningful unless we focus on all aspects of national-state development. This means bread, arms, *and* social aspirations. By strengthening these footholds in the Middle East, we will not reduce the possibility of obtaining an agreement with the U.S.S.R. on preserving the Shatterbelt characteristics of the

Middle East. On the contrary, the stronger our allies become, the greater will be the opportunity to gain such an agreement.

International alliances are agreements between governments, not between peoples. Consequently, the form of government, the character of its leadership, and the role played in the governmental process by the majority of the inhabitants, are factors that have to be assessed in evaluating the effectiveness of alliances. The preference of the American people is for broadly-based, republican forms of government among its allies. In most parts of the underdeveloped world, such governments do not exist. We are, therefore, forced to deal with alternatives to democratic governments, and should not close our eyes to the realities of these alternatives.

Iran is a good case in point. In Iran, the alternatives to the Monarchy are the landlords, the intellectual-student classes, and the military. At present, the Throne, backed by the military, is attempting to maintain political stability and to press economic progress and reform. If the Shah should fail, then presumably any of the three alternative groups could come to power. The landlord class represents no hope to Iran or to the West because this is the class which is essentially responsible for Iran's current plight. The intellectual-student class consists of both the Iranian National Front—a heterogeneous group that includes individuals with Neutralist and pro-Communist sentiments, and the Communists themselves. For the West to turn to the National Front and to assume that under its leadership Iran would remain an ally would be quite risky. The fact that Iranian hostility toward the U.S.S.R. is traditional, is no guarantee against a sudden turn to neutrality or even to Communism. Moreover, it is unlikely that the very small, urbanized middle class of Iran would have a greater concern for the peasantry than either the Monarchy or the military.

Experience elsewhere suggests that the young officer class may offer hopes for carrying out land reform under a government less tainted with corruption than the present Iranian government. Military government goes against the grain of the United States political tradition. However, the realistic alternative in Iran is not representative government as we know it, but dictatorship in one of its several forms. Iran's best hope appears to lie in a dictatorship benevolent to its own people, genuinely concerned with land reform and industrialization, and interested in creating a grass-roots type of village democracy. Elsewhere in the world, military rule has proclaimed programs dedicated to such ends.

This leads to the consideration of military juntas as a ruling force. From Egypt, the Sudan, Turkey, and Iraq to Pakistan, Burma, Thailand, and South Korea, military groups control national politics with varying degrees of success. Where these groups, usually "The Generals," represent the aristocratic class or the entrenched interests, genuine reform is not possible. Where these groups consist of reform-minded elements with no stake in the economic status-quo (usually the younger officers), they offer an opportunity for progress within a framework of political stability, as has thus far been the case in Egypt, Iraq, and Pakistan. Military rule provides no guarantee of political stability, and countries like Syria and Thailand offer examples of military governments succeeding each other with monotonous regularity. Stability requires a government both firmly in control and dedicated to the welfare of its people.

The initial phases of a promising experiment with the military, have been launched in Burma. There, the armed forces are being used as an educational device to wipe out illiteracy among the recruits, to train men to become modern farmers and technicians, and to use officers as area and departmental administrators. Such programs may become the base from which military rule can be most readily converted to civil controls through the build-up of an articulate farm-labor class and of a responsible civil service.

Keeping in mind the fact that military governments can run the gamut from despotic, self-seeking totalitarianism to more enlightened, reform-directed, dictatorship, we can realistically weigh the power struggle in Iran. If the alternative to the Monarchy should become a choice between a pro-Western military reform group and one of the other groups previously described, the former would warrant our support.

Because petroleum is so significant in the Free World's relations with the Middle East, we shall consider one aspect of this topic. This is the building of pipeline alternatives to the Suez Canal—the trans-Syrian pipelines, and the proposed Pan-Arab pipeline. (See Map 20.) Middle Eastern petroleum production, now about one-fifth of the world's total, is on the rise. The bulk of the oil (70 per cent) is exported to Europe, and as has been noted, pipelines carry over 40 per cent of these exports. When Egypt and Syria were combined, the U.A.R. monopolized the accessways. No wonder, therefore, that Persian Gulf areas were so susceptible to Cairo's influence. Even separated, Egypt's and Syria's control over the oil transit ways is a serious threat to Western security. If we possessed an alternative to these routes we would be in a better position to support our allies and to deal with neutrals and enemies. Two alternatives have been suggested: one, from Qum in Iran, southwest of Teheran, to Iskenderun in Turkey; the second, from Eilat to Haifa in Israel; these would have a combined throughput capacity of over 40 million tons. Building them would strengthen the hands of our allies as well as those of the Western world.

The easiest line to build is Eilat-Haifa. The suggested Iranian terminus at Qum in Central Iran is the site of recent major petroleum discoveries. Until a pipeline is built to Iskenderun (or to the Iranian pipelines to the southwest), Qum's oil cannot be effectively exploited. Because of the time involved in planning and building the Iranian-Turkish line would be considerable, there is even more reason to construct the Eilat-Haifa line as rapidly as possible to give a transportation hedge to southern Iranian oil. Recent indications are that the oft-proposed 16-inch pipeline from Eliat will be built shortly. A thoroughly adequate line, however, would be a 30-inch line, capable of pumping 15 to 20 million tons a year. The current step-up in exploring for alternative sources of petroleum with good water access to Europe, as in Latin America and North Africa, is also bound to help counteract oil-blackmail politics in the Middle East.

The key to the Maritime World's position in the Middle East lies in the selective support of allies and in the general support of neutrals. Fortunately, population pressures within Turkey, Iran, and Israel are not such as to make the task of economic assistance hopeless. Moreover, the physical and human resource base in these countries is sufficiently broad to enable them to achieve economic stability.

What is crucial about the strategic location of the Middle East is its relationship to North Africa and Africa south of the Sahara.

Petroleum and the Suez Canal are secondary elements. We can increase Iranian petroleum production or exploit alternative sources of petroleum in such parts of the world as Latin America, Canada, and North Africa. We can use the circum-African route and our position in the Turkish Straits as checks against Soviet manipulations in Suez. If the U.S.S.R. should obtain direct control of Persian Gulf petroleum and seek to dump it upon the Free World, we can counter this most dangerous cold war weapon by rigid embargoes and far-reaching measures of cooperation in Free World oil production and distribution. But we cannot find substitute political and miiltary positions for our Middle East footholds. Without such positions of strength and counterweights, the Middle East's Shatterbelt character cannot be maintained. With such positions, the Free World will not see itself swept out of the Middle East or find itself confronted with a hostile world power perched on the southern Mediterranean and West African coasts. It is for this reason, above all, that the Maritime World must seek positions of strength through Middle Eastern footholds. The only way to maintain these footholds is to base them upon mutual aspirations and interests—not on expediency, accident, and intrigue.

Southeast Asia

Southeast Asia is new to the regional map of the world. Prior to the Second World War, when only one sovereign state (Thailand) existed there, what is now Southeast Asia was a mixture of colonies with little sense of internal identification. So great was regional diversity that even the term "Southeast Asia" was not generally accepted.[5] In less than two decades, however, the picture has changed. Seven new states have emerged, and there is a groping by all of the region's components for some new role on the international scene.

In surveying the region we find that every single state is plagued with problems that touch upon the very existence of the state. Far more than with economics, these problems have to do with centralization of government, securing of borders, and basic foreign policy orientation.

Every one of the states, with the exceptions of Cambodia and

[5] Ginsburg, ed., *op. cit.*, p. 290.

Thailand, has had to contend with serious internal rebellions. Every one has a boundary dispute or a territorial problem on its hands. Three of the countries concerned—Thailand, Malaya, and South Vietnam—are allied with the West; four—Burma, Indonesia, Cambodia, and (for the moment) Laos—are neutral—and one—North Vietnam—is Communist. There are no strong blocs within the region. Even an attempt by Thailand and South Vietnam to achieve greater internal co-operation has to be made in association with a peripheral nation—the Philippines.

So rapidly must the focus of our attention shift from problem area to problem area that we quickly forget past preoccupations. Burma, Indonesia, and Malaya have been eclipsed, as danger spots, by Laos and Vietnam. All that we can say with confidence is that no part of Southeast Asia is an island of calm within the troubled seas.

The instability and unrest that is prevalent reflects the Shatterbelt nature of Southeast Asia, with the deep-rooted diversities that both attract outside interference and prevent internal cohesion.[6]

These diversities in Southeast Asia are the result of the cross-currents that have shattered the region into fragments in the past, the internal physical and cultural barriers that have frozen these fragments into separate political entities, and the external pressures that intensify these differences.

Southeast Asia has lain in the path of Indian, Chinese, European, American, Australian, and Japanese pressure. Indian influence was first felt through the spread of Hinduism and Buddhism into Burma, Thailand, Laos, and Cambodia nearly 2,000 years ago. Some of the great empires of the past, like those centered at Ankor, were cultural outliers of Indian civilization. Bali is a "relict" area of Hinduism. The Chinese, moving along the coast and down the river valleys of the interior, were the forefathers of the Annamese, Lao-Thai, and Thai. The cultural influence of the Chinese is strongest among the Annamese, and has been established in the Tonkin Delta for 2,000 years. Muslim merchants from India, in the fourteenth century, established trade centers in Malaya, throughout the Indies, and up to the southern

[6] Jan Broek, "Diversity and Unity in Southeast Asia," *The Geographical Review*, XXXIV, No. 2 (1944), pp. 175-95.

Philippines. Their religious stamp has been indelibly etched upon insular Southeast Asia. Then came the recent colonialists: the British in Burma, Malaya, and Borneo; the Dutch in Indonesia; and the French in Indochina. They have left strong marks in the economic and political field and lesser ones in the religious field. Encouraged by the Europeans, Indians migrated as plantation workers to Burma and Malaya. During the colonial era the various countries had their main contacts with European or Asian states, not with one another. Since the end of the Second World War there have been no really significant regional attempts to find solutions to common economic and political problems. And this is understandable. Low national incomes, lack of industrialization, limited production, and uneven distribution of population do not by themselves provide a framework for regional thought and action.

Actually, the separateness and isolation of national ecumenes, religions, cultures, and peoples; the differing national orientations to separate parts of the world—these are the diversities that have made it so difficult for Southeast Asia to find common economic, political, and military expressions.

Economic differences exist, partly because Southeast Asian states are so isolated from one another and partly because their products are similar and therefore competitive in the world export markets. The Malaysian or insular Southeast Asian portion is highly competitive in its plantation crops and minerals. And Mainland Southeast Asia, from Burma through Vietnam, with similar physical environments, subsistence agriculture, and export rice, has little basis for internal interchange.

One of the clearest indications of the fragmented nature of Southeast Asia is the restricted extent of its various national ecumenes, without even the hint of the development of a regional ecumene. (See Map 24.)

Only the Tonkin Delta, the northwest coast of Java, and Lower Burma (heavily settled in the past century) are moderately developed economic and population cores within their national frameworks. To envisage a regional ecumene, we should have to consider the Annamese coast, Northern Java, the lands bordering the Straits of Malacca, and the Gulf of Martaban as the best possible framework. The current gaps in both population and

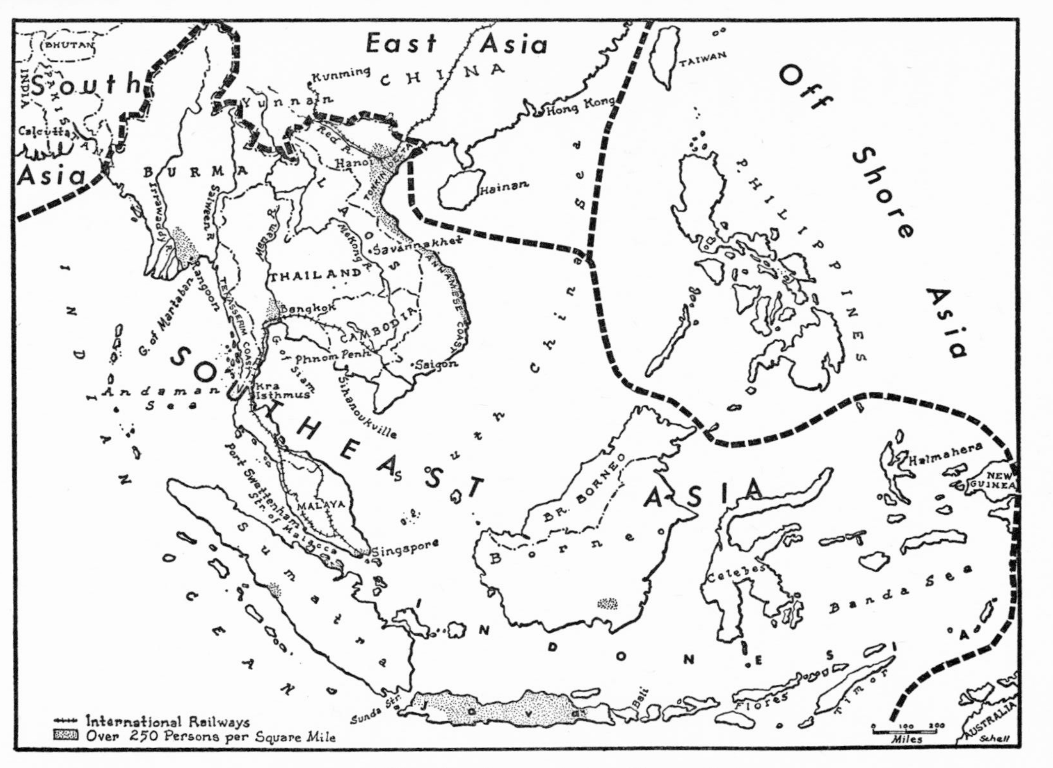

MAP 24. The Southeast Asian Shatterbelt

movement links and the extra-regional orientation of each of these areas suggest that the emergence of such a framework will be a long time in coming. Absence of a regional core makes regional co-operation difficult and weakens the ties of peripheral areas to Southeast Asia.

Uneven distribution of population is characteristic of most of Southeast Asia. The physical framework of lowlands and mountain festoons, as well as the development of plantation crops and minerals for the outside world, has concentrated the population of this Shatterbelt on such river plains as the Red, Mekong, Menam, Salween, and Irrawaddy, and on such coastal lowlands as western Malaya and south-central Java. Where soils are periodically renewed, as are the river flood plains, or are unusually rich intrinsically, population densities attain great heights, and the areas tend to serve as political cores for national states. The Volcanic belts that extend across the southern island arc from Sumatra to Flores (Banda Sea), and northward to Halmahera, the Celebes, and up through northern Luzon in the Philippines, provide the best soils and attract coastal populations. But in most parts of Southeast Asia the soils are poor, either because they are intensely leached lateritics or swamps along the coasts (New Guinea, Borneo, Sumatra, Malaya) or because they are thin, acidic, and mountainous. The result is underpopulation throughout most of the region. Only 8.5 per cent of all of Southeast Asia is under cultivation. The central dry zone of Burma, the seat of ancient Burmese civilization, is now only sparsely settled. The same is true for the central valley of Thailand, and for the flood plain of the Mekong in Cambodia—once centers of great civilizations, but now empty. The populations of most of these valleys, today, are concentrated along the deltas, rather than along middle valley portions.

In over-all terms, the average population density of Southeast Asia (slightly over 100 persons per square mile) is only one-third that of India or China, and one-sixth that of Japan. But the full story of maldistribution of population emerges when we consider that rural parts of Lower Thailand have densities of over 1,000 persons per square mile, while northwest of Bangkok and on the grassy plains of Cambodia the density is only 2 to 25 persons per square mile; or that the gross population density of Vietnam is three times that of such countries as Burma and Cambodia.

Absence of water control and fertilizers, overemphasis on paddy rice, especially where Chinese settled in the Red River Delta and Annam and where plantation agriculture created a need for labor and food for this labor in Java, shifting cultivation in the uplands, problems of land tenancy, soil erosion, the spread of deep-rooted grasses—these are all factors in the limited productivity of the lands of Southeast Asia.

Differences within and between states are sharpened by the absence of extensive transportation links. The only rail lines that exist to tie countries together are the two between China and North Vietnam, one between Cambodia and Thailand (the "Cambodian Gateway"), and one between Thailand and Malaya. Road connections are poor everywhere outside the major cities. Shipping within the region is slow and spotty, the more modern services being oriented to Europe, South Asia, or the United States, and reflects external orientations. If the Kra Canal project to link the Andaman Sea and the Gulf of Siam should ever materialize, it would probably enhance external trade even more than it would intra-regional shipping (although the latter would be a factor that would strengthen internal bonds). A by-product of such a canal would be to press Burma and Thailand to joint economic action.

One of the basic weaknesses of Southeast Asia's states is that their revolutions have been carried out within the political frameworks laid down by European colonialism. The national boundaries that exist are mostly the heritage of empire building and accommodations between rivals. Despite boundary disputes within the region, the European-designed political boundaries are the basic lines that new states have accepted. With nationhood have come desires for self-sufficiency. Singapore, the trading entrepôt for the Indies and Malaya, is losing ground in its share of the rubber and tin trade. Port Swettenham in Malaya and Sumatran ports have been developed in response to national pressures to take business away from Singapore. Cambodia, rather than relying on the Mekong or the Thai Railway, has developed its first deepwater port at Sihanoukville on the Gulf of

Siam and has connected this port to Phnom Penh by a modern highway. These are steps that intensify regional fragmentation, rather than interdependence. Moreover, many minorities have entered the scene because of the need of plantations or mines for outside labor. Some of these minorities are so prominent, and antagonisms are so acute, that the drive of national majorities to centralize governmental functions has threatened to split countries like Malaya and Indonesia. Major cities like Rangoon (half Indian) and Singapore (three-quarters Chinese) are largely directed by national minorities.

A basic problem is that some national states are too large and contain too many minorities to warrant a strongly centralized state, or are too small and lacking in the earmarks of the modern national state to be able to function as such. Real national unity in Southeast Asia will have to come about through the help of diverse cultures and peoples, not in spite of them. In some cases, these can only mean federated units.

In this context, one must take special note of the Overseas Chinese. Other sizeable minorities exist—the Shans of Burma; the Outer Islanders of Sumatra, the Celebes, and the Moluccas; the Javanese of Sumatra; the Malayans and Vietnamese in Thailand; the Indians in Malaya and Burma; the Annamese in Cambodia. But the 15 million Overseas Chinese—by their numbers, their economic vitality, their cultural and political ties to either Peiping or Taipei, and their failure to secure acceptance from the peoples among whom they have settled—pose a serious threat to national stabilities in Southeast Asia. Malaya, with 40 per cent Chinese, and Thailand, with 20 per cent Chinese, have especially difficult problems to solve. But even Burma, which is 70 per cent Burman and has only 300,000 Chinese, finds problems in the fact that many of its Chinese are concentrated along the northeast border or the Tenasserim coast—both far removed from the Lower Burmese core.

Frequently the Overseas Chinese problem is regarded in the light of competition between Communist and Nationalist China for the allegiance of this community. But the problem has to be viewed in another light, as well. The Overseas Chinese must be assimilated within the mainstream of the respective national movements of the various countries, especially Malaya, Vietnam,

Thailand, and Indonesia, to avoid the possibility of forced repatriation. Economic restraints against the Chinese in Thailand and Indonesia are particularly strong. In Malaya the restraint has been political so long as Singapore has remained separate from the Malay Federation because its inclusion would create a Chinese majority within the state as a whole. The recent decision has been to offset this increase in Chinese population that would result from the inclusion of Singapore, by also bringing into the Federation the Malaysian peoples of British Borneo. Certainly without such a political resolution, Singapore and its Chinese inhabitants would have a gloomy economic future.

It is difficult to view Southeast Asian national problems from a purely national vantage point, because in almost every instance complications arise from relations with neighboring states or with extra-regional states.

For example, Burma, with a lower population density than that of its neighbors, a broad agricultural base, and some minerals, including oil, has hopes for substantial economic progress. Her problems are essentially political, not economic, since political unification has been Burma's biggest stumbling block. But relations with China and India are also factors in explaining some of Burma's problems. Statehood found Burma devoid of a strong civil service, because Indians had pre-empted so many of the jobs. And creation of a Kachin autonomous state on the Chinese side of the border, unchecked movement of former Chinese Nationalist troops in the north, and dispute over the boundary with Communist China have all weakened the effectiveness of the central government in northern Burma.

Thailand appears uniquely capable of acting as a cohesive political entity. Bangkok is an excellent focus for rivers and coastal routes. It is a good rail and air hub. It is unchallenged as the country's primate city. The rural populace is almost exclusively Thai and the country has never been dominated by European imperialism. On the other hand, Thailand has its internal Chinese problem and has had recent frontier disputes with Laos, Cambodia, Burma, and Malaya. The most depressed part of its country, the Nam Mun Basin, adjoins Laos and Cambodia, and is therefore exposed to subversive action. Finally, the Communist "Free Thai" movement is based in Chinese Yunnan, and will be capable of operating much more freely against Thailand if Northern Laos should go Communist.

Indonesia's control over Sumatra is complicated by the orientation of much of that island to Singapore. While culturally Malaya, Indonesia, and the Philippines are part of the Malaysian world, and voices for forging a Pan-Malayan Union are not completely mute, the extra-regional economic and military ties of both Malaya and the Philippines dim any prospect of such a union.

Finally, has it not proven impossible for Laos to solve its problems without outside contact? Physically and culturally, Laos is closely related to Thailand. Indeed, Pan-Thai proposals have sometimes raised the prospects of a Buddhist bloc to include Thailand, Cambodia, Laos, and Burma. But the best route linking Laos with the outside has been via Savannakhet to South Vietnam—the product of the transport pattern that was forged during French rule. And today, the routes—land and air—from North Vietnam to North Laos are increasing its outside orientation and dependence in that direction.

Can any sort of regional economic or political pattern be foreseen that will give some hope for the harmonious development of Southeast Asia as a region? Do such ideas as the Buddhist bloc of the north and the Malayan bloc of the south offer realistic prospects for some sort of long-term economic and political balance for Southeast Asia? We doubt it, because of the strength of those elements that make of Southeast Asia the Shatterbelt that it is.

Two rings of external pressure surround Southeast Asia: Inner and Outer. The Inner Ring consists of India, Mainland China, Japan, and Australia. Its interests are economic, cultural, ideological, and strategic. The Outer Ring consists of the Soviet Union, Western Europe, and the United States—the Soviet Union operating in association with Mainland China; the others with Australia and Japan. Outer Ring interests are economic and global strategic.

National sovereignty and various forms or espousals of neutralism have not freed Southeast Asia of these encircling pressure rings. On the contrary, the struggle between East and West has made each Southeast Asian nation the scene of internal struggle, the more acute because it is now a "brother against brother" conflict rather than the former conflict between native nationalism and European or Japanese colonialism.

In assessing the external relations of Southeast Asia, we can observe four trends since the recent Western European withdrawal:

1) A weakening in international trade;

2) Greater Western interests in adjoining parts of Offshore Asia (Japan, Taiwan, the Philippines, and Australia);

3) Direct penetration of Communist China into the region via Viet Minh;

4) Closer involvement of Southeast Asia in Asian affairs.

Southeast Asian trade has not kept pace with the general increase of international trade. Its current proportionate share of world exports is only half of what it was in 1938. Both Maritime Europe and the United States have redirected much of their former commerce with this region to tropical Africa and tropical Latin America. In part, the weakened international trade position of Southeast Asia stems from local economic pressures against Western trading interests; in part it has been occasioned by desires to broaden and diversify national economies at the expense of specialized international trade commodities; and in part it is the result of less well-developed regions of the tropical world beginning to catch up with Southeast Asia. Certainly, the desire of independent Southeast Asian states to turn partly from industrial crops to food crops, and to divert some investment in plantations and mines to consumer industries, is to be understood within the context of national ambitions and goals. Its effect upon the international trade picture is cited, therefore, not as a criticism, but rather as the result of basic national forces.

With the political and military retreat of Europe from Southeast Asia, and with the shift of the arena of conflict to the Northwest Pacific, the United States and its allies have put their major emphasis upon developments in Japan and the entire Offshore Asian line from the Aleutians to Australia. Western political and economic interests in Southeast Asia have, in this sense, been proportionately reduced.

The direct penetration of Communist China into northern Vietnam has since been followed by successes in Laos and by a resolution of the border dispute with Burma. Strengthened economic and military postures in eastern Tibet and Yunnan enhance Communist China's ability to intervene in Southeast Asia.

The location of the Shatterbelt foreshadows its greater involvement in Asian affairs, as surrounding regions seek ties with one another. Thus Southeast Asia can be expected to assume new importance as a land and sea link between the U.S.S.R. and China, as a land link between China and India, and as a sea link between the northern and southern portions of Offshore Asia.

We have described Southeast Asia as a Shatterbelt, internally fragmented and externally pressured. The region is not an inert body, but a zone of contact. The maintenance of key Free World alliances within the region through SEATO helps to insure that the Communist world will not swallow up the entire region, thus radically affecting events in the western Pacific and Indian ocean areas. They also make it clear that the Maritime World has no intention of withdrawing to positions so rigid and crucial as to leave no alternative but nuclear war. They enable economic and political competition to serve as alternatives to military competition. Finally, they make it strategically possible for the West to encourage neutralism elsewhere within Southeast Asia. But the alliances that we have forged must be with willing partners, with governments that know how to use military and economic aid for the good of their peoples, not for the aggrandizement of the few. As for neutralism, what we refused to recognize as a sound principle for Laos in the past has now been turned against us. It is not likely that genuine neutrality can be maintained in Laos, in the light of what has occurred. We must now turn our attention to Indonesia, Cambodia, and Burma—where popularly supported governments desire to be neutral and where our backing of such desires can have fruitful results; and Thai neutrality, a deep-rooted tradition for this country, may re-emerge as foreign policy, if events in adjoining areas should dictate such a discretionary attitude.

Southeast Asia is not strictly comparable with the Middle East from the following standpoints: (1) The region lacks near-monopolistic control over an export commodity such as the Middle East holds over petroleum. Rubber and tin, Southeast Asia's strategic exports, can be replaced by synthetics and by other raw materials, or can be extracted from other parts of the world. (2) Independent and competing Southeast Asian centers of power did not persist over such lengthy periods as did the Middle Eastern power cores. This was because of Southeast Asia's exposure to Indian, Chinese, and European land and sea movement. (3) The U.S.S.R. and the major Western allies do not meet directly in Southeast Asia, as they do in the Middle East. Rather, China and Offshore Asia represent the direct contacts with the Shatterbelt in the struggle between the Maritime and Communist worlds.

As a consequence, it is difficult to project key sites or states which should be sought as the Maritime World's Southeast Asian footholds. But the securing of Malaya, because of its Western orientation, its raw material base, its central, narrow, seas-dominating location with respect to the rest of the region, and its record of victory against Communist guerilla warfare is of first-rank priority. Expansion of independent Malaya to include the Borneo territories and Singapore, will enhance that state's significance as a foothold.

Burma, also, warrants our wholehearted protection against Communist encroachments, because of its prospects for economic development, its relative physical isolation from China, its non-xenophobic attitude towards contacts with the West, and its location astride the land and sea approaches to South Asia.

South Vietnam, because its government has already identified itself with the West in the struggle with the Soviet-Chinese bloc, and because of its location in relation to China and Offshore Asia, is an important foothold and a justifiable battleground. But a distinction must be drawn between battles and wars. We can lose the battle for South Vietnam without losing the war for Southeast Asia. The same can be said for our position in Thailand—a position that should be maintained as long as it is ideologically and militarily feasible to maintain it, and as long as the Thais wish to remain identified with the West in the Cold War struggle. But loss of Thailand and South Vietnam would not make retention of Offshore Asia strategically impossible. Nor would this loss make it impossible for the United States to maintain the Shatterbelt status of Southeast Asia through footholds in Malaya and Burma.

A neutral Burma is not to be equated with the military type of foothold that is represented by countries that belong to the Western Alliance. Burma is, however, a foothold for Maritime World security in that it contributes to the maintenance of the Shatterbelt status of Southeast Asia and to the security of South Asia. Genuine neutrals, such as Burma, can remain neutrals because of direct Western military positions in Southeast and South Asia. Burmese recognition of this factor, as well as Western recognition of the significant contribution of Burmese neutrality to the warding-off of Communist pressures, can inject greater realism into the West's relations with Burma.

Recently, both proponents and opponents of SEATO have raised serious doubts about the efficacy and utility of the organization, owing to its failure to take action in the Laotian crisis. We must recognize that SEATO today cannot play the same role that was envisaged for it during its formulative years of 1953-54. Then, under the shadow of the Geneva Conference on Indo-China, SEATO was organized to counter existing or feared Communist uprisings in Malaya, the Philippines, Burma, and non-Communist Indochina. It was, in fact, a hastily put together "fire fighting" brigade. Since then, conditions have stabilized throughout most of Southeast Asia, save in Laos and Vietnam. Those states that are not members of SEATO have raised strong objections to being included within its joint defense-planning framework, and it is probably futile, as well as presumptuous, for SEATO to try to continue to regard itself as responsible for the security of non-members.

Thus, first the organization's responsibilities should be focused directly upon its members. Second, non-members of SEATO that have bilateral treaties with Western nations, such as Malaya, but that do not wish to join SEATO, cannot and need not be forced to do so. Co-ordination of military activities in such cases can be achieved on an informal basis. Third, and perhaps most important, SEATO's treaty area may warrant redefinition.

As defined, the treaty area includes the general area of the Southwest Pacific, but excludes the Pacific areas north of latitude 21° 30″. A joint defense organization without Taiwan, Japan, and Korea ignores the realities of Western Pacific security problems. Indian representatives who have criticized SEATO as "a Southeast Asian Alliance without Southeast Asia" have a telling point.

What SEATO needs, as a long-range goal, is to seek inclusion within a broader Maritime Asian Treaty Organization—("MATO"?). Such an alliance of Offshore Asia and key portions of the Southeast and South Asian littoral, would constitute a more realistic approach to the Maritime World's defense needs. NATO and MATO could well become the twin cornerstones of the Trade-Dependent Maritime Region.

Southeast Asia will never be completely realigned with the West. Nor dare we let it fall in its entirety to the Communist world. What we must do is encourage a combination of alliances and neutrality within part of the region and recognize the Sino-Soviet interests elsewhere. Hard and fast lines need not, and should not, be drawn. Southeast Asia is likely to remain a zone of contention for decades to come—in the military, economic, and political fields. The alternative to its present Shatterbelt status is broad regional bufferdom or a sharp, three-way split that will be produced from Communist, Maritime World, and Indian interests. Such a split may well take place with the military and economic maturing of China, India, and Offshore Asia. Or most of the region may be able to adopt political neutrality, as mutually defined and guaranteed by the contending great powers. For the present, however, the threat of Chinese or local Communist pressures, with or without Soviet help, makes any guarantees of neutrality meaningless. The Maritime World has two possible courses—to side with its allies where Western orientation is domestically acceptable and strategically tenable, or to encourage Neutralism. Such a policy will help to maintain the plasticity of the Southeast Asian Shatterbelt.

In this context, a Chinese break with the U.S.S.R. might prove disastrous to hopes for the preservation of the Shatterbelt status. Admittedly, China's military position would be severely damaged by such a break. But its ability to sponsor far greater subversion efforts in Southeast Asia would probably not be curtailed. As a gesture to its people and the Communist world as a whole, Communist China might take considerable risks to subvert Southeast Asia. In so doing, China could assume that the threat of direct Western retaliation would be nullified by the threat of Soviet counter-retaliation. For the U.S.S.R. would not be likely to countenance a Western attack upon China that might topple a Communist regime, regardless of the gulf between the two Communist power centers.

Therefore, if the Shatterbelt can be maintained in its present form, the region will best be able to serve as a safety valve that provides both East and West with room to manoeuver and to compete without touching off a world explosion.

·8·

THE SOUTHERN CONTINENTS AND OFFSHORE ASIA

Rounding Out the Maritime World

If the geopolitical alignment of this earth should take the rigid north-south orientation suggested by the pan-regionalists, the attendant economic competition and political strife might well touch off the great war that must be prevented at all costs. Pan-America, Euro-Africa, and Pan-Asia are neither desirable nor feasible as geostrategic units.

Thus, we have not placed the South American geopolitical region in any more special association with Anglo-America than with the other portions of the Trade-Dependent Maritime World. Some proponents of Western Hemispheric unity claim that physical connection of the two continents and common colonization experiences provide strong enough bonds for joint economic, political, and cultural activities. Events have proved this assumption invalid. Pan-America cannot stand alone, strategically or economically.

On the other hand, do the east-west axes of geopolitical alignment, along which NATO has been formed (as well as the Warsaw Pact and the Moscow-Peiping axis) satisfy all of our strategic needs? Certainly the supply of raw materials—minerals, fibers, foodstuffs—that are drawn from South America and Africa are essential to the economies of the North Atlantic powers. In fact, then, North Atlantic unity cannot provide strategic self-containment. This can be achieved only by a crisscrossing of lines of orientation within the Atlantic and Pacific basins. Anglo-America and the Caribbean, and South America south of the Amazon, are likely to forge stronger bonds with each other, but not in isolation of the rest of the Trade-Dependent Maritime World. Already the Western Hemispheric units have close ties within this oceanic realm through the links between Canada and the United Kingdom, the British Caribbean islands and the United Kingdom, the United States and Maritime Europe, the United States and Japan, Brazil and Japan, Argentina and Maritime Europe, and the United States and Australia.

South America

It is frequently convenient to divide the Western Hemisphere along the cultural divide of the Rio Grande, separating Anglo-America from Latin America. Another divide is framed by the physical environment—the double line of the Central American-North Andean-Guiana Highland ranges and the Amazon. This is the divide along which we have drawn our geopolitical boundary. South America is a triangle, fronting the ocean, with two physical features of great magnitude that have profoundly influenced the political map. These are the Andes and the Amazon. The Andes, with their adjoining forests and deserts, separate western from eastern South America. The Panama Canal has strengthened this condition of separatism because it has made it easier for western South America to communicate with the Caribbean and the North Atlantic than overland with South American neighbors.

Amazonia acts as an effective barrier between South and Middle America, and reinforces the Andean division between east and west. Only in a very limited sense does the Amazon provide some measure of unity to both east and west coast South American states like Colombia, Ecuador, Peru, and Brazil, in that its resources are a force of attraction to all of these abutters. The centripetal force of such unifying elements as river navigation and petroleum prospects is far less significant, however, than the centrifugal affect of the rain forest barrier.

It is noteworthy that, save between Argentina and Chile, the crests of the Andes do not serve as national boundaries. Here in the south, where they form a single range, they are sufficiently high, narrow, and unpopulated to warrant a barrier boundary function. To the north, with three distinct ranges separated by high valleys, and in the center, with two ranges and one high valley, they form a wide but habitable zone. There the Andes serve as zones of unity, not of separatism. The rain-forested areas on the eastern slopes of the mountains serve as the barriers.

An important facet of the geopolitical structure of South America is its population distribution. On the western side of the continent the populace is highland-oriented. The Spanish settled in the mountains for the minerals. They found the Indians already there, and this coincidence of minerals and labor supply kept the European population in the highlands. Some attempts were made to bring Indians down to the coast to help develop ports. Most of these efforts ended in disaster. Oasis agriculture in the Peruvian desert is a modern attempt to develop the coast, but the population involved is limited. Until Chile is reached, then, the major centers of western South American population—the capital cities and business nodes—are in the highlands, in the Bogota Basin, Quito, the Peruvian Highland, and the Bolivian Plateau. This is an example that is carried over through much of Central America and Mexico, and indicates how higher altitudes cancel out the effects of latitude in tropical and subtropical areas. The population of eastern South America is, in contrast, coast-oriented. This is because of the attraction power of the fertile, well-watered, coastal plains that stretch from northeastern Brazil to Bahia Blanca in Argentina, and the low East Brazilian Highlands. The major population intrusion into the interior, along the Parana estuary, is a strong reflection of the economic orientation of that area to ocean ports and international trade.

While most of South America's population lives in western, coastal-rimming mountains, or on the eastern coastal plain, the interior is a hollow core because of rain forest, dry grassland, or Patagonian desert.

The weight of population and resources is on the eastern side. Brazil, Uruguay, Paraguay, and Argentina, for example, have over 90 million people, while the lands from Colombia to Chile have only 40 million. There is no unified regional ecumene as yet, but the link-up of Brazil's Rio-São Paulo core with the Pampas via southern Brazil's "pioneering fringe" may be anticipated. Sea ties with Chile and land links across the Gran Chaco into Bolivia suggest a further extension of this South American regional ecumene. With it should come greater geopolitical unity.

Trade-orientation of South America reflects two features. First, South America as a whole is not nearly so heavily oriented to the United States as is Middle America. In all, about 35 per cent of South American foreign trade is with the United States. Second, the west coast countries are more closely linked to the United States (45 per cent of their total trade is with the United States) than are the east coast countries (30 per cent of their total trade is with the United States). Europe is a more important trading partner with the east coast countries than is the United States. Intra-continental trade is very limited (only about 10 per cent), both because of the physical barriers to trade and because of the competitive nature of many of the national economies.

One might postulate that the strength of economic orientation, reinforced by the Andes barrier, the subsistence economy, and the basic Indian stock of its population makes of western South America a separate geopolitical entity from eastern South America. A counter to this thesis, however, is the political and economic dominance of the east, as well as the cultural bonds that bind all of South America. The future would appear to hold prospects for greater geopolitical unity for the continent, oriented around the primacy of the east coast ecumene. Such unity is likely to continue to be forged through interdependence with both Anglo-America and Europe, rather than exclusively with the former.

Africa South of the Sahara

Is it overstating the obvious to say that "Africa is *not* South America"? Perhaps. But the temptation to link the fates of these two southern continents is constantly before those who look to such superficial similarities as southern latitudes, tropical climates, triangular shapes, modern export economies that are superimposed on the subsistence base, low population densities (20 persons per square mile), and thin networks of transportation lines that act as feeders to the open seas, rather than as continental interconnectors.

In fact, Africa is quite different from South America. In these differences lies the answer to the absence of geopolitical unity in Africa south of the Sahara. Size, physical structure, and inaccessibility are elements that influence Africa's geopolitical fragmentization. Black Africa is nearly twice as large as South America, and has four times as many states as the latter. Its population is one and one-half times greater. This population is more scattered than South America's, partly because of the uniform spread of arable land throughout the tropical African highlands, and partly because of the restricted extent of Africa's coasts. No single coastal area in Black Africa possesses the population concentrations of the Brazilian coast and the deeply-embayed Pampas. Consequently, Black Africa lacks an incipient regional ecumene which would be capable of achieving geopolitical dominance over the entire continent. No single country or group of countries overshadows all others in population or resources. For example, Nigeria, the most populous state, contains only 18 per cent of Black Africa's population, while Brazil has 56 per cent of all of the population of South America south of the Amazon. Finally, Africa is essentially non-White, with Europeans constituting only two per cent of the populace. About two-thirds of the total South American population claims to be White, and Mestizos are another 25 per cent of the total. Thus South America is dominated by peoples of European descent—a most important aspect of its potential for geostrategic unity with the North Atlantic powers.

While Mackinder first described Africa south of the Sahara

as a "Southern Heartland," and later suggested a possible link with South America as a South Atlantic Basin unit, we are more inclined to expect that Africa will remain a geopolitically fragmentized portion of the Trade-Dependent Maritime World. Two long-term alternatives can be posed: (1) Given the disappearance of the Middle East as a Shatterbelt and the shifting of the Maritime World-Soviet contest to the Maghreb, Africa would become a Shatterbelt. (2) Given the expulsion of White settlement from Southern Rhodesia and the Union of South Africa, the Shatterbelt character of the continent could be increased through the introduction of Indian influence along the eastern side.

Africa is a large continent, but like South America, much of it is not suited to mass settlement. Lack of rainfall, disease, bush, and isolation are responsible for Africa's empty spaces. Most of Africa consists of high plateau that has experienced successive uplifts. This includes the Abyssinian Plateau, parts of the Sahara and West Africa, and the Great Central Plateau. Emerged coastal plains, smooth and narrow, occupy a much smaller proportion of the land area than do the coastal plains of other continents, and afford few good natural harbors. Where these plains are present, they are frequently too dry, and therefore are lightly populated, or quite narrow, being blocked off from the interior by highlands. Some coastal areas were depopulated by slaving activities. Lack of large, coastal-centered populations (save in South Africa, the Cameroons, the mouths of the Niger, the Zanzibar coast, and eastern Malagasy), has limited Africa's ability to create large, urbanized manufacturing centers. So has the inaccessibility of the plateau interior of the continent, which hampers land and waterway penetration.

With much of the African population living in scattered fashion on the interior highlands, and this highland being a barrier to internal movement as well as to accessibility to the sea, the creation of a significant regional ecumene has not been possible. While modern railroads and ports have been built, their purpose has been to carry minerals and commercial crops to the sea and to export them, not to link interior areas. True, such a railroad as the one from the Katanga through the Rhodesias to Lourenço Marques has geopolitical significance, in that it enables the Katanga to orient itself away from the Lower Congo and Matadi.

It thus acts as a counterforce to the centralizing aims of Congo nationalism. But the very fact that this railroad, as well as one from the Katanga to the Atlantic via Angola, was built for economic purposes and regardless of its possible effects upon Congo unity, proves the point that has been made—namely, that transportation lines frequently have no relevance to current national boundaries or hopes of regional unity.

The West's primary interest in Africa's resources has been in terms of their contribution to the raw material base of the Free World's defense structure. This interest is not confined to the need for war materials. It is grounded also in the broader raw material and financial support needs of the economies of many Maritime European countries. The orientation of African trade is essentially to the North Atlantic Basin. Eighty per cent of all of its exports and 75 per cent of its imports are with either Maritime Europe or Anglo-America. The most important trading partners, by far, are France and the United Kingdom. They account for about half of all of Africa's international trade. Intra-African trade is relatively insignificant, amounting to only 12 per cent of total exports. As in the case of South America, this trade is small because exports are mainly primary products that cannot be absorbed by the domestic markets of the continent.

Among the minerals coming from Africa south of the Sahara are uranium, copper, gold, manganese, iron, tin, antimony, chromite, magnesite, lead, vanadium, cobalt, industrial diamonds, columbium, beryllium, and mica. Some of these minerals (like diamonds, uranium, gold, cobalt, manganese, and chromite) account for a large share of the total Maritime World supply. Others, like copper and iron ore, are high on the list of Africa's exports in terms of value. Indeed, copper ranks second in value only to oil seeds among the continent's exports.

Among the foods and fibers that are being exported, mainly to Europe, are: oil seeds (palm, peanut, and sesame), cocoa, coffee, cotton, wool, wines, fruits and nuts, hides, tobacco, cereals, timber sisal, and tea. These have been listed in descending order of value.

Large-scale development of some minerals, especially bauxite and iron ore, hinges upon power, transportation, and politics. One almost untapped African resource is hydroelectric power.

It holds great promise for the future, because it can provide the substitute for fossil fuels in many parts of Africa that do not possess them. Recent hydroelectric developments in the Rhodesias, Uganda, Ethiopia, and the Cameroons, as well as plans for Ghana, reflect the speed-up of the tapping of this resource.

Single crop or mineral economies take advantage of specialized sets of environmental and market conditions, but they leave a people subject to forces beyond their control. To diversify the raw material base, without abandoning the advantages of the specialized materials that are the bases of Africa's modern export economy, is the basic problem from the African viewpoint. In the search for diversification, agriculture appears to be the key. The foodstuffs and fibers that Europe imports from Africa can be expanded. But more cereals, meat, fish (from both the ocean and ponds), vegetables, and dairy products must be produced to check the appalling effects of malnutrition. If the food supply cannot be significantly increased, then overpopulation is likely to become a major African ailment.

From the native African standpoint, the question of whether sufficient attention has been paid to development of small-holders's food crops is of primary importance. Seventy per cent of all Africans depend on the land for their subsistence. This is essentially a primitive agriculture, whose productivity is limited by present techniques, soil infertility and erosion, and inadequacy of transportation. The continued development of mining can employ only a relatively small percentage of the working force. Local manufacturing lacks capital, and labor must be trained. But even if an efficient labor force should be established to enable domestic manufacturers to compete with imports, there is little reason to assume that manufacturing would relieve the poverty of the majority of Africans. Most manufacturing is likely to emphasize the light products that can be readily absorbed within expanding domestic consumer markets, and consumer markets within a subsistence economy are apt to grow slowly.

It is not a question of *either* agriculture *or* mining and industry. It is rather a question of balance of emphasis in the sense of both timing and capital investment. Certainly farming can be improved only as the national funds derived from mining and manufacturing are plowed into agricultural development. And certainly the stimulation of transportation and power projects by mining industries will benefit agriculture as well. But it would be unwise to overemphasize one sector at the expense of the other, and to permit the living-standard gap between the subsistence farmer and city worker to become too great in the forthcoming years of African economic advancement. What Maritime Europe and the United States do with respect to this problem, directly or indirectly, will have much bearing upon whether Africans will continue to feel themselves victims of "exploitation."

Unquenchable desires for political self-expression have reshaped Africa's political map. This process will affect many native and European-imposed features of the cultural landscape. Perhaps the most fundamental question, in the political-geographic sense, is whether the area frameworks for Africa's emerging national states can be based upon existing lines, or whether new boundaries will have to be forged. Many of the present boundaries of Africa hark back to the Berlin Congress of 1885, or to decisions of European states that have been made since that period. These boundaries reflect, to a high degree, the location of European coastal footholds and the building of railroad lines into the interior.

As new national states evolve in Africa, their frameworks are heavily influenced by the European-derived image of the national state and its prerequisites (such as defensive depth, chunkiness, access to the sea, centrality of ecumene, land contiguity, unity of peoples). But complicating this image are existing colonial boundaries, tribal distinctions, and distribution of European and other non-Negro groupings. Will the proposed Nigerian Federation founder for lack of effective centralized authority, because its political framework seeks to embrace all that was British Nigeria and the Northern British Cameroons? Is Ghana going to find that its area is simply too small for it to be able to lead the West African national revolution? Is it possible to conceive of a new national state being formed by Guinea, Ghana, and the Mali Republic? Does the Central African Federation have sufficient national state earmarks, or is it merely a temporary device to serve as a source of, and corridor for, minerals that must be shipped to the sea?

A second basic issue that must be faced is the competition

between Islam and Christianity for influence in Africa. Completely dominant in North Africa and the Sahara, Islam is also embraced by the majority of the population of Gambia, the Cameroons, Northern Nigeria, and the Tanganyika coast. In French West and Equatorial Africa, it has been adopted by about one-third of the population, and by one-fifth the population of Liberia. What makes the spread of Islam so politically significant today is its use by Arab nationalists as a broad anti-Western movement.

The relative weakness of Christianity in most of Africa's urbanized areas (as opposed to its strength in the villages), presents a danger to continued Western influence on the continent. Most political movements are born in the cities, and most revolutions are ignited there. In all likelihood, urbanized Africa will shape African nationalism, and it is in these urban areas that Christianity is particularly weak.

The third and most basic issue revolves upon the manner in which the European and Black African worlds are to work out their final accommodation. In multiracial Africa, the proportion of Whites to total population varies from 22 per cent in the Union of South Africa, to 8 per cent in Southern Rhodesia (and 4 per cent for the entire Central African Federation), to 2 per cent in Kenya. Here the accommodation must be social and political, as well as economic. In those parts of Africa where the European is in the insignificant minority, the problem is no longer political —it is only economic. Investments and trade must take the path of common economic interests between two sets of political equals. Because African leadership throughout most of the continent still is essentially pro-Western, we need not be unduly pessimistic about the prospects. But Africans will only think in Maritime World terms if they meet with rapid, rather than grudging, political accommodation, and with full-scale economic support that takes into account local desires to become secondary and finishing producers.

Maritime Europe can scarcely be accused of ignoring Africa's capital investment needs. On the contrary, the activities by state and privately chartered British, French, Belgian, German, and Common Market institutions are far more significant than United States investments and grants in Africa. In all likelihood the future will bring increased joint European economic activities. Decades late in coming, a partnership towards Africa is emerging within Maritime Europe. This, coupled with the European "presence" in the form of the French Community, the Commonwealth, and the band of White settlement in South Africa and the Rhodesias, should continue to keep Africa within the Maritime Trade-Dependent region.

These forces will not necessarily inspire geopolitical unity. They may, on the contrary, reinforce the divisions between some African states—say, Mali, Guinea, Ghana, and perhaps, soon, Kenya, and their neighbors. The greater the degree of economic co-operation between Maritime Europe and Africa, the more likely it is that Europe's trade with other parts of the world will experience a relative decline. But this is a far cry from saying that a Euro-African unity can or should emerge. It simply says that Europe has held the responsibility for bringing Africa to the threshold of political independence, and that Europe should continue to hold the prime responsibility for integrating independent Africa economically into the Trade-Dependent Maritime World. Logic favors such a course. On the other hand, failure of Europe to find an accommodation with Black Africa over economic and racial issues is still to be feared. In such an event, all of Africa south of the Sahara could become a Shatterbelt, within which the maintenance of footholds in the mineralized Highland South, and in West Africa, would become the minimal strategic requirements of the Maritime World.

Offshore Asia

Offshore Asia is a geopolitical region within the Maritime World that includes Japan, South Korea, Taiwan, the Philippines, Australian New Guinea, Australia, and New Zealand. This region stands in contrast to the East Asian mainland and South Asia. Caught among the three is the Southeast Asian Shatterbelt.

What presents Offshore Asia with the opportunity for geopolitical unity is not only its geographical position in the western Pacific and the pressures of Free World security needs. Economics and ideology are equally important factors. The economies of the Offshore Asian states are sufficiently complementary to provide harmony of interests. The states concerned are in a strong position to help and be helped by one another, and they do not have the overwhelming population problems that threaten to strangle the development efforts of much of the mainland. Offshore Asian peoples, because of their historical associations, are not the victims of the irrational anti-Western, anti-colonial spirit that characterizes other Asian countries.

Present trade within the region is less than may be anticipated. In this respect, we might point out that Australia and Japan, although partly temperate climate countries with strong manufacturing complexes, are not competitive. Their economic and population bases differ. Australia and New Zealand (not a heavy manufacturer) have wool, meat, dairy products, lead, and zinc to export. They purchase fabrics, apparel, machinery, and other metal products. Semitropical northern Queensland and adjoining territories can become a source of rice and plantation crop supply. Even Australian wheat has begun to find a market in Japan, where wheat consumption is already one-fourth of rice consumption.

Intra-regional trade does not dominate the foreign trade of Offshore Asia, nor is it ever likely to do. However, such trade is on the rise. About 15 per cent of Japan's foreign commerce is with other Offshore Asian countries. Taiwan's major trading partner is Japan (if United States grants-in-aid are not counted), and over 20 per cent of the foreign commerce of the Philippines is with Japan. Australia, though less than 10 per cent of its trade is with Offshore Asia, is increasing its regional economic ties. Already it sends Japan one-seventh of its exports. We can foresee, in the very near future, an intra-regional trade that will be at least as important as the region's extra-regional contacts with Anglo-America, Maritime Europe, and South and Southeast Asia. Greater economic interdependence and closer political ties will not only strengthen Offshore Asia as a geopolitical region; it will also enable it to expand its influence in Southeast Asia, thus strengthening the over-all position of the Maritime World in this Shatterbelt.

Placing the Philippines within Offshore Asia and not the Southeast Asian Shatterbelts, may warrant explanation at this point. While many of the geographical features of Southeast Asia also characterize the Philippines, this latter island-state has a uniqueness that justifies its being treated as part of the Offshore Asian geopolitical unit. True, the Philippines have in common with much of Southeast Asia such elements as monsoonal climate, rice and export crop emphasis, soil infertility, shifting agriculture, high percentage of idle farm land, Malaysian race, and wide gaps between present and optimum land-use standards. Because of these elements, the Philippines serve as a bridge to Southeast Asia.

But the orientation of the archipelago to other Pacific lands is stronger than to the Shatterbelt. In terms of sheer distance, Taiwan is its closest neighbor. Japan and Australia are nearer and more accessible than Burma and Java. The Westernized outlook of the people, stemming from half a century's contact with the United States, finds counterpart attitudes in Japan and Australia, not in Southeast Asia. Neither Buddhist nor Muslim, but Christian, their political institutions are modelled along the lines of those of the United States. Three quarters of all foreign trade is with the United States, and most of the remainder is with Japan. Finally, the islands' major military ties are not with Southeast Asia, but with the United States. These ties, fixed through common war, are firm and mutually desired. In the light of the above, the inclusion of the Philippines within Offshore Asia, appears geopolitically warranted.

The *status quo* that prevailed prior to the emergence of the Soviet Union as a great nuclear power can never be regained. We now search for new global dividing lines. In this search we should be mindful of the need to disengage ourselves from areas that are "relicts" of our past situation. One such area is the Quemoy and Matsu islands grouping, overlooking the ports of Amoy and Foochow. These islands can be won by the Mainland Chinese without the use of nuclear weapons. Eventually, then, we are likely to be confronted by the prospect of either defeat or resort to nuclear warfare against the islands' attackers. If the United States continues to procrastinate, it runs the risk of losing, not only the islands and their military manpower, but all of Taiwan. We are not suggesting that these "relicts" simply be handed over to Red China. They should, however, be used as a basis for negotiations aimed at securing the independence of

Taiwan. Other steps in these negotiations between the United States and Mainland China might well involve diplomatic recognition, shipment of United States surplus foods, and normalization of trade relations.

Military defeat in the Offshore Chinese islands could mean the shattering of Nationalist China's will and capacity to hold out on Taiwan. The basic goal of the Maritime World should be to integrate Taiwan into the Offshore Asian framework. Such integration might well be pursued through an independent Taiwan, rather than through a two-China policy. The island is militarily defensible under all conditions save those of nuclear warfare, and the emergence of a genuine form of Taiwanese nationalism, free of Mainland Chinese ambitions, is probably the best assurance of its safety.

Like Taiwan, New Guinea is strategically important to the integrity of Offshore Asia. New Guinea is not a mere enclave, like Hong Kong or Macao; it is the link between Australia and the island states to its north. Indonesian claims upon western New Guinea constitute a long-term threat against the island as a whole. Support of the concept of western New Guinea as a Maritime World protectorate, and eventually as a unit federated with Australia, would have been sounder than support of proposals to place the area first under the United Nations and eventually under Indonesian supervision. Regardless of whether Indonesia ultimately absorbs the former Dutch territory, or whether Papuan independence is achieved, the line has now been drawn between Offshore and Southeast Asia. Offshore Asia cannot afford to see the extension of Indonesian power to eastern New Guinea.

South Asia

China, India, and Southeast Asia are often treated as one great physical and cultural world—Monsoonal Asia. Geopolitically, however, they are quite distinct. This is not to say that a geostrategic merger is an impossibility. In this context, any Western efforts to split the Sino-Soviet bloc might have the adverse effect of directing China toward such a geostrategic framework. Absence of Soviet restraints on Chinese regional ambitions, or the Chinese desire to take over the mantle of militant Communism from the U.S.S.R., could result in a direct attempt by the Chinese to unify the Monsoonal world. Were China to absorb Offshore Asia and the Southeast Asian Shatterbelt, South Asia would be hard pressed to remain outside the new framework. It is far more likely, however, that South Asia will retain its separate geopolitical identity, perhaps some day extending its influence across the Indian Ocean to create a new geostrategic region embracing East Africa and parts of Southeast Asia.

So long as South Asia remains politically divided, geopolitical unity remains a goal, not a reality. It is not necessary to erase national lines to forge a geopolitical region. However, economic and military co-operation, as well as a common approach to world problems, is a prerequisite for such a unity.

Separation from the rest of Asia, and cultural and human similarities, enhance South Asia's prospects for geopolitical distinctiveness. The Indian subcontinent stands aloof from its neighbors, behind a rimming barrier of desert, mountain, and monsoonal forest. Its best connections to the outside are via the Indian Ocean. Both the western and eastern littorals of this basin have absorbed considerable numbers of South Asians in the past century.

Within South Asia, the population follows such river valleys as the Brahmaputra, Ganges, and Indus, and the east and west coasts, to form an almost continuous ring around the Deccan, or South Indian plateau. Although population on the plateau is dense, it is far less so than that of the valleys and coastal plains, which also contain the bulk of the region's industry and transportation. This population core crosses national boundary lines in both Bengal and Punjab to further intertwine the fates of Pakistan and India.

What gives to South Asia geopolitical distinctiveness, apart from physical and cultural qualities, is its inward economic orientation. Though surrounded by water, the region is not a maritime one. Trade with other nations for industrial raw materials and consumer goods is of secondary concern. The major problem is agriculture. South Asia's 550 million people are mostly farmers. Regardless of the success of efforts to industrialize and urbanize, it is clear that most Indians, Pakistani, and Ceylonese will continue to be agriculturists, and in all probability their major efforts will go toward feeding themselves—not toward feeding the big cities.

Considerable political significance is attached to the relative performance of India and China in the resolution of economic problems. China's industrial strides, stemming from a richer mineral base, earlier Japanese efforts, forced industrialization, and recent Soviet assistance, have been much more dramatic than those of India. But it is to the agricultural competition that we must look to judge the relative prospects of these two powers.

In any comparison with Chinese agriculture, Indian agricultural performance lags far behind. Yields per acre are considerably less, and there is relatively little application of fertilizer (India's animal manure has less organic value because of the poor fodder that is available, and human waste is not used). Farming methods are more backward, irrigation is less developed, and religious practices still maintain a high surplus cattle population. Indian food staple production amounts to about 40 per cent of that of China. Specifically, paddy rice production is 50 per cent of China's, wheat is 40 per cent, coarse grains are 36 per cent, and potatoes are 17 per cent. India's population is 63 per cent of China's.

But India's prospects are more encouraging than China's in the sense that she can achieve a relatively greater increase in agricultural productivity through her own efforts, with the set of resources available to her. Most of the country's farm areas have a longer growing season than has China. Because the temperatures are higher, there is less pressure on fuels and fibers for domestic use. About one-third of India's total land area is under some form of cultivation (520,000 square miles), and over one-fifth of this is under irrigation. Indian planners have hopes of eventually doubling their irrigated land, as have their Pakistani counterparts. Even if this target is not actually reached, there is little doubt that food production can be substantially increased. The elements that are required for such an increase—electricity, fertilizers, better seeds, livestock control, reforestation, and land reform—are all within the production capacity of the Indian peoples. Moreover, industrial and commercial crops, like jute, cotton, sugar cane, tea, tobacco, and peanuts, are well advanced, and serve both an export and manufacturing function.

With better land transportation facilities than those possessed by China, and a more realistic approach in its planning through emphasis upon agriculture, India has good prospects of improving its lot as a self-contained farm nation—that is provided that a strong national drive towards that end can be mounted and maintained.

The greatest obstacle to progress at present is the inability of both India and Pakistan to slow down their rates of population growth. The population census for 1961 revealed that population increase over the past decade has averaged about 2 per cent per annum. At such a rate, India's population will rise to nearly 550 million by 1970, and Pakistan's to 115 million. Food production is not increasing at a perceptibly faster rate than the rise in population. Moreover, industrialization is not likely to reach enough of the population to effect a decrease in the rate of growth. Without far greater outside assistance to control this population growth as well as a massive, internally directed program, South Asia is likely to fall behind in its development progress.

The Indian subcontinent is politically divided. Behind the boundaries, each country is working out its destiny in the manner that it sees fit. New patterns of population distribution, of movement, and of internal administrative boundaries are emerging within both countries. But neither India nor Pakistan can devote all of its efforts to internal development as long as the political boundaries serve as economic barriers. The high cost of consumer goods in East Pakistan, because of transportation costs from West Pakistan, is one problem. The high cost of transportation of tea from Assam to Calcutta is another. India's duplication of East Pakistan's jute production is a third. These economic problems, and the problems of joint use of waterways, and of common defense of the Karakorum border, all await solution. Such a solution will not come easily, not even if and when an agreement is reached on Kashmir. But one would expect that a final accommodation will be reached between India and Pakistan, as well as closer political and economic ties with Ceylon. When such a time arrives, the present orientation of Pakistan to the Maritime World will, in all likelihood, change. We should anticipate such an eventuality, not with trepidation, but with optimism.

For greater geopolitical unity on the Indian subcontinent is the best means of preserving its current independence, and of preventing the absorption of the region within a possible Monsoonal Asian geostrategic realm that would in all likelihood be dominated by China.

From the Western point of view, Australia has already replaced South Asia as the strategic guardian of the southern waters that unite the Trade-Dependent Maritime World. It is in the maintenance of a strong, more populous, more industrialized Australia—oriented to the rest of Offshore Asia, as well as to Anglo-America and Maritime Europe—that our primary concern lies, not in the retention of the Indian Ocean as a "Maritime World Lake."

CONCLUSION

The divided world is a geopolitical reality. To ignore the political consequences of the earth's physical and cultural environmental distinctions would be to ignore fact. No form of international government is likely to be able to fulfill all of the needs of various national states and regional associations, from their specialized points of view. For the present, the world is divisible into two major geostrategic regions and their geopolitical components. But change is an essential feature of geopolitical life. As certain of the underdeveloped areas mature economically and politically they may well shift their external allegiances.

There is a growing tendency on the part of some American policy-makers to divide the world into three neat frameworks—East, West, and Neutral—and to project neutrality as a desirable goal for emergent states, regardless of what they are and where they are. This attitude is a reaction to the "era of containment," when we tried to maintain a blanket of American influence over all parts of the globe in the vain hope of confining Soviet influence. In the past, we attempted to extend our influence over too broad a sphere. Today, we are in danger of going to the other extreme and of disengaging ourselves from too many areas. It is fallacious to assume that the underdeveloped world must remain neutral if only it is allowed to grow strong economically. Once a state attains a truly independent posture, there is no guarantee that it will want to continue to remain neutral or that it will be capable of fighting off Communist subversion. From the Western point of view, therefore, not all parts of the politically emergent world should be encouraged to seek an independently neutral course. Such a policy should be reserved for those areas that do not directly affect our security. Where our global security is involved, strong alliances remain our only possible course.

Within the framework of our system of alliances, we must be prepared to maintain bases throughout the world. Bases manned by soldiers of the Western alliance are more than simply offensive-defensive weapons against the Soviet bloc. They are props for friendly governments, and a "presence" that helps to forestall Soviet-inspired Communist subversion. These bases should not represent an "American" presence, however; they should be the reflection of the concern of the entire Trade-Dependent Maritime geostrategic region for the security of key areas. As such, outside of the NATO framework, bases should be manned jointly by the Atlantic powers in concert with host forces.

In isolation of others, the United States cannot remain the world's leading power. In association with others, we can retain our position. We constitute the core of the Trade-Dependent Maritime World, and hold the main responsibility for its economic development and strategic security. Maritime Europe has evolved as a second core. Such a realm, including Europeans, Asians, Latin Americans, and Africans, provides a strategic, economic, and cultural framework for interdependent action. Unity within this framework will avoid the partition of the earth along strictly economic or racial lines.

The Soviet Union has welded together a powerful geostrategic union within this divided world, and China has become the region's second core. We have not been able to confine Soviet influence to the historic Heartland. Now we must gear our own policies, not only to the primacy of Soviet interests in Eastern Europe and to its stakes in East Asia, but also to its ambitions in the Middle Eastern and Southeast Asian Shatterbelts. We must also be on guard lest our efforts to exploit the Sino-Soviet ideological gulf boomerang. Complete orientation of Mainland China toward Monsoonal Asia could have, as its long-term result, the creation of a geostrategic region within this part of the world.

A better understanding of the geographical setting provides us with the basis for a contemporary geopolitical view of the divided world. While change is inevitable, we have tried to present a framework that anticipates the geographic dynamism of our times.

Appendix

INTERNATIONAL RELATIONS: CONCEPT AND APPLICATION

by Andrew Gyorgy

INTERNATIONAL RELATIONS
Concept and Application

by Andrew Gyorgy, *Boston University*

There is no major and definitive key outlook on world affairs. Instead of viewing human life and history from the perspective of a single "outlook," the hazy discipline of international relations consists more of a series of "vantage points" or "approaches." These attempt to interpret the various facets of world politics and to systematize the loosely related forces and factors that have characterized the recent development of the relations of nations. Prior to the twentieth century it would have been premature and erroneous to talk in terms of a well-defined discipline of International Relations. Indeed, the history of the subject is surprisingly brief, vague, and frequently irrational. In the nineteenth century it had largely bogged down in super-sophisticated, highly legalistic, and philosophically oriented dissertations, which only occasionally revealed brief glimpses of international relations and dealt with practical political materials in a purely haphazard and incidental manner. Until the pioneering work of such political geographers as Ritter and Ratzel, who successfully injected notes of down-to-earth realism into nineteenth-century social science, international relations was more or less compelled to hide behind the cloak of some other discipline. This "portmanteau complex" was evident even in the brilliant writings of Mahan, whose significant pronouncements on international political matters were carefully camouflaged behind layers of diplomatic history or international law.

The turning point came with the new century, which brought a tremendous upsurge of interest in international affairs as well as a healthier and more realistic approach to problems of modern diplomacy. In retrospect it is obvious that the climactic age of *total wars* has helped to usher in what Dean Acheson so aptly described as the age of "total diplomacy." The revitalizing influence asserted itself from two different and wholly unrelated sources. On the one hand, certain notable Anglo-American writers sparked this progress. Singling out two representative names from among the many pioneers, one must mention Mackinder and T. Parker Moon, whose massive *Imperialism and World Politics,* first published in 1904, served as a useful general textbook and who for the first time in American educational history held the title of "Professor of International Relations."

Simultaneously, a number of Marxist writers, some closely linked to Western European forms of socialism, others clearly the forerunners of Russian Bolshevism, began to expound Communist doctrines on international politics and offered concrete applications of Marxist dogmas to the realities of twentieth-century world politics. No student of this discipline can afford to neglect the early writings of Lenin, Trotsky, and Stalin, or the differently oriented literary products of Kautsky or Bergson.

For American purposes, the first truly systematic and penetrating study of the entire field was prepared by Frederick L. Schuman, whose monumental *International Politics* first appeared in 1933. This work had a broad impact on the teaching and research of international relations in the United States.

Four Major Approaches to International Politics

1. THE LEGALISTIC SCHOOL

This approach is derived from the study of international law and is imbued with legal systems, juridical values, and expectations. Its principal emphasis is on the peaceful settlement of international disputes, and its overriding objective, the maintenance and perpetuation of regional and global peace. It optimistically sets out to survey international relations primarily as a set of restraints imposed upon the individual nation-state by the community of civilized nations. This attitude assumes exceptionally high standards of international behavior and methods of day-by-day operation even when there seems to be little ground or few practical reasons for making such starry-eyed assumptions.

In order to insure a peaceful *status quo*, exponents of this school urge individual nation-states, as participants in international disputes or crises, to resort to certain complex and highly developed techniques of conflict resolution. The three methods most frequently discussed in the literature are arbitration, adjudication, and—last but not least—negotiation. Arbitration in this context implies the voluntary submission of disputes by the individual states to a judge or group of judges of their own choice. It further implies the unanimous acceptance of the judicial award as binding and postulates a continuing deep respect for the law. Important methods "approaching arbitration" have developed as parallel procedures of dispute resolution. These involve the use of Mixed Commissions, Commissions of Inquiry and of Conciliation, and have been widely employed throughout the nineteen-twenties and -thirties.

Adjudication assumes that the dispute is submitted to a permanent international court, which, acting as the strong arm of a truly international judiciary, has firm powers of imposing sanctions upon the participating governments. Unhappily, both the Permanent Court of International Justice of pre-World War II vintage, and more recently the International Court of Justice, are merely pale replicas of the forceful image of a strong and independent seat of international judicial power.

Of overriding importance are the well-established settlement techniques of international negotiation, which—at their best—can be defined as diplomatic bargaining processes based on the mutual assumption of successful settlement. Within the framework of such "Conference Diplomacy," whether secret or open, each side will strive to attain maximum national advantages with minimum concessions to the other side. Nevertheless, diplomacy by conference also presumes a friendly and constructive atmosphere in which workable international solutions can readily be hammered out without violations of that untouchable "taboo" of world affairs, the selfish national interest.

This last point leads to the most relevant criticism of the legalistic school. Its exponents tend to live in the clouds, hopefully anticipating both high moral standards of international conduct and selfless law-abiding patterns of national behavior. It is safe to state that the era of such high expectations disappeared irretrievably on June 28, 1914, when the tragedy at Sarajevo set off the new age of total wars. Other approaches to international politics had to emerge from the holocaust of World War I, as logical aftereffects and consequences of world-wide sentiments of disillusionment and despair.

2. THE ORGANIZATIONAL-IDEALISTIC APPROACH

As a reaction to the tragedy of World War I, this school of thought expressed a growing sense of the need for collective action against aggressor states. Steeped in the spirit of international organization, it carried the earlier and strictly legalistic approach a long step further by advocating the "firming up" and invigoration, first of the League of Nations, and later of the United Nations. At its best, this approach also placed emphasis on such regional organizations as the Pan-American Union, the OAS, and more recently on NATO and SEATO. Its exponents engaged in a continuing argument concerning the primacy of *regional* vis-à-vis *universal* types of organization, an argument that could not be properly resolved in view of the many intangible considerations on both sides.

The idealism of this school was most apparent when it professed that the *mere existence* of a broad international organization was a sufficient safeguard for the maintenance of peace and harmony. It thus tended to ignore the impact of the nation-state and the many complicating ethnic, religious, demographic, or geopolitical forces which—whether divisive or cohesive in character—certainly have a large determinant share in the make-up of the relations of nations.

Proceeding on the unexamined assumption that everything international was per se better than anything national, adherents of this approach overstudied such issues as disarmament or the pacific settlement of disputes, while the problems of national security, national interest, and legitimate national policy objectives were largely ignored. Coupled with this omission was the broadly shared feeling that deplorable nationalistic attitudes were responsible for producing such vague evils as imperialistic foreign policies and conspiratorial groups of "munitions makers" or oil interests. Nationalism, equated with moral evil, was therefore to be exorcised from the realm of international relations.

In the interwar period, researchers imbued with this approach concentrated primarily on four major study areas: international organization, international law, international trade and finance, and recent diplomatic history. On the whole, as William T. R. Fox observed in *World Politics*, the analytical model these scholars used for their case-study investigations was the image of a "world commonwealth" characterized by permanent peace.

In the course of the past fifteen years the organizational approach placed a great deal of well-justified emphasis on analyzing the unsung and unpublicized but tremendously important work of such technical U.N. agencies as UNESCO, IRO, ILO, WHO, FAO, and the Human Rights Commission. Numerous useful and comprehensive surveys have ably presented the great humanitarian achievements of these agencies, which have succeeded in cutting across national boundaries and promoting world peace—if not by solving the deadlocks on the most vital political or military issues, at least by "nibbling away" at the edges of international tensions or conflict areas. To the extent that this recent literature keeps analyzing the specific, well-defined, and substantive functions for which these technical agencies have been established, it can well be described as the *functional* method or perspective of international politics.

3. THE STRATEGIC-REALISTIC APPROACH

Moving from the relatively simple exposé to the more complicated, this approach must be viewed from a double perspective: first a comment on methodology is in order, then its principal areas of concern have to be analyzed. The strategic-realistic school relies on the *pragmatic* method which postulates that the value of all political institutions is relative, and that the ultimate test of every government lies in its ability to rule effectively *regardless of its political philosophy*. Pope's famous couplet is conveniently cited in this context:

> For forms of government let fools contest;
> Whate'er is best administered, is best.

The pragmatic method has a basically antitheoretical orientation. As Morgenthau observed, it seeks to "meet the day-by-day issues of international politics by trial and error," and devises a pattern of international relations more in keeping with an *empirical* image than an abstract ideal. Its importance to the student lies precisely in that *practical concern* which wants to grapple directly with cases and issues rather than with an explicit theory of international politics.

Writing a 1958 editorial for *Borba,* the Belgrade daily of the Communist party, a Yugoslav social scientist summarized this approach in the following manner: "Politics is neither an abstraction nor a science. Its objectives and its methods must be carefully fitted for a world which constantly changes . . . Politics and political doctrines come and go, but only peoples live forever."

The combination of practical concern and abhorrence of theory logically propels this mode of thought toward power concepts and ideas. It stresses the importance of the political power of individual states in order to insure their survival, which thus becomes both a goal and a technique of diplomatic operation. Pragmatism in international relations postulates that the fundamental source of almost all the tension that arises between nations is fear, based on insecurity. Thus the entire history of international politics may well be viewed as a continuing series of attempts by individual nation-states to meet their need for security and allay their institutional fears. The obvious device to accomplish this objective has been the formation of alliances which in turn produced counteralliances, and eventually led to various balance-of-power systems.

The historic balance-of-power theories of the eighteenth and nineteenth centuries fit perfectly into the framework of strategic-realistic thinking on international politics. In a more primitive era of world affairs, the object of bilateral alliances was to bring preponderant strength to bear on a third party as a deterrent; it was then the normal state of affairs for European countries to be divided into two antagonistic groups. While balancing power in this haphazard manner may have focused a great deal of attention on the security interests of states and on the strategically vulnerable regions of world politics, it also multiplied tensions and fears, rather than reducing them.

As described by Desmond W. Crowley, the balance-of-power system could be effective only under two seriously limiting conditions:

a. If the opposing alliances generally settled down at approximately equal strength, and thus produced a political-military deadlock, which helped to preserve peace, at least temporarily, or

b. If it was possible for the leaders of the two major alliance systems to agree on some workable compromise. As long as the governments involved were of an absolute, dictatorial character, implying that the leaders were free to act largely as their own desires or calculations directed, such agreements seemed to be generally feasible. As long as "the leaders came to know each other personally, and were often able to develop relations of mutual personal trust," remarks Crowley, the delicately tuned balance-of-power system seemed to be adequate enough.[1]

In the long run, it is of course obvious that this pragmatic "by touch and by feel" operation of international diplomacy would prove to be insufficient and unsatisfactory. The horror of modern warfare, the rise of belligerent twentieth-century nationalism, and the emergence of a new form of "total diplomacy" combined to cause a temporary fade-out of other approaches and schools of thought, and helped to push Cold War concepts and maneuvers into the foreground.

4. CONTEMPORARY APPROACHES TO COLD WAR PROBLEMS

In the main, current approaches to the political problems of the Cold War have two common characteristics: they focus on the great, all-transcending problems of war and national policy,

[1] See Desmond W. Crowley, *The Background on Current Affairs* (London: Macmillan, 1958), p. 110.

and they are usually based on narrowly constructed and wholly negative initial definitions. All of them assume, however, that war—which in this particular context becomes "hot" or "shooting" war in contradistinction to "cold" war type conflicts—is the supreme exercise of national power. In certain situations, so the reasoning runs, there is no obvious substitute for resorting to war. War settles a number of problems that are primarily in the political-diplomatic sphere. War determines which combatant shall have the chance to write the peace treaty, and it will also crystallize the nation's relative position in the postwar power-balance on the regional, continental, and intercontinental levels.

"Cold War" concepts are concerned with the nature and identifying characteristics of total war. In general terms they suggest that the major techniques which have transformed modern war into an *ad horrendum* last resort, or ultimate weapon in a nation's political and military arsenal, are the following:

(1) its dependence on the complex scientific discoveries of contemporary technology,
(2) its incredibly high degree of industrialization and mechanical complexity,
(3) the compelling factor of popular mass participation, and
(4) its enormously increased total cost.

This is the modern monster that has to be avoided, circumvented or, in turn, chained down by a vigorous assortment of diplomatic, economic, and political weapons. These weapons must then be employed as parallel means of national action and policy. The principal feature of the Cold War is thus a *negative* assertion: War must be avoided at almost all cost! Here one enters the twilight (the double negative world) of Leon Trotsky's original remark about a peculiar kind of in-between situation: "No peace, no war!"

Most recent definitions are merely variations on this negative theme. In Hans J. Morgenthau's opinion: "The political relationship called the Cold War signifies the absence of peace between the two blocs in that there has been no moral and legal agreement upon their relationships and, more particularly, upon the boundaries between them. *Rather these political relationships are the result of the provisional de facto settlement established at the end of the Second World War primarily on military grounds.*"[2]

To illustrate the significance of recent Cold War thinking, this study first offers three brief clusters of definitions, and then presents its own appraisal of the multifaceted Cold War process.

MILLIS, MANSFIELD, AND STEIN ON COLD WAR[3]

While big theoretical issues of atomic energy, military unification, and defense budget were being debated on the congressional level, the years 1947 and 1948 began to introduce into American public life many minor but typically Cold War issues. It was a complex pattern with many loose ends. The "new difficulties" implied mostly that major wartime decisions had to be made in times of non-war. Military policy thus had to be hammered out mainly in the conferences of budget officers and the hearing rooms of the military affairs committees. A crucial non-war difficulty was to determine the proper allocation of production between civil and military demands. It is symptomatic of a Cold War period that usually a nation's economic and military policies are badly out of adjustment with the actualities of the perilous world confronted by the protagonists.

The authors rightfully stress that in such a period all great national issues are intimately related. They must be taken together and call for a broad, correlated, and "global" policy; they cannot be handled in a piecemeal and *ad hoc* fashion, which is the luxury token of normal political times. The Cold War era thus clearly demands a newly formulated national political-military strategy different from the routine actions of the previous era.

In the Cold War context, assert the authors, basic policies are obviously neither "purely military" nor "purely civilian" in their inspiration. Many different factors go into the construction of such a Cold War posture, and many men and institutions par-

[2] See Hans J. Morgenthau, *Dilemmas of Politics* (Chicago: University of Chicago Press, 1958), pp. 199-200. Italics added.

[3] This is a summary of Chapter 5 (*Cold War*) from *Arms and the State* by Walter Millis, Harvey C. Mansfield, and Harold Stein, published as a volume in the Project on Civil-Military Relations by *The Twentieth Century Fund,* New York, 1958.

ticipate in the result—soldiers, diplomats, administrators, economists, congressmen, the press, and public opinion.

The authors' approach is particularly helpful in focusing attention on the multiple impact of the Cold War era on the decision-making process in government. Non-war circumstances surrounding wartime measures, and the need for mobilization procedures in the midst of an outwardly calm political atmosphere—these are some of the peculiar characteristics that Millis, Mansfield, and Stein emphasize in *Arms and the State.*

RAYMOND ARON AND THE CENTURY OF TOTAL WAR[4]

In this excellent work, Raymond Aron forcefully asserts that the classical definitions of war are valid but inadequate. As a new development, the Cold War is largely the result of World War II and of the revolutionary actions waged by the Soviet-dominated and -controlled Cominform since 1946. This Cold War situation can be characterized by two closely related background phenomena: the formation of the two opposing camps or blocs, and the depressing fact that these two camps are engaged in a seemingly permanent and irreconcilable struggle.

In this world political context Cold War means limited war—limited, however, not as to the *stakes,* but as to the *means* employed by the belligerents. The mid-twentieth-century Cold War uses four major techniques, namely propaganda, espionage and sabotage, agitation and mass movements, and civil war. These four "typical forms" appear usually in combination with each other. The most salient illustration of the Cold War is the "Soviet program of world conquest," which is anxious to avoid open war or precipitate a serious military incident. While meticulously avoiding a *casus belli,* the U.S.S.R. is intent on building up a military superiority, which *in itself* is one of the major weapons in the Cold War.

Aron also has an important discussion of the objectives of the

[4] *The Century of Total War;* Beacon Contemporary Affairs Series, The Beacon Press, Boston, 1955. See especially Chapter IX, pp. 169-180.

Cold War. In military perspective, the Cold War appears primarily as a quadruple race for:

a. bases,
b. allies,
c. raw materials, and
d. prestige

Bases must be secured from which the antagonists can attack or counterattack. The number and resources of potential allies must be increased and the number and resources of potential enemies reduced. Attempts must be made to retain or regain control of the sources of raw materials that are indispensable to the *technological* operation and upkeep of modern war. And finally, the morale of the hostile world must be shaken and the prestige of one's own ideas and strength vigorously spread, thus implying that "the goddess of history has already decided on the ultimate triumph" of one's own side.

Reaching over to the side of the Free World, Aron then offers a specific illustration for each of the four ingredients of the Cold War as applied to American foreign policy. In its strategy, he claims, the United States has looked to the Pacific for *bases,* to Europe for *allies,* to the Near East for *raw materials,* and "more or less everywhere" in the world for reassurance and *prestige.*

Although the CW = LW (cold war *is* limited war) formula may not be a startlingly novel contribution to the mushrooming literature on the Cold War, it does have the merit of focusing attention on the *limited, but all-out* features of such a pseudo-military situation. In addition, it offers a neat and systematic set of categories for both the components and the objectives of the Cold War. While the four elements analyzed under each heading are truly significant, they do not constitute either an exhaustive or a complete listing of the multiple variables that make up the total, 360-degree view of modern Cold War. However, in stressing the essential functions of such intangibles as propaganda, agitation, and prestige, Aron has performed a useful service in clearing away the underbrush and blazing a new trail in the jungle of semantics and political ideas.

KENNETH W. THOMPSON'S VIEWS ON THE COLD WAR[5]

Kenneth W. Thompson presents an eloquent analysis of the present conflict between the Soviet Union and the United States in several of his recent articles. Being more than a decade old by now, the Cold War—in Thompson's opinion—is plainly visible as a conflict with *at least two dimensions.* At one level, it is a struggle for men's minds involving the conflict between democracy and Communism, with both ideologies claiming vitality and universality. At the other level, "the struggle engages two great configurations of power who by reason either of necessity or of design reach out to influence others."

Thus the author points up the moral aspects of today's Cold War picture, intimately involving the comparative strengths and weaknesses of democracy and Communism. The Cold War, in this context, can readily be viewed as a continuing conflict between morality and the "national interest" factor. The principal issue is this: to what extent can a broader international community (in more precise terms, for example, the United Nations) harness, beguile, or deflect the more limited, narrower national purposes of a single state, a single unit? Or can it ever transcend them? It is obvious that aspiring to justice, to a peaceful international order, implies one set of values, while maintaining a semi-permanent Cold War posture in a deeply troubled political world requires an entirely different set of standards and patterns of behavior.

Fundamentally, these two guide-lines are in irreconcilable conflict. Paraphrasing Thompson's analysis, one perceives that beyond a relatively substantial inner core of the "Vital National Interest" lies the much slimmer and less obvious outer circle of "International Law, Order, and Morality." By necessity, a Cold War situation directs public attention to the more relevant inner core complex of national interests.

Despite this imbalance between the national interest factor

[5] See K. W. Thompson, "Reflections on the Study of Foreign Policy in the Context of the Cold War," in Chapter 1, *Foreign Policy in World Politics,* Roy C. Macridis, ed. (Englewood Cliffs, N. J.: Prentice-Hall, 1962), pp. 21-27, and "The Limits of Principle in International Politics," *The Journal of Politics,* August 1958, pp. 437-67.

and the role of order and morality, Thompson's analysis does not neglect to emphasize the moral aspects of international politics. "Every legal or social reform," he remarks, "that would be successful must take account of the moral infrastructure. The failure of collective security, of the outlawry of war . . . are all examples of thinking that suffers from the illusion that moral foundations are unimportant. *The political community has its roots in moral factors unhappily sometimes missing in many of the areas that have recently become important in American foreign relations.*"[6] The phrase "moral infrastructure" is a felicitous one indeed since it points to the ever present—although occasionally nebulous—ethical criterion of politics without at the same time disputing the primacy of national interest considerations. Thompson thus rightfully views the Cold War situation as a fluctuating combination of purely political (interest) forces vis-à-vis the legal or ethical issues and imponderables that must enter into the national decision-making process.

A FOUR-POINT EVALUATION OF THE CURRENT COLD WAR

Although there are many complex and academically abstract ways of presenting the problems and issues related to the con-

[6] See K. W. Thompson, "The Limits of Principle in International Politics," loc. cit., pp. 437-67, passim.

temporary Cold War, we shall endeavor to single out four major and distinctive phenomena that might help to illuminate and further define the characteristics of the East-West struggle.

1. *An "Agreement to Disagree" Between the Two Superpowers.*

This crucial feature reaches to the core of the Cold War problem and involves a tacit agreement between the two protagonists not to engage in broad, general negotiations or discussions concerning the issues of disagreement. Such a Cold War posture therefore assumes the absence of a formal, full-dress, and across-the-board conference—whether of the "summit" or "below the summit" character—which would engage in a comprehensive review or reappraisal of the basic military and political problems separating the two camps. Particularly such sensitive issues as atomic and conventional disarmament, the unification of Germany, or the renegotiation of the veto in the United Nations would be classified as "untouchable" in this context, automatically reducing the area of negotiation to peripheral problems of far less significance or relevance. Thus, even if a "summit" type conference were held in the near future, it would be largely ineffective and be concerned primarily with empty posturing for global propaganda purposes and for amateur, rather than professional, "consumption."

This process of a hardening of diplomatic arteries will then result in two major and inevitable consequences. It will, first of all, produce a near-permanent, and highly frustrating, stalemate of diplomacy, which subsequently tends to sharpen the further polarization of political and military power. Thus we emerge in a world in which two blocs of nations keep glaring at each other across "iron curtains" and barbed-wire barricades.

2. *Covert Forms of Warfare*

Overt resort to force is quite exceptional in the contemporary context of the Cold War, and limited primarily to geographically marginal, but characteristically Rimlandic areas or to civil-war type revolutionary situations of an unusual emergency character. Such localized although politically not really remote or distant conflicts occur, for example, in Greece, Malaya, Korea, Indochina, Algeria, or Laos. These rimland crises can become extremely significant whenever they directly involve the leaders of power blocs in world affairs. The Cold War generally speaking utilizes all the non-military aspects of war. The entire gamut of highly refined economic, political, and psychological warfare techniques is fully mobilized and used either in a meticulously planned chronological sequence, or—in most cases—paralleling each other and employed in close combinations. In a world of relentless psychological warfare campaigns the Cold War stresses the myriad nonmilitary aspects of what has traditionally been an exclusively military venture. Indeed, the Cold War has successfully demilitarized war itself!

3. *Propaganda, Violence, and the Threat of Terror*

The localized brush fire situations, which characterize Cold War incidents and conflicts, appear to be sharply limited in terms of the space, techniques, and methods of operation involved. They seem to develop and explode on two levels simultaneously. The first level clearly involves the visible impact of mob violence and unruly demonstrations touched off by the unchecked flames of mass propaganda and by the reckless manipulation of modern media of mass communication. The second level is only subtly observable; is based on the invisible impact of a secret police-induced terror situation in which there are two possible alternatives. People are either driven forward by this terror in the direction desired by the government, or the continual threat of terror operates in reverse, and a popular explosion occurs against the hated police apparatus. In the latter case, an angry populace is seeking an outlet for its pent-up emotions and revenge for years of fear, bitterness, and frustration. Although the Cold War history of the Soviet Union and satellite Eastern Europe abounds with illustrations of each type of incident, since 1945 the highest number of mixed-pattern revolutions have actually occurred in the Middle East and Southeast Asia Shatterbelt. Visible and invisible forces have combined, for example, to set off the frightening eruption of July 14 and 15, 1958, in Baghdad, where the King and Prime Minister of Iraq were ruthlessly murdered by irate street mobs.

4. *The International Civil War*

This characteristic carries the previous story a step further by injecting the notion of *externally* fomented and encouraged revolutionary situations. Cutting across national boundaries, local political parties, and regional sets of economic interests, these familiar acts of indirect aggression add up to a veritable "international civil war," to quote Sigmund Neumann's prophetic phrase. In terms of the techniques employed, one witnesses here an immensely broad spectrum of operation with such seemingly minor incidents as individual acts of subversion, fifth column work, and infiltration at one end of the scale, and landing of troops on foreign soil, invasion attempts, temporary seizures of territory and mass riotings encouraged by foreign agents at the other end. The common denominator of unusual interest to the student is the emphasis on *trans-national* acts of aggression, both of a direct and an indirect character.

The revolutions of the modern era, commonly regarded as merely internal upheavals, have become real world phenomena. Their true significance must be measured in terms of their *international* effect. "Radical upheavals, as all great revolutions are," observes Sigmund Neumann, "must be played on an international stage. Every region has become sensitive to the developments of far-distant lands." [7] Areas that have been geographically and historically far apart have now been politically compressed to the point where one major ideological movement immediately provokes revolutionary reactions in seemingly distant and unrelated regions. Cold War situations and contemporary revolutions are inextricably interwoven: they cannot be isolated in neat and separate compartments, since they parallel each other and cut across traditional lines of political demarcation. This pattern of inevitable parallelism is particularly pertinent in areas that directly adjoin the Communist world. Yugoslavia, Greece, Tibet, Laos, and the Congo loom as sharp reminders of the continuous relevance of trans-national or indirect aggression.

This fourth feature of the Cold War spectrum emphasizes the

[7] See Sigmund Neumann, "Toward a Comparative Study of Political Parties," in *Modern Political Parties* (Chicago: University of Chicago Press, 1956), p. 418.

confluence of external and internal factors in a given situation. The Soviet Communist blueprint of such situations is actually based on the scientific mobilization of this "double pincer," in which two forces are employed in joint and overlapping operation: CW = ICW = EX(Iv) + In(V)R, where the Cold War is equated with an international civil war composed of an external (frequently invisible) and an internal (always visible) revolutionary pattern. Where the two patterns meet and overlap, there emerges a full-blown international incident frequently approximating lukewarm or even hot war.

Nobody is more acutely aware of the complexities of the con-

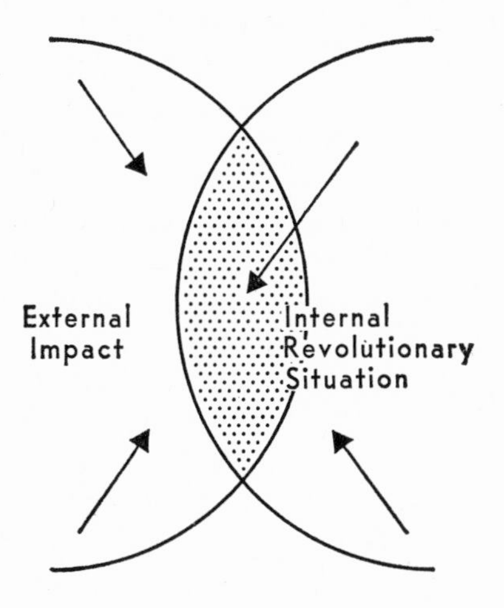

temporary Cold War than our Communist opponents. Not for a moment can the Western public indulge in hopeful illusions concerning the naïveté of Soviet statesmen or the primitive views of Communist political writers in assessing the true character of Cold War situations. If anything, they approach this aspect of world politics probably more realistically and soberly than we do. Writing on "Disarmament and International Tension" in the December 1958 issue of *The Bulletin of the Atomic Scientists*, Soviet Academician A. V. Topchiev made the following illuminating remark: "It is in the interests of international confidence that the 'cold' and the 'psychological' wars be done with, once and for all, with their artificial increase in international tension, propaganda of power politics, and of hatred and animosity toward other countries."

New Factors and Problem Areas in International Politics

There are myriads of more or less latent forces and problems which have directly affected the long-term development of international diplomacy and its day-by-day conduct among individual states. In order to present a profile of these problem areas, four major issues have been selected for brief treatment.

1. THE CHANGING NATURE OF MODERN DIPLOMACY

There have been numerous revolutionary changes in the nature of modern diplomacy—both of a quantitative and a qualitative character. One of the most challenging recent developments has been the gradual decline in the role and importance of the professional diplomat and professional diplomacy itself.

At first blush this broad statement appears to be highly questionable. International politics, after all, is made by men and for men, and since among men the lines of communication and interpenetration can never be drawn sharply or permanently, there would seem to be an ever increasing need for highly skilled and truly professional communicators on the international level. Despite this need, however, there has been a steady and obvious depreciation of professional diplomacy since World War I. Hans J. Morgenthau has offered three primary reasons for this decline. The most obvious factor has been the development of modern communications. Speedy and regular communications in the form of the airplane, radio, telegraph, teletype, and long-distance telephone have immensely broadened the scope of direct negotiations between governments at the expense of the permanent representatives stationed abroad. Often the most sensitive negotiations have been carried on, not by diplomatic representatives, but by special delegates, who may be the foreign ministers themselves or highly placed technical experts.

A related facet has been the world-wide condemnation of secret diplomacy, which forcefully espouses the view that the secret machinations of diplomats shared a great deal, if not the major portion, of responsibility for World Wars I and II. This opinion, as Morgenthau remarks, also stresses that "the secrecy of diplomatic negotiations was an atavistic and dangerous residue from the aristocratic past, and that international negotiations carried on and concluded under the watchful eyes of a peace-loving public opinion could not but further the cause of peace." [8]

Whatever the moral implications, it is clear that a concerted campaign against secret negotiations has been successful in restricting both the formal scope and the substantive range of action of the professional diplomat. "Open covenants openly arrived at" was no empty or ineffective Wilsonian slogan, but one that had a continuing impact on the history of the subsequent thirty years. Secret intergovernmental discussions were thus equated with evil intentions and conspiratorial political techniques. Few experts phrased this public revulsion more forcefully than the professional diplomat and ex-ambassador, Hugh Gibson, who made the following remarks in his *The Road To Foreign Policy:* "As a matter of fact, there is such a thing as secret diplomacy, and it is reprehensible. This might be defined as intergovernmental intrigue for wrongful ends, resulting in obligations for future action of which the people are kept in ignorance . . . There are also secret negotiations between governments to infringe the rights of another." [9]

Interestingly, however, even Ambassador Gibson has to admit that "open diplomacy" is often close to being a contradiction in terms, and that the glare of "pitiless publicity" can wreck the most promising international negotiations. He is also convinced that secret diplomacy might frequently involve the "systematic exploration of a subject *in private by trained negotiators.*" (Italics mine.) This admission, then, brings him around the full circle, and attempts to vindicate the much maligned professional diplomat in his role as secret agent or negotiator for his government.

The third reason for the over-all disintegration of diplomacy

[8] See Hans J. Morgenthau, *Politics Among Nations; The Struggle for Power and Peace,* 3rd edition (New York: Alfred A. Knopf, 1960), p. 547.

[9] See Hugh Gibson, *The Road To Foreign Policy* (New York: Doubleday, 1944), p. 77.

—closely related to the previous two—is the evolution of a new, parliamentary-type diplomacy, which has succeeded in introducing a major qualitative change into the area of international political intercourse. The League of Nations and the United Nations developed this pattern, as ably described by Hans J. Morgenthau. "International problems requiring solution are put on the agenda of the deliberative bodies of these organizations. The delegates of the different governments discuss the merits of the problem *in public debate.* A vote taken in accordance with the constitution of the organization disposes of the matter." [10]

This new diplomacy "by parliamentary procedures" seems to be dedicated to two principles acting in close co-operation: openness of deliberation, and teamwork of technical experts. Both tend to restrict and qualify the traditional, historical scope of diplomatic operations. Even if an occasional screen of transparent semisecrecy is drawn in front of these "newfangled" conferences, world public opinion is still allowed to follow the principal phases of the debate, as reported by the various delegations to the competing media of modern mass communication.

2. EMPHASIS ON POLITICAL FLEXIBILITY

This important attribute of modern international politics injects both the short-lived *human* and the more long-range *ideological* aspects into our discipline. The richness of human nature and the gamut of desires and capabilities it displays gives the statesman an infinite number of opportunities to combine, adjust and realign humanity, thus trying to strike balance between the need for stability and the desire for change.

In a fluid field such a tenuous balance can be accomplished only by utmost flexibility in the focus of research, in the over-all objectives sought for, and in the means employed to reach these goals. Years ago, Harold Lasswell talked in terms of alternating currents of national (or international) attitudes of satisfaction and dissatisfaction as useful units of "thermodynamic measurement" in international relations. Since Lenin's time, Communist revolutionary authors have freely used such military phrases as

[10] See Hans J. Morgenthau, *Politics Among Nations,* p. 548.

"Advance and Retreat," "Strategy and Tactics," etc., denoting the need for diplomatic-political flexibility.

More recently, Quincy Wright attempted to circumscribe the role of the individual as the subject of international politics from a fourfold perspective. Individuals, he suggested, are influenced at the "biological level," the "social level," the "psychological level" and at the "action level." Within this field, the individual choices, decisions, and actions important for international relations must be measured by various and complex political, economic, psychological, sociological, and ethical criteria, in order to arrive at systems of international political action.

Undeniably this formalistic stratosphere is not very useful to the student in search of practical information. More concretely speaking, it is clear that in the contemporary world, beset by the Cold War and a continuing competition between rival power blocs, the focus of international relations must be centered on the concepts of "friend" and "enemy" in the political sense. Our Communist opponent has no staked-out monopoly on the battle cry, "Know Your Enemy!"—closely linked in these times of political warfare to the slogan, "Know Your Friend (or Ally)!"

The flexibility of international politics breaks down at this point. There must be a strong and continuing emphasis on the image of the "enemy" (or opponent) whose built-in picture seems to characterize the contemporary foreign policies of the major powers. Just as the United States has largely replaced Great Britain in the focus of Soviet Russian antagonism, so has our diplomacy centered around the all-pervasive and seemingly permanent image of the Soviet bloc as our arch-opponent in the Cold War. These are truly inflexible categories limiting our field of international vision, our complex political horizon. Only slowly and painfully do these "built-in" national images fade and dissolve. Nicholas Spykman was bitterly criticized in 1942 when he prophetically stated that after World War II, Germany and Japan would become the close allies of the United States while the allies of yesterday might become the mortal enemies of a postwar tomorrow. Despite the obvious geostrategic relevance of Spykman's remarks, it took American public opinion at least six or seven years from the end of the war to familiarize itself with the newly focused images of a friendly, allied West Germany and a Far Eastern bulwark, Japan.

3. SECURITY: THE STRATEGIC FOCUS OF INTERNATIONAL POLITICS

Despite the evident fluidity of subject matter and haziness in problem areas, twentieth-century international politics has a distinct and well-outlined focal point: the concept of national security. In the present age of thermonuclear weapons, security as a truly national goal must be accorded top billing and top primacy in a country's diplomacy. Even the most conflict-ridden leadership groups of a given society must admit that the national community ought to identify itself with the complex requirements of national security, cutting across the fabric of the entire country as a universal goal.

Although theoretically universal within the boundaries of the nation-state itself, security is also a curiously relative concept in many ways. Is it possible to specify more precisely whose security is to be protected against whom? Assuming a primitive "state of nature" for the world, the search for security by each state would be the single dominating factor, and since the search for security by one implies the future insecurity of the others, the search for security by one state would be almost automatically countered by the power policies of other states. Hence the relativity of one nation's security and the inevitability of conflict, as a result of the opposing interests of nations—each searching for its own version of national security.

In other cases, the security concept remains relative if it cannot be equated with the will or the interest of the *whole* nation. Only in theory does the principle of national security always imply unanimous agreement on the immutable needs of the nation. In practice, it is frequently subject to the fluctuating interpretations and understandings of the particular social groups concerned. Security may, therefore, imply the particular conception of interest for given groups in the nation at a given time, but not necessarily for the whole nation for all time. Specific group aims may thus frequently prevent the solid formation or crystallization of broader national interests. In practice there is seldom a permanent, all-inclusive, and universally valid definition of security for any one state over a long period of time.

As the strategic focus of international politics, the concept of national security is apt to create international insecurity. A British author, Desmond W. Crowley, ties the entire history and development of international organization to the ubiquitous phenomenon of political insecurity. Crowley asserts that the traditional and historically acceptable methods used to obtain national security have proved ineffective in recent times.[11] The fundamental source of almost all the tension that arises between nations is fear, based on insecurity. Ever since the emergence of the nation state as a typical form of political organization, nations in small or large groupings have tried to formulate security devices of various types. The author briefly summarizes two major attempts:

a) the "balance of power" system, and b) the concept of the United Nations as a "fresh attempt" to organize internationally against collective insecurity.

a. The balance-of-power system fights insecurity by means of an obvious device—the formation of alliances. But alliances produce counteralliances, and thus lead to a balance-of-power system. It has therefore been the normal state of affairs for European nations to be divided into two antagonistic groups. The result has been to *multiply* tension and fears, rather than to reduce them. This system works only if the opposing alliances are generally of equal strength, thus producing a deadlock, or if the leaders of two alliances agree on some compromise relating to vital issues, such as strategic territories.

b. The emergence of modern nationalism has rendered the process of continual compromise-making between nations much more difficult. Diplomacy has lost its past effectiveness precisely because the conduct and day-by-day shaping of foreign policies has become much more impersonal at a time when the world has become smaller and complicated by many more conflicting national interests.

In this context the real value of the League of Nations and

[11] See Desmond W. Crowley, *The Background to Current Affairs* (London: Macmillan, 1958), Chapter Six, "The United Nations," especially pp. 108-111.

United Nations efforts is seen in terms of replacing the dubious alliance systems by "collective security." This concept has been defined as the deterrent force of an unchallengeable alliance consisting of the great majority of all the nations. Unhappily, this novel-type alliance failed in its principal purpose—that of providing true national security for its member-states. When faced with a crisis, the league was unable to operate the machinery with sufficient vigor and effectiveness. By the middle of the 1930's the individual member nations had reverted to an old-fashioned balance-of-power system. It was World War II that re-emphasized the urgency to devise a better and more meaningful method than the historically discredited balance-of-power system. Thus the decision was taken to project a new world organization, which could approach the haunting dilemma of collective security by attempting to bring the combined resources of all its members to bear against armed aggression. Whether the United Nations has successfully laid the specter of global as well as national insecurity remains to be seen.

4. THE RESTRAINTS ON VIOLENCE—NATIONAL AND INTERNATIONAL

One of the principal and seemingly insoluble problems of international politics is the absence of any legal or institutional restraints on the use of power. Since the application of power leads to violence, both latent and obvious, the crucial issue is to construct tangible restraints on the assertion of violence in international relations. In legal terms this is impossible. It has been frequently stated that the only legal limitation of sovereignty is its duty to admit of no legal limitations.

Side-stepping the permanent dilemma of state sovereignty, the student must search for other instruments acting as restraining forces on the indiscriminate uses of violence. Two major types are worth noting here: ideological and institutional restraints on violence.

Ideological restraints imply a recourse to certain political belief—systems or sets of ideas opposing the limited or unlimited use of force in international relations. Pacifism, for example, has been a major and successful ideology opposing violence. Isolationism, the systematic noninvolvement in the affairs and conflicts of other countries, has operated as an effective deterrent to numerous countries from active participation in wars.

The ideological restraint is most effective when coupled with moral and spiritual considerations. In such situations, aggressors are made to realize that the use of force simply "does not pay," and there are such intensive emotional barriers erected against the assertion of violence that the would-be aggressor shrinks back from open challenge. These restraints are self-contained within the ideologies and myths of the individual nation-states or of the various social groups within the nation. They are never institutionalized or incorporated into specific laws or actual operational principles of political science. Rather, they express the ethical dictate, the voice of national—or group—conscience on the international political level.

Slogans, catchwords, emotionally loaded propaganda phrases, if effectively manipulated, can become significant symbols advocating either restraint on or resistance to violence. Hitler's "Holy War Against Bolshevism!" battle cry was countered by Winston Churchill's "Grand Alliance," by Franklin D. Roosevelt's call for a "War for Survival," for "Unconditional Surrender," and by Joseph Stalin's slogan of "The Russian People's Great Patriotic War." Thus, ideologically motivated symbols can play an enormously important role in organizing or restraining the massive use of violence on the international scene.

Institutional restraints comprise specifically defined procedures by which governments can settle disputes without using their military establishments. In addition to arbitration, mediation, and conciliation, discussed above, one must consider here the institutional aspects of international organization. If any one of the United Nations members chooses to disobey the legal limitations of the Charter, "enforcement action" or sanctions will be applied against it. Force in such a case is not truly restrained, but merely rechanneled or redirected: it is utilized by the society of states rather than by single states.

In successful situations, as in effective UN police actions or in the uses of a UN emergency police force, the institution of international organization is actually able to act as a restraining force against the ready appeal to arms in crises in which the unilateral action of single states would not have deterred the use of violence equally well. In reality, however, institutional restraints are exceedingly weak and mostly, in an embryonic state. The "enforcement actions" of the United Nations have been infrequent and largely ineffective. Behind the façade of "institutional" restraints there hides, not a majority of UN members, but only a few nations, supporting the specific action or sanction for reasons of their own and motivated by their own national interests.

Major Conclusions

One of the principal conclusions to be drawn from our survey is that international politics presents a particularly fluid and dynamic field of study. There are several reasons for this continuing state of flux and for the uncertainties of scope and content. First of all, it seems to be impossible to state concisely or "codify," as it were, the principles and problems of international politics. Vague and somewhat unprecise in character, International Relations has no tangible laws, no closely identifiable body of rules or prescriptions that could be handed down from generation to generation, from student to student. The whole setting of the discipline changes almost continually and the political environment in which it has to operate is steadily exposed to major seismographic shocks and revolutionary upheavals.

It has been frequently, and quite accurately, stated that international politics suffers from chronic exposure to a cultural and political lag, which keeps it approximately twenty-five to fifty years behind the contemporary setting and day-by-day sweep of history. Thus it is clear that the French Army was ready by 1870 to re-fight and win the battle of Waterloo, was set by 1914 to correct the military disasters of 1870-71, and was fully prepared by 1940 to profit from the strategic and tactical lessons of the 1914-18 period. Unhappily, it is also true of world politics that by the time a new military conflict or severe diplomatic crisis arises, it is usually ready to cope with the previous wave of wars or crises, and willing to apply several years later the lessons derived from past difficulties. While history may teach us a great deal, it obviously cannot offer a complete blueprint for the next wave of problems. Hence the chronic state of semibankruptcy in the academic discipline of international politics!

In addition to this "historic gap," the vagueness of scope and content must be stressed again. In the field of international diplomacy, two and two seldom add up to four, but seem to vacillate in a truly quixotic manner anywhere between three and eight. Albert Einstein undeniably spoke his frank opinion when he remarked that "Politics is harder than physics." It was the great fallacy of medieval natural law scholars to concentrate on, and attempt to codify, a set of immutable laws governing the political relations of both individuals and nations. Such unwavering principles do not exist in world politics. Even the experts who keep referring to a "law of political vacuums" (asserting that the place of a weak, practically nonexistent or defunct political system will promptly be taken up and filled by a stronger and more aggressive regime or governing elite) have to qualify and generously footnote their slowly evolving principle in order to give it a degree of relative validity. Even the most modest political generalizations have to be surrounded by defensive "if's and but's" to the point where their pedagogical value and historic significance may rightly be questioned by student and scholar alike.

One of the few tenable generalizations, which ought to be formulated here, is that every facet, aspect, and operational detail of international politics is focused today on the climactic and all-pervasive struggle between democracy and totalitarianism. The global conflict between these two opposing ideologies affects every analysis, discussion, and research project in this field. While Cold War studies may be only incidental and somewhat peripheral phases in the sweep of history, the emergence of totalitarianism itself is truly a historically unique and *sui generis* political form, and quite possibly the most distinctive single contribution of the twentieth century to the world of politics.

The all-pervasive conflict lies between the challenge of Free World democracy on the one hand and totalitarian dictatorships on the other. The challenge is complicated by the political fact that this monster is a "beast of many spots." All fascist and Communist totalitarian dictatorships are basically alike, or at any rate, more nearly like each other than like any other system of government. Thus a new, revolutionary type of political ideology, subject to a single power center, moves into the realm of international affairs with a systematic and ruthless challenge of any other way of life or personal belief. The ensuing global struggle casts a deep and dark shadow over the New World, the Old World, and the Soviet Communist bloc; over international conferences, whether in the United Nations or outside of it, over military and political negotiations, whether top-secret, highly sensitive or open to public knowledge; and, most importantly, it tends to be of a truly divisive character, giving our political world an unnatural black-and-white coloring on a seemingly permanent basis.

BIBLIOGRAPHY

Alexandersson, Gunnar, "Changes in the Location Pattern of the Anglo-American Steel Industry: 1948-1959," *Economic Geography,* Vol. 37, No. 2 (April 1961).

Aristotle, *Politics,* trans. by B. Jowett, New York: The Modern Library, 1943.

Banse, Ewald, *Germany Prepares for War,* trans. by Alan Harris, New York: Harcourt, Brace, 1941.

Baransky, N., *Economic Geography of the U.S.S.R.,* trans. by S. Belsky, Moscow: Foreign Language Publishing House, 1956.

Boggs, S. Whittemore, *International Boundaries,* New York: Columbia University Press, 1940.

Bowman, *The New World,* Yonkers-on-Hudson: World Book, 1922.

Broek, Jan, "Diversity and Unity in Southeast Asia," *The Geographical Review,* XXXIV, N. 2 (1944).

———, "The Problem of 'Natural' Frontiers," *Frontiers of the Future,* University of California, 1940.

Cressey, George, *Asia's Lands and Peoples,* New York: McGraw-Hill, reviewed, 1951.

———, *The Basis of Soviet Strength,* New York: McGraw-Hill, 1945.

———, *How Strong Is Russia?* Syracuse: Syracuse University Press, 1954.

de Gaulle, Charles, Fifth Press Conference, Paris, September 5, 1961.

de Salles, Raoul de Roussy, *The Making of Tomorrow,* New York: Reynal & Hitchcock, 1942.

de Seversky, Alexander P., *Air Power, Key to Survival,* New York: Simon & Schuster, 1950.

———, *America: Too Young to Die,* New York: McGraw-Hill, 1961.

Fairgrieve, James, *Geography and World Power,* University of London Press, 1915.

Finley, M. I., ed., *The Greek Historians,* New York: Viking, 1959.

Frankel, S. Herbert, *The Concept of Colonization,* Oxford: The Clarendon Press, 1949.

Ginsburg, Norton, ed., *The Pattern of Asia,* Englewood Cliffs: Prentice Hall, 1958.

Gottmann, Jean, *A Geography of Europe,* New York: Holt, 1954.

———, "Geography and International Relations," *World Politics,* III, No. 2 (January 1951).

———, "Political Partitioning of Our World" *World Politics,* IV, No. 4 (July 1952).

Guyot, Arnold, *The Earth and Man,* New York: Scribner, 1889.

Gyorgy, Andrew, *Geopolitics,* University of California, 1944.

Harris, Chauncey, "Ethnic Groups in the Soviet Union," *The Geographical Review,* July 1955.

Harris, Norman, *Intervention and Colonization in Africa,* Boston: Houghton, Mifflin, 1914.

Hart, J. F., "Changing Distribution of the American Negro" *Annals of the Association of American Geographers,* September 1960.

Hartshorne, Richard, "The Functional Approach in Political Geography," *Annals of the Association of American Geographers,* XL, No. 2 (June 1950).

———, *The Nature of Geography,* Lancaster, Pa.: The Association of American Geographers, 1939.

———, *Perspective on the Nature of Geography,* Chicago: Rand McNally, 1959.

———, "Political Geography," in James & Jones (q.v.).

———, "Political Geography in the Modern World," *Journal of Conflict Resolution,* IV, No. 1 (March 1960).

———, *Suggestions on the Terminology of Political Boundaries,* Leipzig, 1936.

Jackson, W. A. Douglas, *Russo-Chinese Borderlands,* Princeton: Van Nostrand, 1962.

James, Preston, and Jones, Clarence, eds., *American Geography—Inventory and Prospect,* Association of American Geographers, Syracuse University Press, 1954.

Jones, Stephen, "Global Strategic Views," *The Geographical Review,* XLV, No. 4 (July 1955).

———, "A Unified Field Theory of Political Geography," Annals of the Association of American Geographers, XLIV, 1954).

Jorré, Georges, *The Soviet Union,* translated & revised by E. D. Labords, London: Longmans, 1960.

Kant, Immanuel, "The Principle of Progress," *Eternal Peace and Other Essays,* Vol. 3, World Peace Foundation, 1914.

Kennan, George, *Russia and the West under Lenin and Stalin,* Boston: Little, Brown, 1960.

Kimble, George, *Geography in the Middle Ages,* London: Methuen, 1938.

Kropotkin, Pierre, *Orographie de la Siberie,* Institut Geographique de Bruxelles, Publication 9, 1904.

Luethy, Herbert, *France Against Herself,* New York: Praeger, 1955.

Lyde, Lionel W., *The Continent of Europe,* London: Macmillan & Co., Ltd., 1926.

Mackinder, Halford J., *Democratic Ideals and Reality,* New York: Holt, 1942.

———, "The Geographical Pivot of History," *Geographical Journal,* XXII, 1904.

———, "The Round World and the Winning of the Peace," *Foreign Affairs,* XXI, No. 4 (July 1943).

Mahan, Alfred T., *The Problem of Asia and its Effect upon International Policies,* Boston: Little, Brown, 1900.

Malin, James, "Mobility and History," *Agricultural History,* 17, October 1943.

———, "Space and History," Part 2, *Agricultural History,* 18, July 1944.

The Middle East—A Political and Economic Survey, London: Royal Institute of International Affairs, 1950.

Morrison, John, "Russia and the Warm Waters," *U. S. Naval Institute Proceedings,* 1952.

Nasser, Gamel Abdel, *Egypt's Liberation,* Washington: Public Affairs Press, 1955.

Newbegin, Marion, *The Mediterranean Lands,* New York: Knopf, 1924.

Nicholson, Norman, *The Boundaries of Canada, Its Provinces and Territories,* Ottawa: Department of Mines and Technical Surveys, 1954.

Parkins, Almon E., *The South,* New York: Wiley, 1938.

Ratzel, Friedrich, *Politische Geographie,* Munich, Berlin, 1897.

Renner, George T., "Peace by the Map," *Colliers,* CXIII (1944).

Schnitzer, E. W., *German Geopolitics Revived: A Survey of Geopolitical Writing in Germany Today,* The Rand Corporation, March 1954.

Semple, E., and Jones, C., *American History and Its Geographic Conditions,* Boston: Houghton, Mifflin, 1933.

Slessor, John, *The Great Deterrent,* New York: Praeger, 1957.

Sprout, Harold & Margaret, "Geography and International Politics in Revolutionary Change," *The Journal of Conflict Resolution,* IV, No. 1.

———, "*Man—Milieu Relationship Hypothesis in the Context of International Politics,*" Center of International Studies, Princeton University, 1956.

Spykman, Nicholas, *America's Strategy in World Politics,* New York: Harcourt, Brace, 1942.

———, *The Geography of the Peace,* New York: Harcourt, Brace, 1944.

Stamp, L. Dudley, *Applied Geography,* London: Penguin Books, 1960.

Strabo, *The Geography of Strabo,* trans. by H. C. Hamilton & W. Falconer, Vol. I, London: Bohn, 1854-57.

Thomson, J. Oliver, *History of Ancient Geography,* Cambridge University Press, 1948.

Ullman, Edward, *American Commodity Flow,* Seattle: University of Washington Press, 1957.

U. S. Army War College, *Power Analysis of the Nation-State,* Discussion Topic 2-B, Carlisle Barracks, Pa., 1960.

van Loon, Hendrik, *Van Loon's Geography,* New York: Garden City Publishing Company, 1940.

Wanklyn, H. G., *The Eastern Marchlands of Europe,* London: Philip, 1941.

Weigert, Hans *et al.*, *Principles of Political Geography*, New York: Appleton-Century-Crofts, 1957.

Whittlesey, Derwent S., *The Earth and the State*, New York: Holt, 1944.

———, *German Strategy of World Conquest*, New York: Farrar & Rinehart, 1942.

———, "The Regional Concept and the Regional Method," in James & Jones (q.v.).

Wolfe, Bertram, *Khrushchev and Stalin's Ghost*, New York: Praeger, 1957.

INDEX

INDEX

ABOUT THE AUTHOR

SAUL BERNARD COHEN has specialized in political geography in his teaching career as Professor of Geography at Boston University. He has lectured extensively in this field before various governmental agencies, particularly at the United States Naval War College where he was the first Visiting Professor of Geography in 1957. He is a graduate of Harvard College and Harvard University (A.M., Ph.D.) where he worked under Derwent S. Whittlesey, and has been a visiting lecturer in political geography at Yale. His specific regional interests lie in Anglo-America, Europe, and the Middle East.

Professor Cohen's researches in economic geography have brought him additional recognition as a marketing geographer and he is a consultant in this field to leading American corporations. He is the author of numerous professional articles and one book.